We dedicate this book

with the highest

reverence

to

Ghost O.T.

a little

snow in summer

and

Mazda

(the car for

people who can hear)

PATTERNS

OF THE

HYPNOTIC TECHNIQUES

OF

MILTON H. ERICKSON, M.D.

Volume I

BY
RICHARD BANDLER
AND
JOHN GRINDER

Meta Publications
Cupertino, California 95014
1975

Library of Congress Card Number 75-24584

ISBN 0-916990-01-X

Typography by Penguin ≈ Santa Clara, California 95050

Cover illustration by Robert B. Dilts

Table of Contents

PART II (continued)

PART III

EPILOGUE

APPENDIX

Preface

An attack of anterior poliomyelitis in 1919, shortly after my graduation from high school, rendered me almost totally paralyzed for several months, but with my vision, hearing and thinking unimpaired. Since I was quarantined at home on the farm, there was little diversion available. Fortunately, I had always been interested in human behavior, and there was that of my parents and eight siblings, and also that of the practical nurse who was taking care of me, available for observation. My inability to move tended to restrict me to the intercommunications of those about me. Although I already knew a little about body language and other forms of non-verbal communication, I was amazed to discover the frequent, and, to me, often startling contradictions between the verbal and the non-verbal communications within a single interchange. This aroused so much of my interest that I intensified my observations at every opportunity.

The discovery that "double takes" were perceptions at two different levels of understanding, often based upon totally different experiential associations, opened a new field of observation. Then, when I discovered that a "triple take" could occur, I began mentally rehearsing the phrasing of a single communication to cause differing perceptions, even contradictory in character, at differing levels of understanding. These efforts led to the recognition of many other factors governing communication such as tonalities, time values, sequences of presentation, near and remote associations, inherent contradictions, omissions, distortions,

redundancies, over- and under-emphases, directness and indirect-
ness, ambiguities, relevancies and irrelevancies — to name a few.
Also, it became apparent that there were multiple levels of perception and response, not all of which were necessarily at the usual or
conscious level of awareness but were at levels of understanding
not recognized by the self, often popularly described as "instinc-
tive" or "intuitive."

Perhaps the best simple example is the instance of Frank
Bacon's achievement during his starring role in the stage play
"Lightnin'," in which, by the utterance of the single word *no* at
various times, he conveyed at least sixteen different meanings.
These meanings included an emphatic *No*, a subtle *Yes*, an implied
promise of *Not yet*, an amused *Don't be ridiculous*, and even the
exquisite negative *Not even if all hell freezes over!* Altered tone of
voice can constitute an actual vocabulary of transformation of
verbal communication, as can body language.

Then, I was introduced to experimental hypnosis by Clark L.
Hull, and I became aware of the possibilities both of decreasing
the number of foci of attention and of selecting and maneuvering
specific foci of attention. This led to the combining of my aware-
nesses of the complexities of communication with my understandings of hypnosis, for experimental and psychotherapeutic
purposes.

Although this book by Richard Bandler and John Grinder, to
which I am contributing this Preface, is far from being a complete
description of my methodologies, as they so clearly state it is a much
better explanation of how I work than I, myself, can give. I know
what I do, but to explain how I do it is much too difficult for me.
A simple example of this may be cited from the experience of my
daughter, Kristina, as a medical student. She happened to pick up
a paper by Ernest Rossi and myself, on the double bind, and, after
reading it, amusedly commented, "So that's how I do it!" Dr.
Rossi, who was present, immediately asked, "So that's how you
do what?" She explained, "Every patient has the right to refuse
permission for a rectal and hernial examination, and many patients
do. But when I have reached that part of the physical examination, I tell my patients, sympathetically, that I know they are tired
of having me peer into their eyes, and peak into their ears and up
their noses, and poking and thumping here and there, but that, as
soon as I complete the rectal and hernial examinations, they can
say good-bye to me. And they always wait patiently to say that

good-bye."

While I would like still further analyses of the complexities of communication for hypnotic purposes, which would require much more than this book by Bandler and Grinder can encompass, I would also like an analysis of how and why carefully structured communications can elicit such extensive and effective patient responses, often not actually requested. Unquestionably, such additional studies will eventually be made. I look forward to Volume II in this series, by Richard Bandler and John Grinder.

It has been a pleasure and a privilege to write the Preface to this book. I say this, not because it centers around my hypnotic techniques, but because long overdue is the fulfillment of the need to recognize that meaningful communication should replace repetitious verbigerations, direct suggestions, and authoritarian commands.

Milton H. Erickson, M.D.
1201 East Hayward Avenue
Phoenix, Arizona 85020

Acknowledgments

We gratefully thank Milton H. Erickson, M.D., for permission to quote his articles in this volume and the American Society of Clinical Hypnosis which holds the original copyright on much of the quoted material.

We also acknowledge the greatest debt to Jeanne Nixon and *The Penguin People, Artists and Typographers,* of Santa Clara, California, for the design and skillful typography of this book.

We would also like to thank Ernest Rossi for providing us with tapes and manuscript material.

Guide to Volume I of
Patterns of Erickson's Work

Milton Erickson is internationally acclaimed as the leading practitioner of medical hypnosis. He has written more than a hundred professional articles on hypnosis and has taught and practiced hypnosis since the 1920's. He, more than any other human being in this field, has been able both to explore and to demonstrate the vast potentials that hypnosis has to offer humanity. His ability baffles the scientific mind, and his accomplishments, typically, are either viewed as miracles or denounced as impossibilities, although first-hand experience presents him as an undeniable reality, a striking contrast to what most people believe is possible for the mind to accomplish. Furthermore, few of his students have learned to exercise the skills in hypnosis that Milton Erickson uses so easily. The behavior Milton Erickson demonstrates while both inducing and utilizing hypnotic states of consciousness is extremely complex. Yet he is very systematic; that is, his behavior has distinctive patterns.

Our skill is in building explicit models of complex human behavior. What this means is that we build maps of these complex patterns of behavior and these maps then allow other people to learn and use these behavior patterns. We quote Noam Chomsky's remarks[1] concerning his initial formulation of a model for modern transformational linguistics.

> . . . forms part of an attempt to construct a formalized general theory of linguistic structure and to explore the foundations of such a theory. The

search for rigorous formulation in linguistics has a much more serious motivation than mere concern for logical niceties or the desire to purify well-established methods of linguistic analysis. Precisely constructed models for linguistic structure can play an important role, both negative and positive, in the process of discovery itself. By pushing a precise but inadequate formulation to an unacceptable conclusion, we can often expose the exact source of this inadequacy and, consequently, gain a deeper understanding of the linguistic data. More positively, a formalized theory may automatically provide solutions for many problems other than those for which it was explicitly designed.

This volume represents our effort to perform this same service for the field of hypnosis.

When Erickson recognized this skill, he expressed the hope that this volume would be constructed so that other practitioners of hypnosis would have available to them his powerful tools and techniques. It is the authors' intention in this first volume to present to you some of the patterns of Erickson's behavior in hypnosis. We intend to give you, in an easily learnable, step-by-step manner, an explicit model which will make these skills available to you in your own work. This book has three stages or levels of modeling, each represented by a separate part.

Part I contains several of Erickson's articles, exciting examples of his own work. We will present a parallel commentary that will identify the patterns in his behavior. The patterns we will identify do not, by any means, exhaust what is present in Erickson's work. This volume is designed only to begin this process, and, at the same time, to present the most essential elements of Erickson's language patterns.

In Part II we will take these patterns and sort them into natural groupings. Hopefully, this will provide you with an overall way of both understanding Erickson's work and organizing your own experience in hypnosis. Our purpose is to familiarize you with these patterns, and to show examples in which they occur in Erickson's work. This will be accomplished by excerpting small portions of various published articles about his work, most of them of a transcriptual nature.

Part III of this volume is a step-by-step, explicit presentation of the patterns identified in Parts I and II. This Part is intended to give you the skills necessary to construct each pattern through an understanding of its formal characteristics. Our belief is that in this way the patterns of Erickson's behavior will be made available to you for use in your own work.

We strongly recommend that you read this volume carefully and that you spend some time experimenting with each pattern. This book is designed primarily as a training manual, not as a novel. Careful use and re-use will reap the best rewards for you.

FOOTNOTE

1. *Syntactic Structures,* Mouton & Co., The Hague, 1957, p. 5.

PART I

IDENTIFICATION
OF
PATTERNS
OF ERICKSON'S
HYPNOTIC WORK

Introduction:
The Map Is Not the Territory

In the authors' experience, people who use hypnosis for medical, dental, or psychotherapeutic purposes seem more than any other single group to understand that we, as human beings, do not operate behaviorally *directly* upon the world, but rather we operate through a map or model (a created representation) of what we *believe* the world to be. A thorough understanding of how people in general, and each client in particular, create a representation of the world in which they live will yield the practitioner of hypnosis many advantages. Among these will be greater speed in trance induction, more success with a greater number of subjects, and deeper trances. For additional study of the processes by which people create models of the world, we recommend *The Structure of Magic I* and *II*.[1] For our purposes here, we wish now to provide you with only a basic model of the processes by which people create models of the world.

First, the models that we as humans create will differ from the world of reality in three major ways. Some parts of our experience will be deleted, not represented in our model. This is both a necessary and sometimes impoverishing aspect of our modeling processes. If we tried to represent every piece of sensory input, we would be overwhelmed with data. However, when we fail to represent an important or vital aspect, the results can be devastating. In any event, we do delete parts of our experience when creating models of the world. These deletions, and all of the processes of modeling, go on all the time and, for the most part, without our conscious awareness.

The second way in which our model of the world will be different from the world itself is through **distortions**. Distortion is a modeling process which allows us to make shifts in our experience of sensory data. For example, we can fantasize a green cow, even though we have never experienced one with our senses. We can distort our experience and plan the future by imagining that it is now. This modeling process can be an asset or a liability, depending upon how it is used.

The third process of modeling is **generalization**. This is the process by which one element of our model of the world comes to represent an entire category of which it is only an example. This allows us to know that when we read a book, by moving our eyes from left to right, we will be able to extract the content. When we are confronted with a door just like any other door, even though we have not seen this particular door before, we make the assumption it will open by the same process we have used before. Generalizations in our model of the world allow us to operate more efficiently from context to context. Generalization also allows us to keep recoding our experiences at higher levels of patterning. This makes possible the advances in knowledge and technology — in all areas of human functioning.

To this date, the most thoroughly studied and best understood of the human representational systems (models) is natural language. Transformational grammar is explicit, formal, and the most complete model of human language systems. Transformational grammarians have extracted some of the patterns of this representational system which are common to all languages. Therefore, transformational grammar is a Meta-model; that is, a model of a model, or a model of language. Transformational grammarians have built an explicit representation of the intuitions which people demonstrate when communicating and understanding natural language. For example, each sentence of every natural language has two distinct representations: the representation of the way it actually sounds (or, if written, by the way it actually appears), called the **Surface Structure**, and the representation of its meaning which is called the **Deep Structure**. When a person utters the sentence:

The window was broken

the Surface Structure is the representation of the actual sounds made by the person speaking or, in the case of a written representation, the words written out above. In addition to this representation, this sentence is associated with another representation which is the meaning it has — Deep Structure. In this case, the Deep Structure can be represented as:

PAST (BREAK [someone, window, with something])

This Deep Structure representation is designed to capture the intuitions which each of us have as native speakers of English when we hear the Surface Structure presented above. We understand that:

(a) Some event occurred in the past;
(b) The event was a complex event;
(c) It consisted of the following parts:
    (1) An action, *break*, which occurred between:
        a. The agent — some person or thing doing the breaking, here represented by *someone*, and
        b. The object — some person or thing being broken, here represented by *the window*, and
        c. The instrument — the thing used to do the breaking, here represented by *with something*.

Notice that, even though not all of the parts of the Deep Structure represented appear in the Surface Structure (in this case the agent and the instrument are not represented in the Surface Structure), the native speaker of English has that information available in his understanding of the sentence. The statement *The window was broken* implies to native speakers that not only was the window broken but *someone* or *something* had to break the window *with something*. The ways in which Surface Structures can differ from their associated Deep Structure meanings is the research domain of transformational linguists. They have postulated a series of formal mapping operations called transformations which precisely specify how Deep and Surface Structures may differ. The entire process which links a Deep Structure to its Surface Structure(s) is called **derivation** (see page 10).

Explicit, formal models of each Surface Structure—Deep Structure relationship can be made on the above model. (You

```
derivation              deep structure  ⎫
                                     •   ⎪
transformation   1                   •   ⎪
      "          2                   •   ⎬  derivation
      "          3                   •   ⎪
      "          N . . .             •   ⎪
                                     •   ⎪
                 surface structure       ⎭
```

must make this important distinction in order to understand the unconscious processing of language that occurs in hypnosis.) Transformational linguists, therefore, have taken an incredibly complex area of human behavior and built a formal model of it which explicitly represents the rules of behavior which are intuitively demonstrated, although not consciously understood, by native speakers of that language.

The authors (Bandler/Grinder) have used the approach of formalizing intuitions to build an explicit, formal model of the language exchange in psychotherapy. What we did was to create a formal representation of the intuitions which effective therapists from every school of psychotherapy use in their work, although they are not necessarily conscious of it. (This Meta-model of therapy is fully explained in *The Structure of Magic I.*)

We used our formalization techniques to explore and understand the other representational systems used by human beings to organize and create models of their experience. These kinesthetic, visual, auditory, olfactory, gustatory maps of experience were then used as a basis to expand our model of therapy. The results were both fascinating and useful.

We found, first of all, that most people have a most highly valued representational system, one that they use more than any other to organize their experience, and that this most highly valued system can be identified quickly by listening to the predicates (adjectives, adverbs, verbs) used in anyone's speech. For example, a person with a most highly valued representational system which is *visual* will describe his experience with predicates which presuppose a visual system such as: *I see what you are saying, clearly, looking at this work will show you how to improve your work, Imagine how this appears to be dull reading.*

People whose most highly valued representational system is kinesthetic will use predicates which presuppose kinesthetic representations. For example, *I want you firmly to grasp this concept; I feel you can overcome some hard problems; Can you get in touch with, and get a handle on, what this means.*

A person whose primary representational system is auditory will use predicates which presuppose auditory representations. For example, he will say, *Sounds interesting to me; I will talk to you later; I will be hearing from him soon; so in other words we will all get together and be sounding boards for these ideas.*

We also found that those therapists and hypnotists who were most effective in their work had a systematic, though not always conscious, way of utilizing a client's most highly valued representational system. Understanding how a client organizes his experience in terms of these representational systems has great rewards for both the psychotherapist and the practitioner of hypnosis. We make a distinction in our formalization of these patterns of behavior between input channels, representational systems, and output channels. A person can hear (input) words, make a picture (representational system), and express it by pounding his fist (output channel). (The formal model of this aspect of behavior is the substance of *The Structure of Magic II,* which you should read if you wish further study.)

It is enough to say at this point that each of us as human beings creates models of the world which differ from the world. Each of us creates a model of the world which is different from every other person's model of the world. Furthermore, formal models — Meta-models — can be built which represent the patterns of modeling which are at work when we as humans create these maps. Meta-models can be built which represent the rules, whether conscious or unconscious, governing how therapists and hypnotists work with these modeling principles.

Milton Erickson's work with hypnosis is in one such area of complex human behavior. His ability to both induce and to utilize hypnosis is extremely effective. Unfortunately, few people have been able to learn this skill. Even more tragic is the fact that the lack of formal understanding of hypnosis and its induction has resulted in a diminishing of interest, research, and practice of this profoundly useful therapeutic tool. The authors' ability to understand and represent the patterns of Erickson's skill has made it possible for us to learn and to use those patterns. Realizing the special skills we have to create formal representations of complex human behavior, he has made available to us his writings and video and audio tapes, in the hope that the formal model of his work which follows in this book will make it possible for more of us to share his skills, and, thus, to spur greater interest in research and clinical use of hypnosis.

The strategy we have employed in this book is to take each of Erickson's techniques apart piece by piece. First we extracted the small components. For instance, his interspersal technique has a series of special uses of language; when these components, which include use of presupposition, imbedded commands and sentence fragments, are put together with special use of voice tempo and tonality, a larger pattern called **interspersal** results. We have chosen a series of articles which represent a wide range of Erickson's work with hypnosis. We hope the result will be both educational and useful to you in your own specific area of work. The focus of this first Volume will be to give you the language skills at the first level of patterning used so effectively by Erickson.

Our strategy has three steps: First, to identify these patterns in the context of Erickson's work. Second, to familiarize you with each pattern, its form and use. And, third, to give you formalizations that will enable you to construct and utilize these patterns in your own work.

In the past three decades, a great deal has been learned about how human beings function in regard to language, behavior, and consciousness. The fields of linguistics and neurology, have made substantial progress in understanding human behavior. There is, however, much to be learned; the processes at work in the organism called a human being constitute an as yet uncharted universe of complexity. We intend in this volume to take some of what is known about these fields and apply it to the study of hypnosis in a way that will help you to organize your experience to better understand the work of Milton Erickson and the phenomenon of hypnotism. One of the major contributions of neurology that helps us to understand hypnotic behavior is the study of split-brain patients.[2] Observations regarding hemispheric differences made of split-brain patients, and brain-damaged patients (Gardner) reveal that the two cerebral hemispheres of the brain in humans serve different functions. Erickson's behavior in hypnosis seems to demonstrate an intuitive understanding of these differences.

The field of linguistics offers us a vast resource for understanding how humans process complex segments of language at non-conscious levels.[3] The research in these two fields raises the long overdue question: What is an unconscious mind? We, as yet, have no complete answer to this question; however, we do believe that when Erickson uses the term *unconscious mind* he is referring to more than just some term left over from the Freudian foundations of psychology. We believe he is referring partially to the functioning of the dominant cerebral hemisphere that occurs below the level of awareness, and also to the functioning of the non-dominant cerebral hemisphere. He is probably referring to more than these two aspects of mental processing, but we are sure that his use of this term includes these two functions. His overall strategy while conducting trance inductions appears to have these three dimensions.

(1) Pacing and distraction of the dominant (language) hemisphere;
(2) Utilization of the dominant hemisphere, language processing which occurs below the level of awareness;
(3) Accessing of the non-dominant hemisphere.

Further readings in these areas are presented in the bibliography for the interested reader.

It is our intention in the rest of Part I to help you to identify how Erickson operates in a way that accomplishes and utilizes these three strategies for trance induction. A more explicit analysis will be presented in Part II.

Preview of Patterns

In the remaining portion of Part I of this volume, we will present examples of Erickson's work in trance induction and suggestion. As we stated previously, we will focus on simply identifying the patterns in his work. The latter parts of this volume concern themselves with the formalization and construction of these patterns, thus making them available for you in your work. If we first present some overview of these patterns, it will assist you in attempting to understand the complex use to which Erickson puts them.

In all trance induction work, the hypnotist must be sensitive to the particular way in which the client organizes his experience — that is, to the client's model of the world and the modeling processes which the client uses to construct that model. The hypnotist's ability to identify and utilize the client's model and the client's modeling processes will determine to a large extent his ability to successfully *pace* the client. The notion of pacing is central to any discussion of successful trance induction and trance suggestion. Here we restrict ourselves to verbal pacing. A hypnotist has successfully paced a client verbally when the hypnotist's verbalizations are accepted by the client as an accurate description of the client's ongoing experience.

In verbal pacing, there are two general categories of description which will be effective:

(1) Descriptions of the client's ongoing, observable

experience;
(2) Description of the client's ongoing, non-observable experience.

The first category of verbal description depends primarily on the hypnotist's ability to make acute visual and auditory distinctions as he observes and listens to the client and to incorporate these distinctions into his ongoing description of the client's behavior. As mentioned in the commentary on the Huxley article, at the end of Part I, in standard inductions the hypnotist will frequently use descriptions such as:

. . . breathing in and out . . .
. . . hand lifting, lifting . . .

where these descriptions, in fact, are timed so that they are accurate descriptions of the client's experience — that is, uttered as the client is, in fact, breathing in and out, as the client's hand is, in fact, lifting. In this type of pacing there is no substitute for the hypnotist's ability to make refined visual and auditory distinctions. We mention here that while Erickson's ability to make these refined visual and auditory distinctions is phenomenal and he skillfully incorporates the distinctions he makes into his ongoing descriptions, this is not the only use that he makes of these distinctions. In the process of pacing, the hypnotist is making himself into a sophisticated bio-feedback mechanism. He may do this primarily verbally. In addition, however, and dramatically effective both from our observations of Erickson and in our own work, the hypnotist may use his own body posture and movements, his own tonality and tempo as pacing mechanisms. More specifically, Erickson frequently adopts the client's tonality, syntax and tempo of speech, will adjust his body position, breathing rate and gestures to match the client's. Thus, the client feels his own breathing, the rising and falling of his chest, and simultaneously sees Erickson's body moving with the same rhythmic motions. Erickson extends these principles in every way. He not only matches his breathing to that of the client, but will also match the tempo of his voice to the client's breathing or pulse rate by watching the client's veins expand and contract. He will use words and phrases he has heard the client use and voice inflections used tonally by the client. He, in essence, makes all his own output channels a feedback mechanism that will match his client's subjective experience on both conscious and unconscious levels. Rarely are clients aware of the complex ways in which Erickson is pacing them. This lack of awareness on the part of the client seems to be an essential ingredient in rapid, effective trance induction. The result of this complex type of pacing is a complete bio-feedback loop for the client. The client's outputs and the corresponding experience he has of his body and his auditory output is matched by Erickson's output:

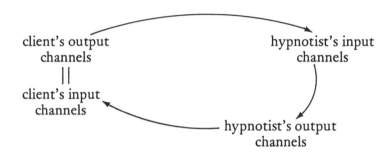

We will treat this complex type of pacing at length in Volume II of Patterns; here we focus on the verbal dimensions of Erickson's work.

This first type of pacing, then, involves the hypnotist's ability to verbally match the client's ongoing experience. It includes both the obvious — for example:

. . . as you sit there, listening to the sound of my voice . . .

and the less obvious types of observable behavior pacing. For example, in the following discussion of a hand levitation with Jay Haley (H) and John Weakland (W),

W: *. . . I'm not sure whether you took no response as a response, or the tiniest response and said, "It's lifting." There were a*

Here Erickson gives instructions in the induction being discussed for the client's hands to lift. He does this at the time the client is breathing in. If *number of times there when you said it when I couldn't quite detect whether anything was happening or not.*

E: *There was one thing that happened. Put your hand on your thigh, take a deep breath. What happened to your hand?*

W: *It lifts!*

E: *You time the inspiration. And they haven't got an opportunity to deny it. . . . Later on I thought I would emphasize that, by taking every other inspiration to say "lifting."*

your hands are on your thighs and you breathe in, you will have the sensation that your hands are lifting. His directions verbally match what he knows will be the client's experience. This is another example of pacing.

In pacing the client's ongoing experience, the hypnotist's objective is to so successfully pace that he may begin to lead the client's experience. In other words, once the client has accepted (usually unconsciously) the hypnotist's description as an accurate account of his ongoing experience, the line between the hypnotist's description of the client's actual behavior and what the client will experience next becomes blurred. Typically, Erickson will make a series of pacing statements which are immediately verifiable by the client and link these to a statement which is a description of the behavior which he desires to elicit from the client. The strength of these links will vary. The weakest linkage is **Simple Conjunction** — the use of the word *and* as in:[4]

> *. . . you are sitting there, listening to the sound of my voice and relaxing more and more . . .*

A somewhat stronger link is that which we call the **Implied Causative**,[5] shown in sentences such as:

> *. . . as you sit there, listening to the sound of my voice, you will relax more and more . . .*

The strongest form of the linkage occurs with what we call **Cause-Effect** (semantic ill-formedness; see *Magic I,* Chapters 3 and 4):

> *. . . sitting there, listening to the sound of my voice, will make you relax more and more . . .*

The important feature of these types of linkages is not whether the logic of the statement is valid, but simply whether they constitute a successful link between the client's ongoing behavior and what the client experiences next. Erickson's use of these linkage principles is an excellent example of his ability to employ the client's own modeling principles in pacing and leading the client into new and medically, dentally, or psychotherapeutically beneficial directions. Particularly in the case of the stronger forms of linkage, Implied Causatives and Cause-Effect statements, the important issue is not logic but the modeling principles by which the client organizes his experience. Specifically, since clients accept Implied Causatives and Cause-Effect as principles in organizing their experiences, Erickson is simply making use of these modeling principles to achieve the trance goals.

The second type of pacing statements are descriptions of the client's ongoing, non-observable experience. This may strike the reader as something of a paradox. How is it possible accurately to describe someone else's experience unless that person's experience is observable? Here we encounter Erickson's exquisite sense of language use. He makes extensive use of the linguistic modeling principles to present the client with a series of statements which are vague and ambiguous yet, to the untrained ear, sound quite specific. Erickson may say, for example:

> *. . . and you may be aware of a certain sensation . . .*

The client sitting there, listening to the sound of Erickson's voice, certainly is experiencing some sensation, and as he hears Erickson say the phrase *a certain sensation,* he understands the phrase to refer to one of his present sensations, thereby, the statement is an accurate description of the client's ongoing, non-observable experience. The phrase *a certain sensation* fails to pick out a specific sensation, thereby leaving the client the freedom to attach it to some portion of his ongoing experience. Phrases which fail to pick out specific portions of the listener's experience are said to have no **referential index**. Thus, by using phrases which fail to have referential indices, Erickson is able to successfully pace the client. There are a number of linguistic modeling principles which Erickson uses systematically in his work which allow him to pace and lead non-observable behavior. The following is a brief overview of some of these.

Erickson often uses a technique which is closely related to the lack-of-referential-index technique. For example, he may say:

> *. . . the tomato plant can feel good . . .*

For many native speakers of English, this sentence is not well formed. They typically balk at accepting the claim that plants feel anything. Rather, in their model of the world, only animals and humans feel things; to claim that a tomato plant can feel something is to violate what linguists call a **selectional restriction**. When the client hears the sentence with such a selectional restriction violation, the burden of constructing some other meaning for this communication falls upon him. The most frequent outcome of his resulting attempt to make sense of such a sentence is that he comes to understand (unconsciously) a sentence such as:

> *. . . you* (the client) *can feel good . . .*

One of the most powerful of these linguistic modeling techniques is **deletion**, the case in which a portion of the meaning of the sentence (the Deep Structure) has no representation in Surface Structure, that is, in the actual sentence spoken to the client. Erickson may, for example, say:

> *. . . and continue to wonder . . . and really . . .*

The predicate *wonder* is a word which describes the process of someone's wondering about something. However, as it appears in this Surface Structure or sentence, who is doing the wondering and what that unmentioned person is wondering is not specified; those portions of the meaning have been deleted. This leaves the information which is missing to be filled in by the listener.[6]

A linguistic process closely related to the lack of referential index and deletion is the phenomenon called **nominalization**.

Nominalization is the representation of a process word — a predicate — by an event word — a noun.

For example, Erickson may say:

. . . a certain sensation . . .

The word *sensation* is a noun in its use in this phrase, yet it is derived from a predicate which has more information associated with it, specifically:

SENSE (someone *sensing,* someone/something being *sensed*)

That is, the noun *sensation* is the result of the linguistic process of nominalization — the transformation of a predicate *sense* into a noun. In the process of this transformation, the information of who is doing the sensing and who or what is being sensed has disappeared. Therefore, the referential indices of the sensor and the person/thing being sensed are gone, and the resulting nominalization is maximally available for interpretation by the listener as a statement which is applicable to his ongoing experience.

Predicates of natural language systems differ greatly as to their specificity. For example, the predicates:

touch . . . kiss

are successively more specified. The predicate *touch* simply indicates that some people/objects have made physical contact, while the predicate *kiss* adds an additional piece of information, namely, that the person initiating contact made contact with his lips. The predicate *kiss* is still, however, unspecified as to where on the person or object the contact (kiss) was made. Erickson exercises his linguistic skills in pacing a client's non-observable experience by selecting verbs which are relatively unspecified, thereby maximizing the likelihood that the statement that he makes will fit the client's ongoing experience. Predicates such as:

wonder, think, feel, sense, know, experience, understand, become aware of, remember occur frequently in his pacing and leading statements. These are relatively unspecified predicates. In addition, many of these predicates are predicates which simply by their occurrence call the client's attention to some portion of his own experience, thereby successfully both pacing and directing his ongoing experience, as in the example of the phrase *a certain sensation* presented previously.

Erickson frequently employs this class of unspecified predicates with the technique of **mind reading**. Mind-reading statements are statements in which one person claims to have knowledge of the thoughts or feelings of another person without specifying the process by which he came to have that information. In one sense, this entire discussion of the way in which Erickson paces and then leads the client's non-observable behavior is a discussion of his mind-reading ability. An example of this technique is:

> *. . . I know that you are wondering . . .*

Here Erickson is claiming to have knowledge of the internal, non-observable experience of the client without specifying the process by which he has secured that information.

As trance induction proceeds, the amount of pacing as opposed to leading that the hypnotist does shifts dramatically. Trance induction and suggestion to the client in trance are typically a mixture of pacing and leading. We review briefly some of the techniques Erickson uses which typically occur more frequently as leading statements than as pacing statements. In leading the client's experience, Erickson characteristically does not instruct the client directly, rather he makes skillful use of a number of natural language modeling principles. For example, rather than instruct the client to sit down in a chair, he might say:

> *. . . yes, and I wonder whether you have noticed the chair that you will soon find yourself comfortably sitting in . . .*

Here he is using the principle of **presupposition**. In natural language systems, when a relative clause — *that you will soon find yourself comfortably sitting in* — is attached to a noun phrase —*the chair* — in order for the sentence in which it appears to make any sense, the listener must accept as accurate the description given in the relative clause. Presuppositions are the linguistic equivalent of what is more commonly called assumption, basic organizing principles without which the information being presented makes no sense. Another example of the typical use of presuppositions by Erickson is:

> ... I wonder whether you are aware that you are deeply in trance ...

Here Erickson uses the predicate *aware*. This is a **factive** predicate — that is, a predicate which presupposes the truth of the clause which follows it. In order to make sense out of Erickson's communication, the client must accept the clause which follows the predicate *aware* as true, namely, *that you are deeply in trance.* Furthermore, the clause *that you are deeply in trance* itself contains another presuppositional device — the use of an adverb, *deeply.* By using the adverb (a Deep Structure predicate) within the clause, the remainder of the clause is presupposed. If Erickson says to a client:

> ... Are you deeply in trance? ...

the issue is whether the client is *deeply* in trance, not whether the client is in trance — that much is presupposed. Natural languages contain a large number of devices for the communication of presupposition. Thus, in the case of the first example:

> ... I wonder whether you are aware that you are deeply in trance ...

Erickson compounds the presuppositions, making it very difficult for the client to challenge the truth of the statement *you are in trance.*

Another common pattern in Erickson's work is the use of **conversational postulates.** Rather than directly instruct the client to place his hands on his thighs, Erickson, typically, will say:

> Can you place your hands on your thighs?

This communication has the form of a question, a question to which the response which is literally appropriate is either *yes* or *no.* However, this form of yes/no questions typically carry with it the force of the command closely related to it, namely, *put your hands on your thighs.* By using the indirect communication, Erickson bypasses altogether the issue of resistance and control, leaving the client to respond as he chooses.

Erickson make extensive use of a very powerful form of language patterning which is closely related to this last one, the pattern of **lesser included structures.** Erickson may, as an example, say to a client:

> ... *I knew a man once who really understood how to feel good about* ...

Notice that the portion of Erickson's communication in bold type itself is identical with the command *feel good.* As another, slightly different example, Erickson may say:

> ... *I wonder whether you are completely comfortable* ...

Here the lesser included structure is the indirect question, *Are you completely comfortable.* However, since the question is a lesser portion of a statement, there is no direct request on Erickson's part for a reply. Characteristically, the client does make a response, covertly responding to the communication as a question. Lesser included structures are a very powerful way of directing the client's experience and building up response potential. This technique becomes even more powerful when combined with the technique of **analogical marking.**

Analogical marking is the use of non-linguistic modes of communication to identify and sort the linguistic communication into separate message units. Erickson will, for example, shift his tonality (an analogical mark) for the portions of the sentence in bold type:

> ... *knew a man who really understood how to feel good about* ...

Since clients are rarely conscious of such analogical shifts (and, if conscious of such shifts, they are very unlikely to associate them with the simultaneously presented verbal material), the result of Erickson's communication is the double communication — the story Erickson is telling to the conscious mind and the command *feel good* to the unconscious mind. Erickson uses visual as well as auditory cues to analogically mark his verbal communication, fragmenting them into separate message units.

We have presented a brief and sketchy overview of some of the patterns employed by Erickson in his work. There are several additional effects of this type of communication which are important in understanding the powerful effect which Erickson has in his work. By communicating indirectly, he avoids the issue of resistance to a large extent. Furthermore, he leaves the client the maximum freedom to choose (on the unconscious level) to what portions of the communication he will respond. Communicating in this way also engages the client at the unconscious level of communication while simultaneously occupying the client's conscious mind in a way which prevents it from intruding unhelpfully in the process of trance induction and suggestion. Finally, the client is able to participate more actively and creatively (again at the unconscious level of behavior) in the process of hypnotic work.

This completes the overview of some of the patterns which occur frequently in Erickson's trance work. We present now one of Erickson's articles which includes trance work. First, we present the article in its entirety; then we will extract lines of the induction and suggestion which illustrate each of the patterns which we have presented. We wish to emphasize that there are many examples of these patterns in the article; we will extract only enough examples to allow the reader to recognize these patterns as Erickson's. In addition, we are aware that Erickson uses other patterns in his trance work in this article which we will, for the moment, ignore; the presentation here is not exhaustive.

The Interspersal Hypnotic Technique for Symptom Correction and Pain Control[7]

Innumerable Times this author has been asked to commit to print in detail the hypnotic technique he had employed to alleviate intolerable pain or to correct various other problems. The verbal replies made to these many requests have never seemed to be adequate since they were invariably prefaced by the earnest assertion that the technique in itself serves no other purpose than that of securing and fixating the patient's attention, creating in him a receptive and responsive mental state, and thereby enabling him to benefit from unrealized or only partially realized potentials for behavior of various types. With this achieved by the hypnotic technique, there is then the opportunity to proffer suggestions and instructions serving to aid and to direct the patient in achieving the desired goal or goals. In other words, the hypnotic technique serves only to induce a favorable setting in which to instruct the patient in a more advantageous use of his own potentials of behavior.

Since the hypnotic technique is primarily a means to an end while therapy derives from the guidance of the patient's behavioral capacities, it follows that, within limits, the same hypnotic technique can be utilized for patients with widely diverse problems. To illustrate, two instances will be cited in which the same technique was employed, once for a patient with a distressing neurotic problem and once for a patient suffering from intolerable pain from terminal malignant disease. The technique is one that the author has employed on the illiterate subject and upon the college graduate, in experimental situations and for clinical purposes. Often it has been used to secure, to fixate, and to hold a difficult patient's attention and to distract him from creating difficulties that would impede therapy. It is a technique employing ideas that are clear, comprehensible, but which by their patent irrelevance to the patient-physician relationship and situation distract the patient. Thereby the patient is prevented from intruding unhelpfully into a situation which he cannot understand and for which he is seeking help. At the same time, a readiness to understand and to respond is created within the patient. Thus, a favorable setting is evolved for the elicitation of needful and helpful behavioral potentialities not previously used, or not fully used or perhaps misused by the patient.

The first instance to be cited will be given without any account of the hypnotic technique employed. Instead, there will be given the helpful instructions, suggestions, and guiding ideas which enabled the patient to achieve his therapeutic goal and which were interspersed among the ideas constituting the hypnotic technique. These therapeutic ideas will not be cited as repetitiously as they were verbalized to the patient for the reason that they are more easily comprehended in cold print than when uttered as a part of a stream of utterances. Yet, these few repeated suggestions in the hypnotic situation served to meet the patient's needs adequately.

The patient was a 62-year-old retired farmer with only an eighth-grade education, but decidedly intelligent and well-read. He actually possessed a delightful, charming, out-going personality, but he was most unhappy, filled with resentment, bitterness, hostility, suspicion and despair. Approximately two years previously for some unknown or forgotten reason (regarded by the author as unimportant and as having no bearing upon the problem of therapy) he had developed a urinary frequency that was most distressing to him. Approximately every half hour he felt a compelling urge to urinate, an urge that was painful, that he could not control, and which would result in a wetting of his trousers if he did not yield to it. This urge was constantly present day and night. It interfered with his sleep, his eating, his social adjustments and compelled him to keep within close reach of a lavatory and to carry a briefcase containing several pairs of trousers for use when he was "caught short." He explained that he had brought into the office a briefcase containing three pairs of trousers and he stated that he had visited a lavatory before leaving for the author's office, another on the way and that he had visited the office lavatory before entering the office and that he expected to interrupt the interview with the author by at least one other such visit.

He related that he had consulted more than 100 physicians and well-known clinics. He had been cystoscoped more than 40 times, had had innumerable x-ray pictures taken and countless tests, some of which were electroencephalograms and electrocardiograms. Always he was assured that his bladder was normal; many times he was offered the suggestion to return after a month or two for further study; and "too many times" he was told that "it's all in your head"; that he had no problem at all, that he "should get busy doing something instead of being retired, and to stop pestering doctors and being an old crock." All of this had made him feel like committing suicide.

He had described his problem to a number of writers of syndicated medical columns in newspapers, several of whom offered him in his stamped, self-addressed envelope a pontifical platitudinous dissertation upon his problem stressing it as one of obscure organic origin. In all of his searching, not once had it been suggested that he seek psychiatric aid.

On his own initiative, after reading two of the misleading, misinforming and essentially fraudulent books on "do-it-yourself hypnosis," he did seek the aid of stage hypnotists, in all three in number. Each offered him the usual blandishments, reassurances, and promises common to that type of shady medical practice and each failed completely in repeated attempts at inducing a hypnotic trance. Each charged an exorbitant fee (as judged by a standard medical fee, and especially in relation to the lack of benefit received).

As a result of all this mistreatment, the medical no better than that of the charlatans and actually less forgivable, he had become bitter, disillusioned, resentful and openly hostile, and he was seriously considering suicide. A gas station attendant suggested that he see a psychiatrist and recommended the author on the basis of a Sunday newspaper article. This accounted for his visit to the author.

Having completed his narrative, he leaned back in his chair, folded his arms, and challengingly said, "Now psychiatrize and hypnotize me and cure this _____ bladder of mine."

During the narration of the patient's story, the author had listened with every appearance of rapt attention except for a minor idling with his hands, thereby shifting the position of objects on his desk. This idling included a turning of the face of the desk clock away from the patient. As he listened to the patient's bitter account of his experiences, the author was busy speculating upon possible therapeutic approaches to a patient so obviously unhappy, so resentful toward medical care and physicians, and so challenging in attitude. He certainly did not appear to be likely to be receptive and responsive to anything the author might do or say. As the author puzzled over this problem there came to mind the problem of pain control for a patient suffering greatly in a terminal state of malignant disease. That patient had constituted a comparable instance where a hypnotherapeutic approach had been most difficult, and yet, success had been achieved. Both patients had in common the experience of growing plants for a livelihood, both were hostile and resentful, and both were contemptuous of hypnosis. Hence, when the patient issued his challenge of "psychiatrize and hypnotize me," the author, with no further ado, launched into the same technique employed with that other patient to achieve a hypnotherapeutic state in which helpful suggestions, instructions, and directions could be offered with reasonable expectation that they would be accepted and acted upon responsively in accord with the patient's actual needs and behavioral potentials.

The only differences for the two patients were that the interwoven therapeutic material for the one patient pertained to bladder function and duration of time. For the other patient, the interwoven therapeutic instructions pertained to body comfort, to sleep, to appetite, to the enjoyment of the family, to an absence of any need for medication and to the continued enjoyment of time without concern about the morrow.

The actual verbal therapy offered, interspersed as it was in the ideation of the technique itself, was as follows, with the interspersing denoted by dots.

> You know, we could think of your bladder needing emptying every 15 minutes instead of every half hour . . . . Not difficult to think that . . . . A watch can run slow . . . . or fast . . . . be wrong even a minute . . . . even two, five minutes . . . . or think of bladder every half hour . . . . like you've been doing . . . . maybe it was 35, 40

minutes sometimes . . . . like to make it an hour . . . .
what's the difference . . . . 35, 36 minutes, 41, 42, 45
minutes . . . . not much difference . . . . not important
difference . . . . 45, 46, 47 minutes . . . . all the
same . . . . lots of times you maybe had to wait a second or
two . . . . felt like an hour or two . . . . you made
it . . . . you can again . . . . 47 minutes, 50 minutes, what's
the difference . . . . stop to think, no great difference,
nothing important . . . . just like 50 minutes, 60 minutes,
just minutes . . . . anybody that can wait half an hour can
wait an hour . . . . I know it . . . . you are learning . . . . not
bad to learn . . . . in fact, good . . . . come to think of it,
you have had to wait when somebody got there ahead of
you . . . . you made it too . . . . can again . . . . and
again . . . . all you want to . . . . hour and 5 minutes . . . .
hour and 5½ minutes . . . . what's the difference . . . . or
even 6½ minutes . . . . make it 10½, hour and 10½
minutes . . . . one minute, 2 minutes, one hour, 2 hours,
what's the difference . . . . you got half a century or better
of practice in waiting behind you . . . . you can use all
that . . . . why not use it . . . . you can do it . . . . probably
surprise you a lot . . . . won't even think of it . . . . why not
surprise yourself at home . . . . good idea . . . . nothing
better than a surprise . . . . an unexpected surprise . . . .
how long can you hold out . . . . that's the surprise . . . .
longer than you even thought . . . . lots longer . . . . might
as well begin . . . . nice feeling to begin . . . . to keep
on . . . . Say, why don't you just forget what I've been
talking about and just keep it in the back of your mind.
Good place for it — can't lose. Never mind the tomato
plant — just what was important about your bladder —
pretty good, feel fine, nice surprise — say, why don't you
start feeling rested, refreshed right now, wider awake than
you were earlier this morning (this last statement is, to the
patient, an indirect, emphatic, definitive instruction to
arouse from his trance). Then, (as a dismissal but no
recognizable as such consciously by the patient) why don't
you take a nice leisurely walk home, thinking about
nothing (an amnesia instruction for both the trance and his
problem, and also a confusion measure to obscure the fact
that he had already spent 1½ hours in the office)? I'll be

able to see you at 10:00 a.m. a week from today
(furthering his conscious illusion, resulting from his
amnesia, that nothing yet had been done except to give
him an appointment).

A week later he appeared and launched into an excited
account of arriving home and turning on the television with an
immediate firm intention of delaying urination as long as possible.
He watched a two-hour movie and drank two glasses of water
during the commercials. He decided to extend the time another
hour and suddenly discovered that he had so much bladder
distension that he had to visit the lavatory. He looked at his watch
and discovered that he had waited four hours. The patient leaned
back in his chair, beaming happily at the author, obviously
expecting praise. Almost immediately he leaned forward with a
startled look and declared in amazement, "It all comes back to me
now. I never give it a thought till just now. I plumb forgot the
whole thing. Say, you must have hypnotized me. You were doing
a lot of talking about growing a tomato plant and I was trying to
get the point of it and the next thing I knew I was walking home.
Come to think of it, I must of been in your office over an hour
and it took an hour to walk home. It wasn't no four hours I held
back, it was over six hours at least. Come to think of it, that ain't
all. That was a week ago that happened. Now I recollect I ain't had
a bit of trouble all week — slept fine — no getting up. Funny how
a man can get up in the morning, his mind all set on keeping an
appointment to tell something, and forget a whole week has went
by. Say, when I told you to psychiatrize and hypnotize me, you
sure took it serious. I'm right grateful to you. How much do I owe
you?"

Essentially, the case was completed and the remainder of the
hour was spent in social small talk with a view of detecting any
possible doubts or uncertainties in the patient. There were none,
nor, in the months that have passed, have there occurred any.

The above case report allows the reader to understand in part
how, during a technique of suggestions for trance induction and
trance maintenance, hypnotherapeutic suggestions can be interspersed for a specific goal. In the author's experience, such an
interspersing of therapeutic suggestions among the suggestions for
trance maintenance may often render the therapeutic suggestions

much more effective. The patient hears them, understands them, but before he can take issue with them or question them in any way, his attention is captured by the trance maintenance suggestions. And these in turn are but a continuance of the trance induction suggestions. Thus, there is given to the therapeutic suggestion an aura of significance and effectiveness deriving from the already effective induction and maintenance suggestions. Then again the same therapeutic suggestions can be repeated in this interspersed fashion, perhaps repeated many times, until the therapist feels confident that the patient has absorbed the therapeutic suggestions adequately. Then the therapist can progress to another aspect of therapy using the same interspersal technique.

The above report does not indicate the number of repetitions for each of the therapeutic suggestions for the reason that the number must vary with each set of ideas and understandings conveyed and with each patient and each therapeutic problem. Additionally such interspersal of suggestions for amnesia and posthypnotic suggestions among the suggestions for trance maintenance can be done most effectively. To illustrate from everyday life: A double task assignment is usually more effective than the separate assignment of the same two tasks. For example, a mother may say, "Johnny, as you put away your bicycle just step over and close the garage door." This has the sound of a single task, one aspect of which favors the execution of another aspect, and thus there is the effect of making the task seem easier. To ask that the bicycle be put away and then to ask that the garage door be closed has every sound of being two separate, not to be combined, tasks. To the separate tasks, a refusal can be given easily to one or the other task or to both. But a refusal when the tasks are combined into a single task means what? That he will not put away the bicycle? That he will not step over to the garage? That he will not close the garage door?

The very extent of the effort needed to identify what one is refusing in itself is a deterrent to refusal. Nor can a refusal of the "whole thing" be offered comfortably. Hence Johnny may perform the combined task unwillingly but may prefer to do so rather than to analyze the situation. To the single tasks he can easily say "later" to each. But to the combined task, he cannot say, "later" since, if he puts away the bicycle "later," he must "immediately" step over to the garage and "immediately" close the door. This is specious reasoning, but it is the "emotional reasoning" that is common in daily life, and daily living is not an exercise in logic. As a common practice the author says to a patient, "As you sit down in the chair, just go into a trance." The patient is surely going to sit down in the chair. But going into a trance is made contingent upon sitting down, hence, a trance state develops from what the patient was most certainly going to do. By combining psychotherapeutic, amnestic and posthypnotic suggestions with those suggestions used first to induce a trance and then to maintain that trance constitutes an effective measure in securing desired results. Contingency values are decidedly effective. As a further illustration, more than once a patient who has developed a trance upon simply sitting down has said to the author, "I didn't intend to go into a trance today." In reply the author has stated, "Then perhaps you would like to awaken from the trance and hence, *as you understand that* you can go back into a trance when you need to, *you will awaken.* Thus, the "awakening" is made contingent upon "understanding," thereby insuring further trances through association by contingency.

With this explanation of rationale, the problem of the second patient will be presented after a few preliminary statements. These are that the author was reared on a farm, enjoyed and still enjoys growing plants, and has read with interest about the processes of seed germination and plant growth.

The first patient was a retired farmer. The second, who will be called "Joe" for convenience, was a florist. He began his career as a boy by peddling flowers, saving his pennies, buying more flowers to peddle, etc. Soon he was able to buy a small parcel of land on which to grow more flowers with loving care while he enjoyed their beauty which he wanted to share with others, and in turn, to get more land and to grow more flowers, etc. Eventually he became the leading florist in a large city. Joe literally loved every aspect of his business, was intensely devoted to it but he was also a good husband, a good father, a good friend and a highly respected and valued member of the community.

Then one fateful September a surgeon removed a growth from the side of Joe's face, being careful not to disfigure Joe's face too much. The pathologist reported the growth to be a malignancy. Radical therapy was then instituted but it was promptly recognized as "too late."

Joe was informed that he had about a month left to live. Joe's reaction was, to say the least, unhappy and distressed. In addition he was experiencing much pain, in fact, extremely severe pain.

At the end of the second week in October, a relative of Joe's urgently requested the author to employ hypnosis on Joe for pain relief since narcotics were proving of little value. In view of the prognosis that had been given for Joe, the author agreed reluctantly to see him, stipulating that all medication be discontinued at 4:00 a.m. of the day of the author's arrival. To this the physicians in charge of Joe at the hospital courteously agreed.

Shortly before the author was introduced to Joe, he was informed that Joe disliked even the mention of the word hypnosis. Also, one of Joe's children, a resident in psychiatry at a well-known clinic, did not believe in hypnosis and had apparently been confirmed in this disbelief by the psychiatric staff of the clinic, none of whom is known to have had any first-hand knowledge of hypnosis. This resident would be present and the inference was that Joe knew of that disbelief.

The author was introduced to Joe who acknowledged the introduction in a most courteous and friendly fashion. It is doubtful if Joe really knew why the author was there. Upon inspecting Joe, it was noted that much of the side of his face and neck was missing because of surgery, ulceration, maceration and necrosis. A tracheotomy had been performed on Joe and he could not talk. He communicated by pencil and paper, many pads of which were ready at hand. The information was given that every 4 hours Joe had been receiving narcotics (¼ grain of morphine or 100 milligrams of Demerol) and heavy sedation with barbituates. He slept little. Special nurses were constantly at hand. Yet Joe was constantly hopping out of bed, writing innumerable notes, some pertaining to his business, some to his family, but many of them were expressive of complaints and demands for additional help. Severe pain distressed him continuously and he could not understand why the doctors could not handle their business as efficiently and as competently as he did his floral business. His situation enraged him because it constituted failure in his eyes. Success worked for and fully merited had always been a governing principle in his life. When things went wrong with his business, he made certain to correct them. Why did not the doctors do the same? The doctors had medicine for pain so why was he allowed to suffer such intolerable pain?

After the introduction, Joe wrote, "What you want?" This constituted an excellent opening and the author began his technique of trance induction and pain relief. This will not be given in its entirety since a large percentage of the statements made were repeated, not necessarily in succession but frequently by referring back to a previous remark and then repeating a paragraph or two.

Another preliminary statement needed is that the author was most dubious about achieving any kind of success with Joe since, in addition to his physical condition, there were definite evidences of toxic reactions to excessive medication. Despite the author's unfavorable view of possibilities, there was one thing of which he could be confident. He could keep his doubts to himself and he could let Joe know by manner, tone of voice, by everything said that the author was genuinely interested in him, was genuinely desirous of helping him. If even that little could be communicated to Joe, it should be of some comfort, however small, to Joe and to the family members and to the nurses within listening distance in the side room.

The author began:
Joe, I would like to talk to you. I know you are a florist, that you grow flowers, and I grew up on a farm in Wisconsin and I liked growing flowers. I still do. So I would like to have you take a seat in that easy chair as I talk to you. I'm going to say a lot of things to you but it won't be about flowers because you know more than I do about flowers. *That isn't what you want.*
(The reader will note that italics will be used to denote interspersed hypnotic suggestions which may be syllables, words, phrases or sentences uttered with a slightly different intonation.)
Now as I talk and I can do so *comfortably,* I wish that you will *listen to me comfortably* as I talk about a tomato plant. That is an odd thing to talk about. It makes one *curious. Why talk about a tomato plant?* One puts a tomato seed in the ground. One can *feel hope* that it will grow into a tomato plant that *will bring satisfaction* by the fruit it has. The seed soaks up water, *not very much difficulty* in doing that because of the rains that *bring peace and comfort* and the joy of growing to flowers and

tomatoes. That little seed, Joe, slowly swells, sends out a little rootlet with cilia on it. Now you may not know what cilia are, but cilia are *things that work* to help the tomato seed grow, to push up above the ground as a sprouting plant, and *you can listen to me Joe* so I will keep on talking and *you can keep on listening, wondering, just wondering what you can really learn,* and here is your pencil and your pad but speaking of the tomato plant, it grows so slowly. *You cannot see* it grow, *you cannot hear* it grow, but grow it does — the first little leaflike things on the stalk, the fine little hairs on the stem, those hairs are on the leaves too like the cilia on the roots, they must make the tomato plant *feel very good, very comfortable* if you can think of a plant as feeling and then, *you can't see* it growing, *you can't feel* it growing but another leaf appears on that little tomato stalk and then another. Maybe, and this is talking like a child, maybe the tomato plant does *feel comfortable and peaceful* as it grows. Each day it grows and grows and grows, *it's so comfortable Joe* to watch a plant grow and *not see* its growth *not feel* it but just know that *all is getting better* for that little tomato plant that is adding yet another leaf and still another and a branch and it is *growing comfortably* in all directions.

(Much of the above by this time had been repeated many times, sometimes just phrases, sometimes sentences. Care was taken to vary the wording and also to repeat the hypnotic suggestions. Quite some time after the author had begun, Joe's wife came tiptoeing into the room carrying a sheet of paper on which was written the question, "When are you going to start the hypnosis?" The author failed to cooperate with her by looking at the paper and it was necessary for her to thrust the sheet of paper in front of the author and therefore in front of Joe. The author was continuing his description of the tomato plant uninterruptedly and Joe's wife, as she looked at Joe, saw that he was not seeing her, did not know that she was there, that he was in a somnambulistic trance. She withdrew at once.)

And soon the tomato plant will have a bud form somewhere, on one branch or another, but it makes no difference because all the branches, the whole tomato plant will soon have those nice little buds — I wonder if the tomato plant can, *Joe, feel really feel a kind of comfort.* You know, Joe, a plant is a wonderful thing, and *it is so nice, so pleasing* just to be able to think about a plant as if it were a man. Would such a plant *have nice feelings, a sense of comfort* as the tiny little tomatoes begin to form, so tiny, yet so *full of promise to give you the desire to eat* a luscious tomato, sunripened, it's so *nice to have food in one's stomach,* that wonderful feeling a child, a thirsty child, has and can *want a drink, Joe,* is that the way the tomato plant feels when the rain falls and washes everything so that *all feels well* (pause) *You know, Joe,* a tomato plant just flourishes each day *just a day at a time.* I like to think the tomato plant can *know the fullness of comfort each day. You know, Joe, just one day at a time* for the tomato plant. That's the way for all tomato plants.

(Joe suddenly came out of the trance, appeared disoriented, hopped upon the bed, waved his arms, and his behavior was highly suggestive of the sudden surges of toxicity one sees in patients who have reacted unfavorably to barbiturates. Joe did not seem to hear or see the author until he hopped off the bed and had walked toward the author. A firm grip was taken on Joe's arm and then immediately loosened. The nurse was summoned. She mopped perspiration from his forehead, changed his surgical dressings, and gave him, by tube, some ice water. Joe then let the author lead him back to his chair. After a pretense by the author of being curious about Joe's forearm, Joe seized his pencil and paper and wrote, "Talk, talk.)

Oh yes, Joe, I grew up on a farm, I think a tomato seed is a wonderful thing, *think, Joe, think* in that little seed there does *sleep so restfully, so comfortably* a beautiful plant yet to be grown that will bear such interesting leaves and branches. The leaves, the branches look so beautiful, that beautiful, rich color, *you can really feel happy* looking at a tomato seed, thinking about the wonderful plant it contains *asleep, resting, comfortable, Joe.* I'm soon going to leave for lunch and I'll be back and I will talk some more.

The above is a summary to indicate the ease with which

hypnotherapeutic suggestions can be included in the trance induction and trance maintenance suggestions which are important additionally as a vehicle for the transmission of therapy. Of particular significance is Joe's own request that the author "talk." Despite his toxic state, spasmodically evident, Joe was definitely accessible. Moreover he learned rapidly despite the absurdly amateurish rhapsody the author offered about a tomato seed and plant. Joe had no real interest in pointless endless remarks about a tomato plant. Joe wanted freedom from pain, he wanted comfort, rest, sleep. This was what was uppermost in Joe's mind, foremost in his emotional desires, and he would have a compelling need to try to find something of value to him in the author's babbling. That desired value was there, so spoken that Joe could literally receive it without realizing it. Joe's arousal from the trance was only some minutes after the author had said so seemingly innocuously, "want a drink, Joe." Nor was the re-induction of the trance difficult, achieved by two brief phrases, "think Joe think" and "sleep so restfully, so comfortably" imbedded in a rather meaningless sequence of ideas. But what Joe wanted and needed was in that otherwise meaningless narration, and he promptly accepted it.

During the lunch time, Joe was first restful and then slowly restless, another toxic episode occurred, as reported by the nurse. By the time the author returned Joe was waiting impatiently for him. Joe wanted to communicate by writing notes. Some were illegible because of his extreme impatience in writing. He would irritatedly rewrite them. A relative helped the author to read these notes. They concerned things about Joe, his past history, his business, his family and "last week terrible," "yesterday was terrible." There were no complaints, no demands, but there were some requests for information about the author. After a fashion a satisfying conversation was had with him as was judged by an increasing loss of his restlessness. When it was suggested that he cease walking around and sit in the chair used earlier, he did so readily and looked expectantly at the author.

You know, Joe, I could talk to you some more about the tomato plant and if I did you would probably go to sleep, in fact, a good sound sleep.

(This opening statement has every earmark of being no more

than a casual commonplace utterance. If the patient responds hypnotically, as Joe promptly did, all is well. If the patient does not respond, all you have said was just a commonplace remark, not at all noteworthy. Had Joe not gone into a trance immediately, there could have been a variation such as: "But instead, let's talk about the tomato flower. You have seen movies of flowers *slowly, slowly* opening, giving one *a sense of peace, a sense of comfort* as you watch the unfolding. So beautiful, *so restful* to watch. One can *feel such infinite comfort* watching such a movie.")

It does not seem to the author that more needs to be said about the technique of trance induction and maintenance and the interspersal of therapeutic suggestions. Another illustration will be given later in this paper.

Joe's response that afternoon was excellent despite several intervening episodes of toxic behavior and several periods where the author deliberately interrupted his work to judge more adequately the degree and amount of Joe's learning.

Upon departure that evening, the author was cordially shaken by [the] hand by Joe, whose toxic state was much lessened. Joe had no complaints, he did not seem to have distressing pain, and he seemed to be pleased and happy.

Relatives were concerned about post-hypnotic suggestions but they were reassured that such had been given. This had been done most gently in describing so much in detail and repetition the growth of the tomato plant and then, with careful emphasis, *"You know Joe," "Know the fullness of comfort each day,"* and *"You know, Joe, just one day at a time."*

About a month later around the middle of November, the author was requested to see Joe again. Upon arriving at Joe's home, he was told a rather regrettable but not actually unhappy story. Joe had continued his excellent response after the author's departure on that first occasion, but hospital gossip had spread the story of Joe's hypnosis and interns, residents, and staff men came in to take advantage of Joe's capacity to be a good subject. They made all the errors possible for uninformed amateurs with superstitious misconceptions of hypnosis. Their behavior infuriated Joe who knew that the author had done none of the offensive things they were doing. This was a fortunate realization since it permitted Joe to keep all the benefits acquired from the author without letting his hostilities toward hypnosis interfere.

After several days of annoyance, Joe left the hospital and went home, keeping one nurse in constant attendance, but her duties were relatively few.

During that month at home he had actually gained weight and strength. Rarely did a surge of pain occur and when it did it could be controlled either with aspirin or with 25 milligrams of Demerol. Joe was very happy to be with his family and there was considerable fruitful activity about which the author is not fully informed.

Joe's greeting to the author on the second visit was one of obvious pleasure. However, the author noted that Joe was keeping a wary eye on him, hence, great care was taken to be completely casual and to avoid any hand movement that could be remotely misconstrued as a "hypnotic pass" such as the hospital staff had employed.

Framed pictures painted by a highly talented member of his family were proudly displayed. There was much casual conversation about Joe's improvement and his weight gain and the author was repeatedly hard pushed to find simple replies to conceal pertinent suggestions. Joe did volunteer to sit down and let the author talk to him. Although the author was wholly casual in manner, the situation was thought to be difficult to handle without arousing Joe's suspicions. Perhaps this was an unfounded concern but the author wished to be most careful. Finally the measure was employed of reminiscing about "our visit last October." Joe did not realize how easily this visit could be pleasantly vivified for him by such a simple statement as,

> I talked about a tomato plant then and it almost seems as if I could be *talking about a tomato plant right now. It is so enjoyable to talk about a seed, a plant.*

Thus there was, clinically speaking, a re-creation of all of the favorable aspects of that original interview.

Joe was most insistent on supervising the author's luncheon that day, which was a steak barbecued under Joe's watchful eye in the back yard beside the swimming pool. It was a happy gathering of four people thoroughly enjoying being together, Joe being obviously most happy.

After luncheon, Joe proudly displayed the innumerable plants, many of them rare, that he had personally planted in the large back yard. Joe's wife furnished the Latin and common names for the plants and Joe was particularly pleased when the author recognized and commented on some rare plant. Nor was this a pretense of interest, since the author is still interested in growing plants. Joe regarded this interest in common to be a bond of friendship.

During the afternoon, Joe sat down voluntarily, his very manner making evident that the author was free to do whatever he wished. A long monologue by the author ensued in which were included psychotherapeutic suggestions of continued ease, comfort, freedom from pain, enjoyment of family, good appetite, and a continuing pleased interest in all surroundings. All of these and other similar suggestions were interspersed unnoticeably among the author's many remarks. These covered a multitude of topics to preclude Joe from analyzing or recognizing the interspersing of suggestions. Also, for adequate disguise, the author needed a variety of topics. Whether or not such care was needed in view of the good rapport is a debatable question, but the author preferred to take no risks.

Medically, the malignancy was continuing to progress, but despite this fact, Joe was in much better physical condition than he had been a month previously. When the author took his departure, Joe invited him to return again.

Joe knew that the author was going on a lecture trip in late November and early December. Quite unexpected by the author, a long distance telephone call was received just before the author's departure on this trip. The call was from Joe's wife who stated, "Joe is on the extension line and wants to say 'hello' to you, so listen." Two brief puffs of air were heard. Joe had held the telephone mouthpiece over his tracheotomy tube and had exhaled forcibly twice to simulate "hello." His wife stated that both she and Joe extended their best wishes for the trip and a casual conversation of friends ensued with Joe's wife reading Joe's written notes.

A Christmas greeting card was received from Joe and his family. In a separate letter Joe's wife said that "the hypnosis is doing well, but Joe's condition is failing." Early in January Joe was weak but comfortable. Finally, in his wife's words, "Joe died quietly January 21."

The author is well aware that the prediction of the duration of life for any patient suffered from a fatal illness is most questionable. Joe's physical condition in October did not promise very much. The symptom amelioration, abatement and actual abolishment effected by hypnosis, and the freedom of Joe's body from potent medications, conducive only of unawareness, unquestionably increased his span of life while at the same time permitting an actual brief physical betterment in general. This was attested clearly by his improved condition at home and his gain in weight. That Joe lived until that latter part of January despite the extensiveness of his malignant disease undoubtedly attests to the vigor with which Joe undertook to live the remainder of his life as enjoyably as possible, a vigor expressive of the manner in which he had lived his life and built his business.

To clarify still further this matter of the technique of the interspersal of therapeutic suggestions among trance induction and trance maintenance suggestions, it might be well to report the author's original experimental work done while he was on the Research Service of the Worcester State Hospital in Worcester, Massachusetts, in the early 1930's.

The Research Service was concerned with the study of the numerous problems of schizophrenia and the possibilities of solving some of them. To the author, the psychological manifestations were of paramount interest. For example, just what did a stream of disconnected, rapidly uttered incoherencies mean? Certainly, in some manner, such a stream of utterances must be most meaningful to the patient in some way. Competent secretaries from time to time had recorded verbatim various examples of such disturbed utterances for the author's perusal and study. The author himself managed to record adequately similar such productions by patients who spoke slowly. Careful study of these verbal productions, it was thought, might lead to various speculative ideas that, in turn, might prove of value in understanding something about schizophrenia.

The question arose of whether or not much of the verbigeration might be a disguise for concealed meanings, fragmented and dispersed among the total utterances. This led to the question of how could the author himself produce a series of incoherencies in which he could conceal in a fragmented form a meaningful message. Or could he use the incoherencies of a patient and intersperse among them in a somewhat orderly fashion a fragmented meaningful communication that would be difficult to recognize? This speculation gave rise to many hours of intense labor spent fitting into a patient's verbatim, apparently meaningless, utterances a meaningful message that could not be detected by the author's colleagues when no clue of any sort was given to them. Previous efforts at producing original incoherencies by the author disclosed a definite and recognizable personal pattern indicating that the author was not sufficiently disturbed mentally to produce a bonafide stream of incoherent verbigerations.

When a meaning was interspersed in a patient's productions successfully, the author discovered that his past hypnotic experimentation with hypnotic techniques greatly influenced the kind of message which he was likely to intersperse in a patient's verbigerations. Out of this labor came the following experimental and therapeutic work.

One of the more recently hired secretaries objected strongly to being hypnotized. She suffered regularly upon the onset of menstruation from severe migrainous headaches lasting 3 to 4 or even more hours. She had been examined repeatedly by the medical service with no helpful findings. She usually retired to the lounge and "slept off the headache," a process usually taking 3 or more hours. On one such occasion, she had been purposely rather insistently forced to take dictation by the author instead of being allowed to retire to the lounge. Rather resentfully she began her task but within 15 minutes she interrupted the author to explain that her headache was gone. She attributed this to her anger at being forced to take dictation. Later, on another such occasion, she volunteered to take certain dictation which all of the secretaries tried to avoid because of the difficulties it presented. Her headache grew worse and she decided that the happy instance with the author was merely a fortuitous happenstance. Subsequently she had another severe headache. She was again insistently requested by the author to take some dictation. The previous happy result occurred within ten minutes. Upon the occurrence of another headache, she volunteered to take dictation from the author. Again it served to relieve her headache. She then experimentally tested the benefits of dictation from other physicians. For some unknown reason, her headaches only worsened. She returned from one of these useless attempts to the author and asked him to dictate. She was told he had nothing on hand to dictate but that he could redictate previously dictated material. Her headache was relieved within 8 minutes. Later her request for dictation for headache relief was met by some routine dictation. It failed to have any effect.

She came again, not too hopefully since she thought she had "worn-out the dictation remedy." Again she was given dictation with a relief of her distress in about 9 minutes. She was so elated that she kept a copy of the transcript so that she could ask others to dictate "that successful dictation" to relieve her headaches. Unfortunately, nobody seemed to have the "right voice" as did the author. Always, a posthypnotic suggestion was casually given that there would be no falling asleep while transcribing.

She did not suspect, nor did anybody else, what had really been done. The author had made comprehensive notes of the incoherent verbigeration of a psychotic patient. He had also had various secretaries make verbatim records of patient's incoherent utterances. He had then systematically interspersed therapeutic suggestions among the incoherencies with that secretary in mind. When this was found to be successful, the incoherent utterances of another patient were utilized in a similar fashion. This was also a successful effort. As a control measure, routine dictation and the dictation of "undoctored incoherencies" were tried. These had no effect upon her headaches. Nor did the use by others of "doctored" material have an effect since it had to be read aloud with some degree of expressive awareness to be effective.

The question now arises, why did these two patients and those patients used experimentally respond therapeutically? This answer can be given simply as follows: They knew very well why they were seeking therapy; they were desirous of benefiting; they came in a receptive state ready to respond at the first opportunity, except for the first experimental patient. But she was eager to be freed from her headache, and wished the time being spent taking dictation could be time spent getting over her headache. Essentially, then, all of the patients were in a frame of mind to receive therapy. How many times does a patient need to state his complaint? Only that number of times requisite for the therapist to understand. For all of these patients, only one statement of the complaint was necessary and they then knew that the therapist understood. Their intense desire for therapy was not only a conscious but an unconscious desire also, as judged clinically, but more importantly, as evidenced by the results obtained.

One should also give recognition to the readiness with which one's unconscious mind picks up clues and information. For example, one may dislike someone at first sight and not become consciously aware of the obvious and apparent reasons for such dislike for weeks, months, even a year or more. Yet finally the reasons for the dislike become apparent to the conscious mind. A common example is the ready hostility frequently shown by a normal heterosexual person toward a homosexual person without any conscious realization of why.

Respectful awareness of the capacity of the patient's unconscious mind to perceive meaningfulness of the therapist's own unconscious behavior is a governing principle in psychotherapy. There should also be a ready and full respect for the patient's unconscious mind to perceive fully the intentionally obscured meaningful therapeutic instructions offered them. The clinical and experimental material cited above is based upon the author's awareness that the patient's unconscious mind is listening and understanding much better than is possible for his conscious mind.

It was intended to publish this experimental work, of which only the author was aware. But sober thought and awareness of the insecure status of hypnosis in general, coupled with that secretary's strong objection to being hypnotized—she did not mind losing her headaches by "taking dictation" from the author—all suggested the inadvisability of publication.

A second secretary, employed by the hospital when this experimental work was nearing completion, always suffered from disabling dysmenorrhea. The "headache secretary" suggested to this girl that she take dictation from the author as a possible relief measure. Most willingly the author obliged, using "doctored" patient verbigeration. It was effective.

Concerned about what might happen to hypnotic research if his superiors were to learn of what was taking place, the author carefully failed with this second secretary and then again succeeded. She volunteered to be a hypnotic subject and hypnosis, not "dictation," was then used to meet her personal needs. She also served repeatedly as a subject for various frankly acknowledged and "approved" hypnotic experiments and the author kept his counsel in certain other experimental studies.

Now that hypnosis has come to be an acceptable scientific modality of investigative and therapeutic endeavor and there has developed a much greater awareness of semantics, this material, so long relegated to the shelf of unpublished work, can safely be published.

Summary

Two case histories and a brief account of experimental work are presented in detail to demonstrate the effective procedure of interspersing psychotherapeutic suggestions among those employed to induce and to maintain a hypnotic trance. The patients treated suffered respectively from neurotic manifestations and the pain of terminal malignant disease.

We will now consider in more detail how Erickson constructs this interspersal technique and also extract more of his language patterns for inducing hypnosis and giving suggestions. A more basic induction will be presented later, for now we will examine Erickson's account of his experience with Joe for its unique quality of having little co-operation on the part of the client other than trying to understand Erickson's speaking to him. We will see how a story of a tomato plant can evolve into an effective and sorely needed series of suggestions for the relief of pain.

Erickson begins by pacing the client's experiences. Describing what he knows to be true about the client, he also picks a subject of interest to the client to get his attention. This has more than just the advantage of getting the client to listen; it also is a part of the client's experience in which he has a great investment of himself. Erickson wants the client to be able to take the contents of the story and generalize the referential index to himself. He at one point even said to Joe:

> It is so pleasing just to be able to think about a plant as if it were a man.

Joe's affection for plants will make it easier for Joe to select his own referential index as a relevant substitute for *tomato plant.*

Here Erickson begins with a series of pacing statements:

I know you are a florist	=	A
That you like to grow flowers	=	B
I grew up on a farm in Wisconsin	=	C
I liked growing flowers	=	D
I still do	=	E

Each of these five statements is accurate for the client without any question. Now Erickson linkes these statements to behavior which he wants to elicit from the client with the Implied Causative connective *so* in the sentence:

> So I would like to have you take a seat in that easy chair as I talk to you.

The general form of this series, then is:

A, B, C, D, E, $\xrightarrow{\text{so}}$ I would like to have you take a seat in that easy chair as I talk to you

Notice, in addition, that the last statement itself includes an Implied Causative which links an immediately verifiable statement to a piece of behavior which Erickson wishes to elicit from Joe:

I talk to you $\xrightarrow{\text{as}}$ I would like to have you take a seat in that easy chair

Next, note that the behavior which Erickson wishes to elicit from Joe is not requested directly but rather that Erickson uses a conversational postulate, thereby avoiding the direct command *take a seat in that easy chair* as he says:

> . . . I would like to have you take a seat in that easy chair . . .

> I'm going to say a lot of things to you but it won't be about flowers because you know more than I do about flowers. *That isn't what you want.*

Here Erickson uses a series of patterns:

. . . A lot of things . . .	No referential index on *things.*
. . . It won't be about flowers	No referential index on *it.*
Because you know more than I do about flowers	Mind-reading *(you know),* Cause-Effect *(because).*
That isn't what you want	Mind-reading *(that isn't what you want).* Erickson repeats Joe's word (previously written out) *what you want.*

In addition, Erickson uses a meta-communication (communication about communication) technique closely related to the selectional restriction violation technique mentioned previously. Here Erickson comments directly about his intended communication with Joe. He says that he is going to talk to Joe but not about flowers. As the communication develops, however, Erickson superficially talks about a tomato plant — in fact, employing the selectional restriction violation technique. Here Erickson is directly warning Joe that he wants Joe to find some other referential index for the communication about tomato plants.

> Now as I talk and I can do so *comfortably,* I wish that you will *listen to me comfortably* as I talk about a tomato plant.

. . . as . . . . . . as	Implied Causatives.
. . . comfortably . . . listen to me comfortably. . . .	Analogical marking, lesser included structure.
. . . I wish that you will . . .	Use of ungrammatical sentence structure alerting Joe for special message . . . *wish* . . . *will* instead of . . . *wish* . . . *would* . . .

> That is an odd thing to talk about. It makes one *curious.* *Why talk about a tomato plant?* One puts a tomato seed in the ground. One can *feel hope* that it will grow into a tomato plant that *will bring satisfaction* by the fruit it has.

. . . odd thing . . . to talk about . . .	Deletion (odd for whom? talk to whom?).
. . . makes one . . .	Cause-Effect (. . . *makes* . . .).
. . . one . . ., one . . ., one . . .	Lack of referential index.
. . . feel hope . . . will bring satisfaction	Analogical marking of lesser included structures.

. . . satisfaction . . .	Nominalization with accompanying deletions and lack of referential indices.

The seed soaks up water, *not very much difficulty* in doing that because of the rains that *bring peace and comfort* and the joy of growing to flowers and tomatoes.

. . . difficulty . . . peace . . . comfort . . . joy . . .	Nominalization with accompanying deletions and lack of referential indices.
doing . . . bring . . .	Unspecified verbs.
. . . because . . .	Cause-Effect link.
peace . . . comfort . . . joy . . . to flowers and tomato plants	Selectional restriction violation.

In addition, here Erickson's earlier meta-communication . . . *it won't be about flowers* is relevant, since he earlier warned Joe that he wouldn't be talking about flowers and here he is, in fact, talking about flowers, the burden of constructing a meaning for this communication falling upon Joe.

That little seed, Joe, slowly swells, sends out a little rootlet with cilia on it. Now you may not know what cilia are, but cilia are *things that work* to help the tomato seed grow, to push up above the ground as a sprouting plant, and *you can listen to me Joe* so I will keep on talking and *you can keep on listening, wondering, just wondering what you can really learn.*

. . . seed . . . rootlet . . . cilia . . . tomato seed . . . sprouting plant . . .	All nouns whose referential index has already been disqualified by Erickson's earlier meta-communication.
. . . keep on listening . . .	Presupposition that Joe has been listening.

. . . know . . . wonder . . . learn . . .	Unspecified verbs.
. . . wondering what you can really learn . . .	Lesser included structure (the question — What can you really learn?).
. . . and . . . and . . . so . . . as . . .	Links — simple conjunctions, Implied Causatives.
. . . things that work . . .	Lack of referential index.
. . . you can listen to me . . . you can really learn . . .	Conversational postulates.

> . . . and here is your pencil and your pad but speaking of the tomato plant, it grows so slowly. *You cannot see* it grow, *you cannot hear* it grow, but grow it does — the first little leaflike things on the stalk, the fine little hairs on the stem, those hairs are on the leaves too like the cilia on the roots, they must make the tomato plant *feel very good,*. . .

. . . and here is your pencil and your pad . . .	Pacing statement.
. . . but speaking of the tomato . . .	Deletion (who's speaking to whom?).
. . . they must make the tomato plant feel very good . . .	violation

Basic Trance Induction*
with Commentary

This now should begin to give you an idea of the level of complexity of language Erickson employs to create an induction or to give suggestions. Erickson's ability to utilize language in this complex way is the result of experience and creativity plus his courageous belief in people's ability to learn the things they need to know. However, although Erickson himself can generate these language patterns spontaneously, he does not know consciously their formal characteristics. As Erickson has stated:

> *The Structure of Magic I* by Richard Bandler and John Grinder is a delightful simplification of the infinite complexities of the language I use with my patients. In reading this book, I learned a great deal about the things that I've done without knowing about them.

The induction that follows was taped in the author's (Grinder) presence, and is presented verbatim, with commentary on the right.

(1) *Will you uncross your legs?*	Erickson begins induction with a conversational postulate.
(2) *Cont . . .*	*Will you uncross your legs* (a conversational postulate), as

described previously is a question form of one of the presuppositions of the command, "uncross your legs." This move begins the process of having the client operate patterns which aren't ordinarily conscious, at the same time getting her in a position for a trance induction as she has begun already to respond to his suggestion on a waking level.

(3) *And sit with your hands just like this*

And links this conversational postulate to his next command which is also not expressed as a command but a continuance of the preceding pattern of conversational postulate. Here there is an additional ambiguity (scope) of whether it's *will you sit . . .* or simply *sit . . .*

(4) *And look at any one spot there*

(5) *And do not touch it*

Continuing the same process of conversational postulate here.

(6) *And, yes, just keep looking at that spot*

Just keep looking, presupposes that nothing else is required of the client. At the same time "and" connects this statement in a casual way to all that has preceded. Furthermore, the predicate *keep* in the phrase *keep looking* presupposes that the client has been looking.

(7) *Now there is no need to talk*

Conversational postulate with the force of the command

"don't talk" in addition to the deletion (who talks about what to whom?) and the nominalization *need* with its accompanying deletions and lack of referential indices.

(8) *No need to move*

Ungrammatical sequence of words, deletions (who moves where?) and the nominalization *need*.

(9) *You really don't have to pay attention to me because . . .*

Presupposition of remainder of sentence when *really* occurs, nominalization *attention*, and the beginning of a Cause-Effect statement *(because)*, *don't have to pay attention* has the conversational postulate "don't pay attention."

(10) *Your unconscious mind will hear me*

Presupposes that the client's unconscious mind exists and can hear Erickson speaking, lesser included structure *hear me*.

(11) *And it will understand*

Deletion (understand what?), lesser included structure *(understand)*, unspecified verb *(understand)*.

(12) *Really don't even need to pay attention to me*

Use of words *even* and *really*, remainder of communication presupposed. Ungrammatical sentence, conversational postulate, lesser included structure *(pay attention)*, nominalization *need*.

(13) *And while you have been*

Pacing statement linked to

sitting there	previous statements by *and* and Implied Causative *while*.
(14) *You've been doing the same thing*	Lack of referential index *(thing)*, deletion (same as what for whom?), unspecified predicate *doing*.
(15) *That you did when you first went to school*	Deletion (did what?), Implied Causative *when,* age regression suggestion, both mentioning the earlier period of the client's life and the statement that the client is doing the same thing now.
(16) *When you first saw the task of writing*	Nominalizations *task* and *writing* with accompanying deletions and lack of referential indices, age regression suggestion *when* as well as Implied Causative.
(17) *The letters of the alphabet*	The predicate *saw* in (16) plus the reference to the letters of the alphabet are powerful accessing of the non-dominant hemisphere techniques.
(18) *It seemed like an impossible task*	Deletions (seemed to whom, impossible to whom?), nominalization *task*.
(19) *And how do you recognize a "b"*	Lesser included structure (recognize a "b," question asked with no pause, allowing client to respond overtly.
(20) *How is it different from a "d"*	Deletion (different for whom?), children have exactly

this difficulty — thus, age regression suggestion.

(21) *And numbers*

Also stored in non-dominant hemisphere, ungrammatical fragment.

(22) *Is a 6 an upside down 9 . . . 9 is an upside down 6*

Ungrammatical fragments, non-dominant hemisphere accessing, age regression suggestion, deletion (for whom?).

(23) *And while you were mastering those problems — you were forming mental images that stay with you for the rest of your life*

Non-dominant hemisphere accessing, mind-reading, nominalization *problems* with accompanying deletions and lack of referential indices.

(24) *But you didn't know it then*

Suggests amnesia.

(25) *And while you've been sitting there*

Pacing statement, Implied Causative *(while)*.

(26) *The same thing has been happening to you now that happened to you then*

All of the above descriptions are taking place at this moment: regression, amnesia, forming mental images, learning, *the same thing* has no referential index and could be anything — this allows the client to choose. While more likely responding to all the above to some degree, Erickson's phrasing of this sentence also made it an imbedded command, *the same thing is h a p p e n i n g t o y o u NOWWWWWWWW — that happened to you then.* Marking in such a way that tonally implies "do it."

(27) *Your respiration is changed*

(28) *Your blood pressure is changed*

This is pacing. Erickson has watched his client closely and is describing the change he has seen, reinforcing by feedback and also presupposing that it has already occurred.

(29) *Your heartbeat is changed*

(30) *Your eyelid reflex is changed*

(31) *And you've got a mental image, a visual image of that spot and now you can close your eyes NOWWWW*

Mind-reading, conjunction *and* linking mind-reading pacing statement and desired behavior, ungrammatical (two occurrences of *now*), conversational postulate, lesser included structure, unspecified verb *(got)*, analogical marking *Nowwww.*

(32) *And now you can enjoy the comfort of going ever deeper into the trance*

Conjunction link *and,* lesser included structure, conversational postulate, presupposition, nominalizations.

(33) *And I want you to* **enjoy every moment of it**

Lack of referential index *(it)* presupposition *(every moment),* lesser included structure, analogical marking.

(34) *. . . And I don't need to talk to you*

Deletion (talk to you about what?).

(35) *You can have a lot of pleasure*

Lesser included structure, conversational postulate, nominalization *(pleasure)* with accompanying deletions and lack of referential indices, presupposition *(a lot of)*.

(36) *In becoming* **aware** *of the comforts*

Presupposition (*aware* is a factive predicate), nominalization *comforts,* unspecified predicate, analogical marking.

(37) *You can have within yourself*

Lesser included structure, unspecified verb, conversational postulate.

(38) *And one of those is the understanding you can go back*

Lack of referential index *those,* presupposition *(one),* nominalization *(understanding),* lesser included structure, conversational postulate.

(39) *Then perhaps you might* **have the experience**

Implied Causative *then,* lesser included structure, analogical marking, nominalization *(experience).*

(40) *. . . Of not knowing which one of your hands is going to lift first*

Lesser included structure (the question *which one of your hands* . . .), presupposition *which one of your hands* . . . presupposes that one of your hands . . . , presupposition *first* presupposes that one hand will lift and asks which will be first.

A Special Inquiry with Aldous Huxley into the Nature and Character of Various States of Consciousness, with Commentary

The patient's behavior is a part of the problem brought into the office; it constitutes the personal environment within which the therapy must take effect; it may constitute the dominant force in the local patient-doctor relationship. Since whatever the patient brings into the office is in some way both part of him and part of his problem, the patient should be viewed with a sympathetic eye appraising the totality which confronts the therapist.

Milton H. Erickson, *The Use of Symptoms as an Integral Part of Hypnotherapy*

Milton Erickson is generally recognized as the leading practitioner of medical hypnosis and the use of hypnosis in the psychotherapeutic context. He has consistently urged over the years of his continuing research into the nature of hypnosis and the working of the human mind in altered states of consciousness, that hypnotists, psychotherapists, medical doctors and dentists develop a refined ability to identify and meet the special needs and requirements which their clients bring with them to the specific context. Erickson realizes that full communication between two people at both the conscious and the unconscious levels can occur when there is a sensitivity to the other person's model of the world. In the therapeutic context, for example, the therapist assumes the responsibility of both making contact and assisting the client to learn the skills of communication necessary to allow any change in his behavior which he needs. Often this may require that the therapist be skilled in teaching the client to develop a new way of representing his experience — literally teaching the client to have new choices behaviorally (either consciously or unconsciously or both) about the way he represents the world. In the use of hypnosis in medical or dental contexts, the doctor must assist each client in achieving an altered state of consciousness which will allow him to experience the world in a way radically different from that of his normal state of consciousness, in order that otherwise difficult surgical procedures may proceed and the patient be properly cared for. Common to each of these contexts is the client's increased ability to control portions of his experience normally represented as outside his control (e.g., the ability to recall memories of events from the distant past, to dissassociate severe pain, etc.). The client, with the assistance of the hypnotist, literally achieves domination over portions of his nervous system usually considered beyond conscious control — he can succeed in gaining phenomenal command over the ongoing process of his direct experience of the world, his modeling process.

One of the most highly valued skills in western European culture is the experience which we call *creativity* or *the creative act.* Although there is little agreement about the nature of this experience, the investigators of creativity, typically, have characterized it as a state of altered consciousness. In studies of many of the world's most famous mathematicians, for example, the commentators as well as the mathematicians themselves have noticed that their discoveries and inventions often come to them in the form of dreams, of sudden insights into the solution to a problem which they are not working on consciously.[8]

In this first article, Erickson is working jointly with Aldous Huxley exploring the "various states of psychological awareness." Huxley, of course, is recognized as one of the most creative individuals in recent western European history. In this context, we see Erickson's systematic behavior in assisting Huxley to achieve altered states of consciousness with a sensitivity to Huxley's powerful creative resources. The principles of communication which allow Erickson to act so effectively in a psychotherapeutic encounter occur with clarity in this special situation in which the impressive resources of a highly creative individual are being explored with him. It is in this article, perhaps, that the potential which hypnosis offers as a tool both for research into highly valued altered states of consciousness and for the exploration of extending the limits of human experience displays itself most clearly. Not only are Erickson's potent techniques available as a technique to assist in the changing of portions of an individual's normal model of the world in a way which is narrowly therapeutic or medically or dentally useful, but they also provide a complete approach to the mapping of portions of human potential not normally experienced — portions of human potential which we may call *creative acts.*

*A Special Inquiry with Aldous Huxley into the Nature and
Character of Various States of Consciousness*[9]

Introduction

Over a period of nearly a year much time was spent by Aldous
Huxley and by the author, each planning separately for a joint
inquiry into various states of psychological awareness. Special
inquiries, possible methods of experimental approach and investi-
gations and various questions to be propounded were listed by
each of us in our respective loose-leaf notebooks. The purpose was
to prepare a general background for the proposed joint study with
this general background reflecting the thinking of both of us
uninfluenced by the other. It was hoped in this way to secure the
widest possible coverage of ideas by such separate outlines prepared from the markedly different backgrounds of understanding
that the two of us possessed.

Early in 1950 we met in Huxley's home in Los Angeles, there
to spend an intensive day appraising the ideas recorded in our
separate notebooks and to engage in any experimental inquiries
that seemed feasible. I was particularly interested in Huxley's
approach to psychological problems, his method of thinking and
his own unique use of his unconscious mind which we had discussed only briefly sometime previously. Huxley was particularly
interested in hypnosis and previous exceedingly brief work with
him had demonstrated his excellent competence as a deep somnambulistic subject.

It was realized that this meeting would be a preliminary or
pilot study, and this was discussed by both of us. Hence we
planned to make it as comprehensive and inclusive as possible
without undue emphasis upon completion of any one particular
item. Once the day's work had been evaluated, plans could then be
made for future meetings and specific studies. Additionally, we
each had our individual purposes, Aldous having in mind future
literary work, while my interest related to future psychological
experimentation in the field of hypnosis.

The day's work began at 8:00 a.m. and remained uninter-
rupted until 6:00 p.m. with some considerable review of our
notebooks the next day to establish their general agreement, to
remove any lack of clarity of meaning caused by the abbreviated
notations we had entered into them during the previous day's
work and to correct any oversights. On the whole we found that

our notebooks were reasonably in agreement but that naturally certain of our entries were reflective of our special interests and of the fact that each of us had, by the nature of the situation, made separate notations bearing upon each other.

Our plan was to leave these notebooks with Huxley since his phenomenal memory, often appearing to be total recall, and his superior literary ability would permit a more satisfactory writing of a joint article based upon our discussions and experimentations of that day's work. However, I did abstract from my notebook certain pages bearing notations upon Huxley's behavior at times when he, as an experimental subject, was unable to make comprehensive notations on himself, although post-experimentally he could and did do so, though less completely than I had. It was proposed that, from these certain special pages, I was to endeavor to develop an article which could be incorporated later in the longer study that Huxley was to write. Accordingly, I abstracted a certain number of pages intending to secure still more at a later date. These pages that I did remove Huxley rapidly copied into his own notebook to be sure of the completeness of his own data.

Unfortunately, a California brush fire sometime later destroyed Huxley's home, his extensive library containing many rare volumes and manuscripts, besides numerous other treasures to say nothing of the manuscripts upon which Huxley was currently working as well as the respective notebooks of our special joint study. As a result, the entire subject matter of our project was dropped as a topic too painful to discuss, but Huxley's recent death led to my perusal of these relatively few pages I had abstracted from my notebook. Examination of them suggested the possibility of presenting to the reader a small but informative part of that day's work. In this regard, the reader must bear in mind that the quotations attributed to Huxley are not necessarily verbatim, since his more extensive utterances were noted in abbreviated form. However, in the essence of their meaning, they are correct and they are expressive of Huxley as I knew him. It is also to be borne in mind that Huxley had read my notations on the occasion of our joint study and had approved them.

Project Initiations

The project began with Huxley reviewing concepts and definitions of conscious awareness, primarily his and in part those of others, followed by a discussion with me of his understandings of hypnotic states of awareness. The purpose was to insure that we were both in accord or clear in our divergences of understanding, thus to make possible a more reliable inquiry into the subject matter of our interest.

There followed then a review in extensive detail of various of his psychedelic experiences with mescaline, later to be recorded in this book.[10]

Huxley then proceeded with a detailed description of his very special practice of what he, for want of a better and less awkward term which he had not yet settled upon, called "Deep Reflection." He described this state (the author's description is not complete since there seemed to be no good reason except interest for making full notations of his description) of Deep Reflection as one marked by physical relaxation with bowed head and closed eyes, a profound progressive psychological withdrawal from externalities but without any actual loss of physical realities nor any amnesias or loss of orientation, a "setting aside" of everything not pertinent, and then a state of complete mental absorption in matters of interest to him. Yet, in that state of complete withdrawal and mental absorption, Huxley stated that he was free to pick up a fresh pencil to replace a dulled one to make "automatically" notations on his thoughts and to do all this without a recognizable realization on his part of what physical act he was performing. It was as if the physical act were "not an integral part of my thinking." In no way did such physical activity seem to impinge upon, to slow, or to impede "the train of thought so exclusively occupying my interest. It is associated but completely peripheral activity. . . . I might say activity barely contiguous to the periphery." To illustrate further, Huxley cited an instance of another type of physical activity. He recalled having been in a state of Deep Reflection one day when his wife was shopping. He did not recall what thoughts or ideas he was examining but he did recall that, when his wife returned that day, she had asked him if he had made a note of the special message she had given him over the telephone. He had been bewildered by her inquiry, could not recall anything about answering the telephone as his wife asserted, but together they found the special message recorded on a pad beside the telephone which was placed within comfortable reaching distance from the chair in which he liked to develop Deep Reflection. Both he and his wife reached the conclusion that he had been in a state of Deep Reflection at the time of the telephone call, had lifted the receiver and had said to her as usual, "I say there, hello," had listened to the message, had recorded it, all without any subsequent recollections of the experience. He recalled merely that he had been working on a manuscript that afternoon, one that had been absorbing all of his interest. He explained that it was quite common for him to initiate a day's work by entering a state of Deep Reflection as a preliminary process of marshaling his thoughts and putting into order the thinking that would enter into his writing later that day.

As still another illustrative incident, Huxley cited an occasion when his wife returned home from a brief absence, found the door locked as was customary, had entered the house and discovered in plain view a special delivery letter on a hallway table reserved for mail, special messages, etc. She had found Huxley sitting quietly in his special chair, obviously in a state of deep thought. Later that day she had inquired about the time of arrival of the special delivery letter only to learn that he had obviously no recollection of receiving any letter. Yet both knew that the mailman had undoubtedly rung the doorbell, that Huxley had heard the bell, had interrupted whatever he was doing, had gone to the door, opened it, received the letter, closed the door, placed the letter in its proper place and returned to the chair where she had found him.

Both of these two special events had occurred fairly recently. He recalled them only as incidents related to him by his wife but with no feeling that those accounts constituted a description of actual meaningful physical behavior on his part. So far as he knew, he could only deduce that he must have been in a state of Deep Reflection when they occurred.

His wife subsequently confirmed the assumption that his behavior had been completely "automatic, like a machine moving precisely and accurately. It is a delightful pleasure to see him get a book out of the bookcase, sit down again, open the book slowly, pick up his reading glass, read a little, and then lay the book and glass aside. Then some time later, maybe a few days, he will notice the book and ask about it. The man just never remembers what he does nor what he thinks about when he sits in that chair. All of a sudden, you just find him in his study working very hard."

In other words, while in a state of Deep Reflection and seemingly totally withdrawn from external realities, the integrity of the task being done in that mental state was touched by external stimuli, but some peripheral part of awareness made it possible for him to receive external stimuli, to respond meaningfully to them but with no apparent recording of any memory of either the stimulus or his meaningful and adequate response. Inquiry of his wife later had disclosed that when she was at home, Aldous in a state of Deep Reflection paid no attention to the telephone which might be beside him or the doorbell. "He simply depends completely on me, but I can call out to him that I'll be away and he never fails to hear the telephone or the doorbell."

Huxley explained that he believed he could develop a state of Deep Reflection in about five minutes but that in doing so he "simply cast aside all anchors" of any type of awareness. Just what he meant and sensed he could not describe. "It is a subjective experience quite" in which he apparently achieved a state of "orderly mental arrangement" permitting an orderly free flowing of his thoughts as he wrote. This was his final explanation. He had never considered any analysis of exactly what his "Deep Reflection" was nor did he feel that he could analyze it, but he offered to attempt it as an experimental investigation for the day. It was promptly learned that, as he began to absorb himself in his thoughts to achieve a state of Deep Reflection, he did indeed "cast off all anchors" and appeared to be completely out of touch with everything. On this attempt to experience subjectively and to remember the processes of entering into Deep Reflection, he developed the state within five minutes and emerged from it within two as closely as I could determine. His comment was, "I say, I'm deucedly sorry. I suddenly found myself all prepared to work with nothing to do and I realized I had better come out of it." That was all the information he could offer. For the next attempt, a signal to be given by me was agreed upon as a signal for him to "come out of it." A secondary attempt was made as easily as the first. Huxley sat quietly for some minutes and the agreed-upon signal was given. Huxley's account was, "I found myself just waiting for something. I did not know what. It was just a 'something' that I seemed to feel would come in what seemed to be a timeless, spaceless void. I say, that's the first time I noted that feeling. Always I've had some thinking to do. But this time I seemed to have no work in hand. I was just completely disinterested, indifferent, just waiting for something and then I felt a need to come out of it. I say, did you give me this signal?"

Inquiry disclosed that he had no apparent memory of the stimulus being given. He had had only the "feeling" that it was time to "come out of it."

Several more repetitions yielded similar results. A sense of timeless, spaceless void, a placid, comfortable awaiting for an undefined "something" and a comfortable need to return to ordinary conscious awareness constituted the understandings achieved. Huxley summarized his findings briefly as "a total absence of everything on the way there and on the way back and an expected meaningless something for which one awaits in a state of Nirvana since there is nothing more to do." He asserted his intention to make a later intensive study of this practice he found so useful in his writing.

Further experiments were done after Huxley had explained that he could enter the state of Deep Reflection with the simple undefined understanding that he would respond to any "significant stimulus." Without informing him of my intentions, I asked him to "arouse" (this term is my own) when three taps of a pencil on a chair were given in close succession. He entered the state of reflection readily and, after a brief wait, I tapped the table with a pencil in varying fashions at distinct but irregular intervals. Thus, I tapped once, paused, then twice in rapid succession, paused, tapped once, paused, tapped four times in rapid succession, paused, then five times in rapid succession. Numerous variations were tried but with an avoidance of the agreed-upon signal. A chair was knocked over with a crash while four taps were given. Not until the specified three taps were given did he make any response. His arousal occurred slowly with an almost immediate response to the signal. Huxley was questioned about his subjective experiences. He explained simply that they had been the same as previously with one exception, namely that several times he had a vague sensation that "something was coming," but he knew not what. He had no awareness of what had been done.

Huxley is already quite experienced in the ability to enter and leave altered states of consciousness. Notice that in the discussion of the state which Huxley calls Deep Reflection both Huxley and Erickson distinguish his experience of normal state of consciousness from this special state with descriptions such as:

As if the *physical* act were *not* an integral part of my thinking . . .

In *no* way did such *physical* activity seem to impinge . . .

Recalled them only as incidents related to him by his wife but with *no feeling* . . .

Automatic, like a machine moving precisely and accurately . . .

Simply *cast aside all anchors* . . .

To be *completely out of touch* with everything . . .

One of the patterns which connects each of these descriptions is that in each the normal state of consciousness and Huxley's experience of the altered state of consciousness are distinguished by the reduction or complete absence of kinesthetic sensations. If you examine the normal-state descriptions by Huxley of his normal-state experience of the world throughout the article, you will find a definite preference on Huxley's part for kinesthetic predicates — that is, verbs, adjectives and adverbs which are based on (or presuppose) a kinesthetic representational system. In other words, Huxley's most highly valued representational system is kinesthetic. Since the kinesthetic representational system is Huxley's most highly valued one, the altered state of consciousness — Deep Reflection — is characterized as differing from the primary by a reduction or absence of body sensations.

There are two additional patterns which recur in Erickson's work and also occur in this portion of the article. First Huxley's wife states that "The man (Huxley) just never remembers . . . when he sits in that chair." One of the fastest ways of assisting a person who has achieved an altered state of consciousness, whether hypnosis, Deep Reflection, or other states, in re-entering that state is through a full recall of their experience at the time when they achieved that altered state of consciousness. For example, it is a standard Erickson technique to have the client who wishes to re-enter a trance state to re-create the experience which he had on some previous occasion. Huxley, who has trained himself to enter Deep Reflection rapidly, uses one of the most powerful of these recall techniques — kinesthetic recall. In other words, by seating himself in "that chair," he accelerates his process of entering an altered state of consciousness as in that chair he had repeatedly entered that state, and the physical act of seating himself in "that chair" places him in touch with the familiar kinesthetic sensations of sitting in "that chair" — a powerful set of kinesthetic cues associated with the altered state. The recovery of re-experiencing of kinesthetic sensations associated with former altered states of consciousness is one of a set of techniques which Erickson characteristically employs to insure satisfactory future trances.

> The procedure is to get the subject to recall from the beginning in a reasonably orderly, detailed manner the events of a previous successful hypnotic trance. As the subject does this, repetitions of his statements are offered and helpful questions are asked. As he becomes absorbed in this task, the subject revivifies the previous trance state, usually regressing subjectively to that previous situation and developing a special rapport with the operator.
> Milton Erickson, *Utilization Techniques*,
> p. 36.

Precisely this same formal pattern occurs in what psychotherapists call *the enactment technique.* In an enactment the client is asked to recall in its entirety the kinesthetic, visual, auditory, and other sensations which are connected with some experience which is the basis of a block to desired growth and change in his behavior. In this way the past is made present and the client, by re-experiencing this event, comes to have new choices in his behavior (see *Magic I,* Chapter 6, and *Magic II,* Part I, for a detailed discussion of the enactment technique).

Note that Huxley's choice of a particular physical location ("that chair") and the accompanying kinesthetic sensation associated with it are congruent with the fact that Huxley's most highly valued representational system is kinesthetic. Erickson systematically selects cues or signals from the client's most highly valued representational system to assist the client in entering or re-entering trance states. Thus, while the kinesthetic cues are quite effective with Huxley, with a highly visual client a fantasized image of some experience would be more appropriate.

> Another variation of the rehearsal technique is that
> of having the subject visualize himself carrying out
> some hypnotic task and then adding to the visuali-
> zation other forms of imagery such as auditory,
> kinesthetic, etc.
>
> Milton Erickson, *Deep Hypnosis and its
> Induction,* p. 29

He, thereby, uses the person's most highly developed representational system to lead and gain access to the other representational
systems available.

Second, Erickson arranges an "arousal" signal with Huxley
without informing him of his full intentions. Here Erickson is
demonstrating several important points. He chooses a signal which
is in a different modality (auditory) from Huxley's most highly
valued representational system (kinesthetic). Erickson typically
arranges signals or cues for post-hypnotic behavior in modalities
other than the other person's most highly valued representational
system. This allows him to bypass the modality and representational system most frequently connected with conscious mind
activity and to communicate more directly with the unconscious
portions of the person's mind. Erickson then proceeds to test the
effectiveness of the cue by creating a number of signals in the
same modality (auditory — sequences of pencil taps other than the
arranged signal, the crash of a chair Erickson causes to fall, etc.).
Huxley's ability not to respond to these auditory signals demonstrates the depth of Deep Reflection. Erickson, in arranging the
cue for arousal with Huxley, does not give Huxley specific directions *not* to respond to auditory stimulation other than the cue.
Rather, he makes the positive statement that Huxley will arouse to
a specific signal. The way in which Huxley is to respond or not to
respond to other auditory signals is left ambiguous, thereby allowing Huxley to utilize his own vast resources in determining his
behavior. This is an excellent example of Erickson's consistent
pattern of limiting the person he is working with as little as
possible, consistent with the demands of the context. By making a
positive suggestion about a specific signal, Erickson allows Huxley
maximum freedom to respond or not as he (Huxley) decides.

> In trance induction, the inexperienced hypnotist
> often tries to direct or bend the subject's behavior
> to fit his conception of how a subject "should"

behave. There should be a constant minimalization of the role of the hypnotist and a constant enlargement of the subject's role.

Milton Erickson, *Deep Hypnosis and its Induction*, p. 18

In this way Erickson makes use of the full resources which the person he is working with has available.

Further experimentation was done in which he was asked to enter Deep Reflection and to sense color, a prearranged signal for arousing being that of a handshake of his right hand. He complied readily and when I judged that he was fully absorbed in his state of reflection, I shook his left hand vigorously, then followed this with a hard pinching of the back of both hands that left deep fingernail markings. Huxley made no response to this physical stimulation, although his eyes were watched for possible eyeball movements under the lids and his respiratory and pulse rates were checked for any changes. However, after about a minute he slowly drew his arms back along the arms of the chair where he had placed them before beginning his reflection state. They moved slowly about an inch and then all movement ceased.

He was aroused easily and comfortably at the designated signal.

His subjective report was simply that he had "lost" himself in a "sea of color," of "sensing," "feeling," "being" color, of being "quite utterly involved in it with no identity of your own, you know." Then suddenly he had experienced a process of losing that color in a "meaningless void," only to open his eyes and to realize that he had "come out of it."

He remembered the agreed upon stimulus but did not recall if it had been given. "I can only deduce it was given from the fact that I'm out of it," and indirect questioning disclosed no memories of the other physical stimuli administered. Neither was there an absent-minded looking at nor rubbing of the backs of his hands.

This same procedure in relation to color was repeated but to it was added, as he seemed to be reaching the state of Deep Reflection, a repeated, insistent urging that, upon arousal, he discuss a certain book which was carefully placed in full view. The results were comparable to the preceding findings. He became "lost," . . . "quite utterly involved in it," . . . "one can sense it but not describe it," . . . "I say, it's an utterly amazing, fascinating state of finding yourself a pleasant part of an endless vista of color that is soft and gentle and yielding and all-absorbing. Utterly extraordinary, most extraordinary." He had no recollection of my verbal insistences nor of the other physical stimuli. He remembered the agreed-upon signal but did not know if it had been given. He found himself only in a position of assuming that it had been given since he was again in a state of ordinary awareness. The presence of the book meant nothing to him. One added statement was that entering a state of Deep Reflection by absorbing himself in a sense of color was, in a fashion, comparable to, but not identical with, his psychedelic experiences.

In this portion of the article Erickson is presenting an important description of the process of assisting Huxley in shifting to a representational system other than the one primarily associated with his normal state of awareness — in this case, visual. The experience of color, which Erickson requests Huxley "sense" as he re-enters Deep Reflection, is an experience which is usually based on a visual representational system. Erickson's choice of words here again show his refined sense of the use of language and his principle of allowing the person he is working with maximum freedom to respond. Erickson states, ". . . was asked to enter Deep Reflection and to *sense* color." Notice, not to see color but to sense color. Huxley, in fact, responds creatively with expressions such as:

> . . . Lost himself in a "sea of color" . . .

> Of sensing, feeling being color . . .

> An endless vista of color that is soft and gentle and yielding . . .

Here Huxley's choice of predicates in these descriptions shows that he is in a transition state between his primary representational system — kinesthetic (*lost, feeling, soft, gentle, yielding*) — and the representational system for the experience indirectly requested by Erickson — visual (e.g., *color, vista, color*). Again, by allowing Huxley a maximum flexibility in having this experience, Erickson uses Huxley's resources more fully than would be possible if he (Erickson) were more directive. Huxley is here, by his use of mixed predicates, demonstrating a phenomenon often associated with creative activity — synesthezia, cross modality experiences. That these neural circuits are, in fact, available as the basis for this behavior has been established (see *Magic II*, Part III, and Bach-y-Rit work referenced in the Bibliography).

As a final inquiry, Huxley was asked to enter the reflection state for the purpose of recalling the telephone call and the special-delivery letter incidents. His comment was that such a project should be "quite fruitful." Despite repeated efforts, he would "come out of it" explaining, "There I found myself without anything to do so I came out of it." His memories were limited to the accounts given to him by his wife and all details were associated with her and not with any inner feelings of experience on his part.

A final effort was made to discover whether or not Huxley could include another person in his state of Deep Reflection. This idea interested him at once and it was suggested that he enter the reflection state to review some of his psychedelic experiences. This he did in a most intriguing fashion. As the reflection state developed, Huxley, in an utterly detached, dissociated fashion, began making fragmentary remarks, chiefly in the form of self-addressed comments. Thus he would say, making fragmentary notes with a pencil and paper quickly supplied to him, "most extraordinary . . . I overlooked that . . . How? . . . Strange I should have forgotten that (making a notation) . . . fascinating how different it appears . . . I must look. . . ."

When he aroused, he had a vague recollection of having reviewed a previous psychedelic experience but what he had experienced then or on the immediate occasion he could not recall. Nor did he recall speaking aloud nor making notations. When shown these, he found that they were so poorly written that they could not be read. I read mine to him without eliciting any memory traces.

Huxley's choice of predicates while in Deep Reflection reveal a complete shift to the visual representational system:

I *overlooked* that

. . . how different it *appears*

I must *look* . . .

In Erickson's inductions as well as in our own trance induction work, we notice a consistent pattern of the emergence of the visual representational system as primary as the client achieves more and more depth of hypnosis. One fascinating explanation of this pattern is that in a hypnotic induction the hypnotist is attempting to communicate with the client's unconscious mind. One of the ways in which the two cerebral hemispheres of humans differ is in their language and visual functions. In general, the hemisphere which has the language faculty is less developed with respect to making visual distinctions:

> Each side of the brain is able to perform and chooses to perform a certain set of cognitive tasks which the other side finds difficult, distasteful or both. In considering the nature of the two sets of functions, it appears that they may be logically incompatible. The right (non-language, in most of the population) hemisphere synthesizes over space. The left (language, in most of the population) analyzes over time. The right hemisphere notes visual similarities to the exclusion of conceptual similarities. The left hemisphere does the opposite. The right hemisphere perceives form, the left hemisphere, detail. The right hemisphere codes sensory input in terms of images, the left hemisphere in terms of linguistic descriptions. . . . This description of hemispheric behavior suggests that the Gestalt Laws of Perceptual Organization pertain only to the mute hemisphere.
>
> Jerre Levy, *Psychobiological Implications of Bilateral Assymetry in Hemispheric Function in the Human Brain*, Dimond and Beaumont, p. 167.

In a more recent review of cerebral assymetry, Gardiner (1975) comments:

> . . . that each half of the brain controls the movements of the opposite part of the body. When the

left foot, the left hand, or fingers of the left hand are moved, impulses have been sent from the right half of the brain; when the individual looks to the left, the impulses (or connections) again go to the right half of the brain; and impulses conveying information from the left ear tend to go to, or "favor," the right half of the brain. This principle of *contralateral* ("opposite-side") representation applies equally well to the right limbs of the body; functioning of the right hand or leg, and other organs on that side, is controlled by the left half of the brain.

Gardiner, 1975, *The Shattered Mind*, p. 351.

If, when Erickson refers to "the unconscious part of the mind," he is referring to the mute or non-dominant hemisphere, then the pattern of emergence of the visual representational system which we have noted in Erickson's work as well as our own is understandable. There are several other patterns which we have noticed in our work which support this interpretation.

First, in doing double inductions (trance inductions in which each of the authors is speaking to the client simultaneously), the style of speech which each of us uses varies by the ear into which we are speaking. Specifically, if John is speaking into the ear which transmits information to the languge hemisphere, he will speak in a style of syntax which is complex, using ambiguity, for example, as a key technique, while Richard speaks to the mute hemisphere in a style of syntax which is maximally simple — a style of syntax which is not well-formed *adult* English but is well-formed *baby* English. (We discuss this in more detail later.) Double trance inductions are more rapid and the depth of trance more profound when we make this hemispheric distinction than when we do not.

Secondly, one of the more reliable indications that a client is entering a satisfactory state of trance is the coordinated appearance of movements of the side of the body controlled by the non-dominant hemisphere.

Third, in the course of our therapeutic work, we have developed a number of techniques to assist clients in rapidly developing representational systems other than their most highly valued one.

Many times, in the course of teaching a client who has a most highly valued representational system other than visual, we have noticed the client making a distinction between "imaging a picture" and "seeing a picture." In the first case, the client, typically, reports vague, relatively unfocused, schematized and unstable visual images, while in the second case, the images have the focused, stable, full, rich, vivid properties of direct visual input. In every case to date, the experience of "imaging a picture" has associated with it a verbal, internal dialogue, while the vivid visualization has no internal verbal dialogue associated with it. Apparently, the first case is one in which the client is constructing a picture using his language system as the lead system, while the second is a direct accessing of pictures residing in the non-dominant hemisphere. Thus, one way which we have developed to assist the client in coming to have the ability to visualize vividly is to teach him to shut down his internal verbal dialogue. Very often his first experiences with shutting down his internal dialogue leads to what appears to us to be trance behavior.

Fourth, in different places in Erickson's work, he makes very effective use of melodies as part of his induction. Melodies are stored in the non-dominant hemisphere.

Fifth, in the context of therapy one of the most effective techniques of assisting a client in changing his model of the world is the Guided Fantasy (see *Magic I*, Chapter 6, and *Magic II*, Part I, for a detailed presentation) in which the client is typically asked to close his eyes and visualize a particular experience which will then assist him in changing. Our initial interest in hypnosis springs from our realization that our clients' behavior during a Guided Fantasy was indistinguishable from descriptions of patients in medium and deep trance states. Next, and again in the therapeutic context, specifically when working with polarities — polarities are the expression of two conflicting models of behavior which the client has (see *Magic II*, Part III) — we have noted that one of the most immediate and effective ways of assisting the client in fully expressing and integrating his polarities is to insure that one of the polarities is using a visual representational system and the other either a kinesthetic or an auditory representational system.[11]

Finally, we have observed that clients executing post-hypnotic suggestions often shift the predicates which they normally use to visual predicates as they re-enter the trance state to execute the post-hypnotic suggestions.

A repetition yielded similar results with one exception. This was an amazed expression of complete astonishment by Huxley suddenly declaring, "I say, Milton, this is quite utterly amazing, most extraordinary. I use Deep Reflection to summon my memories, to put into order all of my thinking, to explore the range, the extent of my mental existence, but I do it solely to let those realizations, the thinking, the understandings, the memories seep into the work I'm planning to do without my conscious awareness of them. Fascinating . . . never stopped to realize that my Deep Reflection always preceded a period of intensive work wherein I was completely absorbed. . . . I say, no wonder I have an amnesia."

Later when we were examining each other's notebooks, Huxley manifested intense amazement and bewilderment at what I had recorded about the physical stimuli and for which he had no memory of any sort. He knew that he had gone into Deep Reflection repeatedly at my request, had been both pleased and amazed at his subjective feelings of being lost in an all-absorbing sea of color, had sensed a certain timelessness, spacelessness and had experienced a comfortable feeling of something meaningful about to happen. He reread my notations repeatedly in an endeavor to develop some kind of a feeling of at least a vague memory of subjective awareness of the various physical stimuli I had given him. He also looked at the backs of his hands to see the pinch marks but they had vanished. His final comment was, ". . . extraordinary, most extraordinary, I say, utterly fascinating."

When we agreed that, at least for the while, further inquiry into Deep Reflection might be postponed until later, Huxley declared again that his sudden realization of how much he had used it and how little he knew about it made him resolve to investigate much further into his "Deep Reflection." The manner and means by which he achieved it, how it constituted a form of preparation for absorbing himself in his writing and in what way it caused him to lose unnecessary contact with reality were all problems of much interest to him.

Huxley then suggested that an investigation be made of hypnotic states of awareness by employing him as a subject. He asked permission to be allowed to interrupt his trance states at will for purposes of discussion. This was in full accord with my own wishes.

He asked that first a light trance be induced, perhaps

repeatedly, to permit an exploration of his subjective experiences. Since he had briefly been a somnambulistic subject previously, he was carefully assured that this fact could serve to make him feel confident in arresting his trance states at any level he wished. He did not recognize this as a simple, direct hypnotic suggestion. In reading my notebook later I was much amused at how easily he had accepted an obvious suggestion without recognizing its character at the time.

He found several repetitions of the light trance interesting but "too easily conceptualized." It is, he explained, "a simple withdrawal of interest from the outside to the inside." That is, one gives less and less attention to externalities and directs more and more attention to inner subjective sensations. Externalities become increasingly fainter and more obscure, inner subjective feelings more satisfying until a state of balance exists. In this state of balance, he had the feeling that, with motivation, he could "reach out and seize upon reality," that there is a definite retention of a grasp upon external reality but with no motivation to deal with it. Neither did he feel a desire to deepen the trance. No particular change in this state of balance seemed necessary and he noted that a feeling of contentment and relaxation accompanied it. He wondered if others experienced the same subjective reactions.

Huxley requested that the light trance be induced by a great variety of techniques, some of them non-verbal. The results in each instance, Huxley felt strongly, were dependent entirely upon his mental set. He found that he could accept "drifting along" (my phrase) in a light trance, receptive of suggestions involving primarily responses at a subjective level only. He found that an effort to behave in a direct relationship to the physical environment taxed his efforts and made him desire either to arouse from the trance or to go still deeper. He also, on his own initiative, set up his own problems to test his trance states. Thus, before entering the light trance he would privately resolve to discuss a certain topic, relevant or irrelevant, with me at the earliest possible time or even at a fairly remote time. In such instances, Huxley found such unexpressed desires deleterious to the maintenance of the trance. Similarly, any effort to include an item of reality not pertinent to his sense of subjective satisfaction lessened the trance.

At all times there persisted a "dim but ready" awareness that one could alter the state of awareness at will. Huxley, like others with whom I have done similar studies, felt an intense desire to explore his sense of subjective comfort and satisfaction but immediately realized that this would lead to a deeper trance state.

When Huxley was asked to formulate understandings of the means he could employ by which he could avoid going into more than a light trance, he stated that he did this by setting a given length of time during which he would remain in a light trance. This had the effect of making him more strongly aware that at any moment he could "reach out and seize external reality" and that his sense of subjective comfort and ease decreased. Discussion of this and repeated experimentation disclosed that carefully worded suggestions serving to emphasize the availability of external reality and to enhance subjective comfort could serve to deepen the trance even though Huxley was fully cognizant of what was being said and why. Similar results have been obtained with other highly intelligent subjects.

In experimenting with medium deep trances, Huxley, like other subjects with whom I have worked, experienced much more difficulty in reacting to and maintaining a fairly constant trance level. He found that he had a subjective need to go deeper in the trance and an intellectual need to stay at the medium level. The result was that he found himself repeatedly "reaching out for awareness" of his environment and this would initiate a light trance. He would then direct his attention to subjective comfort and find himself developing a deep trance. Finally, after repeated experiments, he was given both post-hypnotic and direct hypnotic suggestion to remain in a medium deep trance. This he found he could do with very little concern then. He described the medium trance as primarily characterized by a most pleasing subjective sense of comfort and a vague, dim, faulty awareness that there was an external reality for which he felt a need for considerable motivation to be able to examine it. However, if he attempted to examine even a single item of reality for its intrinsic value, the trance would immediately become increasingly lighter. On the other hand, when he examined an item of external reality for subjective values, for example, the soft comfort of the chair cushions as contrasted to the intrinsic quiet of the room, the trance became deeper. But both light and deep trances were characterized by a need to sense external reality in some manner, not necessarily clearly but nevertheless to retain some recognizable awareness of it.

For both types of trance, experiments were carried out to discover what hypnotic phenomena could be elicited in both light and medium deep trances. This same experiment has been done with other good subjects and also with subjects who consistently developed only a light trance and with those who consistently did not seem to be able to go further than the medium trance. In all such studies, the findings were the same, the most important seeming to be the need of light and medium deep hypnotic subjects to retain at least some grasp upon external reality and to orient their trance state as a state apart from external reality but with the orientation to such reality, however tenuous in character, sensed as available for immediate utilization by the subject.

Another item which Huxley discovered by his own efforts unguided by me and of which I was fully aware through work with other subjects, was that the phenomena of deep hypnosis can be developed in both the light and the medium trance. Huxley, having observed deep hypnosis, wondered about the possibility of developing hallucinatory phenomena in the light trance. He attempted this by the measure of enjoying his subjective state of physical comfort and adding to it an additional subjective quality, namely, a pleasant gustatory sensation. He found it quite easy to hallucinate vividly various taste sensations while wondering vaguely what I would think if I knew what he was doing. He was not aware of his increased swallowing when he did this. From gustatory sensations he branched out to olfactory hallucinations both pleasant and unpleasant. He did not realize that he betrayed this by the flaring of his nostrils. His thinking at the time, so he subsequently explained, was that he had the "feeling" that hallucinations of a completely "inner type of process," that is, occurring within the body itself, would be easier than those in which the hallucination appeared to be external to the body. From olfactory hallucinations he progressed to kinesthetic, proprioceptive and, finally, tactile sensations. In the kinesthetic hallucinatory sensation experience he hallucinated taking a long walk but remaining constantly aware that I was present in some vaguely sensed room. Momentarily he would forget about me and his hallucinated walking would become most vivid. He recognized this as an indication of the momentary development of a deeper trance state which he felt obligated to remember to report to me during the discussion after his arousal. He was not aware of respiratory and pulse changes during the hallucinatory walk.

When he first tried for visual and auditory hallucinations, he found them much more difficult and the effort tended to lighten and to abolish his trance state. He finally reasoned that if he could hallucinate rhythmical movements of his body, he could then "attach" an auditory hallucination to this hallucinated body sensation. The measure proved most successful and again he caught himself wondering if I could hear the music. His breathing rate changed and slight movements of his head were observed. From simple music he proceeded to a hallucination of opera singing and then finally a mumbling of words which eventually seemed to become my voice questioning him about Deep Reflection. I could not recognize what was occurring.

From this he proceeded to visual hallucinations. An attempt to open his eyes nearly aroused him from his trance state. Thereafter he kept his eyes closed for both light and medium deep trance activities. His first visual hallucination was a vivid flooding of his mind with an intense sense of pastel colors of changing hues and with a wavelike motion. He related this experience to his Deep Reflection experiences with me and also to his previous psychedelic experiences. He did not consider this experience sufficiently valid for his purposes of the moment because he felt that vivid memories were playing too large a part. Hence he deliberately decided to visualize a flower but the thought occurred to him that, even as a sense of movement played a part in auditory hallucinations, he might employ a similar measure to develop a visual hallucination. At the moment, so he recalled after arousing from the trance and while discussing his experience, he wondered if I had ever built up hallucinations in my subjects by combining various sensory fields of experience. I told him that that was a standard procedure for me.

He proceeded with this visual hallucination by "feeling" his head turn from side to side and up and down to follow a barely visible, questionably visible, rhythmically moving object. Very shortly the object became increasingly more visible until he saw a giant rose, possibly three feet in diameter. This he did not expect and thus he was certain at once that it was not a vivified memory but a satisfactory hallucination. With this realization came the realization that he might very well add to the hallucination by adding olfactory hallucinations of an intense "unroselike" sickeningly sweet odor. This effort was also most successful. After experimenting with various hallucinations, Huxley aroused from his trance and discussed extensively what he had accomplished. He was pleased to learn that his experimental findings without any coaching or suggestions from me were in good accord with planned experimental findings with other subjects.

Here we find Erickson presenting one of the clearest examples of the systematic understanding and use of representational systems. Huxley is interested in determining whether he can experience hallucinatory phenomena in both light and medium trance. Huxley himself is behaving consistently with the principles mentioned above. First, being in a light/medium trance, his initial behavior is still in large part conscious — he correspondingly utilizes his most highly valued representational system, kinesthetic, as the lead representational system to assist himself in developing hallucinations in the other representational systems.

> . . . Enjoying his subjective state of physical comfort and adding to it.

> an additional subjective quality, namely, a pleasant gustatory sensation.

> . . . From gustatory sensations he branched out to olfactory hallucinations . . .

> From olfactory hallucinations he progressed to kinesthetic, proprioceptive and finally tactile sensations.

Further, Huxley spontaneously arrives at a technique which we have formalized in the context of assisting people in developing additional maps or representational systems for organizing their experience — specifically, using a lead representational system to develop another representational system by finding a point of overlap or intersection between the two.

Mary Lou, a woman in her middle 40's, was working in a Therapist Training Group. In the process of expressing her difficulties, the therapist noticed that each time that she expressed some comment which was critical of her own behavior, Mary Lou's voice quality (tonality) changed. She literally spoke with a different voice. The therapist then asked Mary Lou to repeat a number of the critical remarks. As she did, the therapist asked her to be aware of her voice. As she finished repeating the critical remarks, the therapist leaned forward and asked her whose voice that was. She replied at once that it was her father's voice. At this point the therapist asked her to close her eyes and to hear that same voice inside her head. She was able to do this easily. Next, the therapist instructed her as she listened to her father's voice to see her father's mouth moving, the lips forming the words. As she accomplished this, she was then instructed to see the remainder of her father's face. The therapist continued to work with Mary Lou, using her father's voice to lead her in constructing a full visual representation which matched the voice she continued to hear inside her head. Once the visual and auditory representations were coordinated, the therapist used the material as a basis for an enactment in which Mary Lou played both herself and her father. Thus, in this final phase, all three of the representational systems were brought into play — auditory, visual and kinesthetic. The enactment technique, based on using an auditory representation initially and then adding the other representational systems (visual and kinesthetic) to it — that is, Meta-Tactic III — enabled Mary Lou to confront and overcome some formerly severe blocks to her further growth.

This experience with Mary Lou shows the use of Meta-Tactic III. The therapist notices a sudden shift in a client's behavior. Making use of the representational system in which this sudden shift occurs as a basis from which to build a more complete reference structure (see Chapter 6, *Magic I*), the therapist finds a point of overlap between the representational system in which the shift took place and the representational system which the therapist chooses to add. In this case, since the initial representational system was auditory (specifically, the voice of another person), the therapist had the client form a visual image of the mouth which was creating that voice. Once a portion of the new representational system is tied to the initial representational system, the therapist can work with the client to fully develop the new representational system. The consequence of this Meta-Tactic is dramatically to expand the client's representation of the experience which is causing her difficulty. This expanded representation allows the client an expanded model of the world and, from this, more choices in coping in her life.

Huxley is systematically applying Meta-Tactic III to assist himself in developing hallucinations in representational systems other than his primary ones, as the description indicates:

> . . . reasoned that if he could hallucinate rhythmic movements of his body he could then "attach" an auditory hallucination to this hallucinated body sensation . . . even as a sense of movement played a part in auditory hallucinations, he might employ a similar measure to develop a visual hallucination.

Equally remarkable, in our opinion, is Erickson's finely developed ability to make visual distinctions and to understand, with a minimum of cues, the experience which Huxley is having:

> . . . hallucinate vividly various taste sensations while wondering vaguely what I would think if I knew what he was doing. He was not aware of his increased swallowing when he did this . . . branched out to olfactory hallucinations. . . . He did not realize that he betrayed this by the flaring of his nostrils.

Erickson's ability to identify and understand the meaning of the detailed movements of Huxley's body leaves no doubt about his (Erickson's) explicit understanding of the use and power of representational systems as an organizing principle in human experience. As he states:

> . . . he [Huxley] wondered if I had ever built up hallucinations in my subjects by combining various sensory fields of experience. I told him that that was a standard procedure for me.

This discussion raised the question of anesthesia, amnesia, dissociation, depersonalization, regression, time distortion, hypermnesia (an item difficult to test with Huxley because of his phenomenal memory) and an exploration of past repressed events.

Of these, Huxley found that anesthesia, amnesia, time distortion, and hypermnesia were possible in the light trance. The other phenomena were conducive to the development of a deep trance with any earnest effort to achieve them.

The anesthesia he developed in the light trance was most effective for selected parts of the body. When generalized anesthesia from the neck down was attempted, Huxley found himself "slipping" into a deep trance.

The amnesia, like the anesthesia, was effective when selective in character. Any effort to have a total amnesia resulted in a progression toward a deep trance.

Time distortion was easily possible and Huxley offered the statement that he was not certain but that he felt strongly that he had long employed time distortion in Deep Reflection, although his first formal introduction to the concept had been through me.

Hypermnesia, so difficult to test because of his extreme capacity to recall past events, was tested upon my suggestion by asking him in the light trance state to state promptly upon request on what page of various of his books certain paragraphs could be found. At the first request, Huxley aroused from the light trance and explained, "Really now, Milton, I can't do that. I can with effort recite most of that book, but the page number for a paragraph is not exactly cricket." Nevertheless, he went back into a light trance, the name of the volume was given, a few lines of a paragraph were read aloud to him, whereupon he was to give the page number on which it appeared. He succeeded in definitely better than 65 percent in an amazingly prompt fashion. Upon awakening from the light trance, he was instructed to remain in the state of conscious awareness and to execute the same task. To his immense astonishment he found that, while the page number "flashed" into his mind in the light trance state, in the waking state he had to follow a methodical procedure of completing the paragraph mentally, beginning the next, then turning back mentally to the preceding paragraph and then "making a guess." When restricted to the same length of time he had employed in the light trance, he failed in each instance. When allowed to take whatever length of time he wished, he could reach an accuracy of about 40 percent, but the books had to be ones more recently read than those used for the light trance state.

Here, again, we find behavior supporting the pattern discussed previously. In the light trance state, Huxley has access to functions which are localized in the non-dominant hemisphere:

> . . . The page number "flashed" (a visual predicate) into his
> mind in the light trance state.

However, when the same task is attempted in the waking state or
the normal state of awareness — in Huxley's case, in the state in
which the kinesthetic representational system is dominant — no
visual images are available:

> . . . In the waking state he had to follow a mechanical
> procedure of completing the paragraph mentally,
> beginning the next, then . . .

Notice that, in general, Huxley is unable to match his performance
in the light trance state when in the waking state. The task, of
course, is one of visual recall — a function of the non-dominant
hemisphere.

Huxley then proceeded to duplicate in the medium trance all
that he had done in the light trance. He accomplished similar tasks
much more easily but constantly experienced a feeling of
"slipping" into a deeper trance.

Huxley and I discussed this hypnotic behavior of his at very
considerable length with Huxley making most of the notations
since only he could record his own subjective experience in
relation to the topics discussed. For this reason the discussion here
is limited.

We then turned to the question of deep hypnosis. Huxley
developed easily a profound somnambulistic trance in which he
was completely disoriented spontaneously for time and place. He
was able to open his eyes but described his field of vision as being
a "well of light" which included me, the chair in which I sat,
himself and his chair. He remarked at once upon the remarkable
spontaneous restriction of his vision, and disclosed an awareness
that, for some reason unknown to him, he was obligated to
"explain things" to me. Careful questioning disclosed him to have
an amnesia about what had been done previously, nor did he have
any awareness of our joint venture. His feeling that he must
explain things became a casual willingness as soon as he verbalized
it. One of his first statements was, "Really, you know, I can't
understand my situation or why you are here, wherever that may
be, but I must explain things to you." He was assured that I

understood the situation and that I was interested in receiving any explanation he wished to give me and told that I might make requests of him. Most casually, indifferently he acceded, but it was obvious that he was enjoying a state of physical comfort in a contented, passive manner.

He answered questions simply and briefly, giving literally and precisely no more and no less than the literal significance of the question implied. In other words, he showed the same precise literalness found in other subjects, perhaps more so because of his knowledge of semantics.

He was asked, "What is to my right?" His answer was simply, "I don't know." "Why?" "I haven't looked." "Will you do so?" "Yes." "Now!" "How far do you want me to look?" This was not an unexpected inquiry since I have encountered it innumerable times. Huxley was simply manifesting a characteristic phenomenon of the deep somnambulistic trance in which visual awareness is restricted in some inexplicable manner to those items pertinent to the trance situation. For each chair, couch, footstool I wished him to see, specific instructions were required. As Huxley explained later, "I had to look around until gradually it [the specified object] slowly came into view, not all at once, but slowly as if it were materializing. I really believe that I felt completely at ease without a trace of wonderment as I watched things materialize. I accepted everything as a matter of course." Similar explanations have been received from hundreds of subjects. Yet experience has taught me the importance of my assumption of the role of a purely passive inquirer, one who asks a question solely to receive an answer regardless of its content. An intonation of interest in the meaning of the answer is likely to induce the subject to respond as if he had been given instructions concerning what answer to give. In therapeutic work I use intonations to influence more adequate personal responses by the patient.

With Huxley I tested this by enthusiastically asking, "What, tell me now, is that which is just about 15 feet in front of you?" The correct answer should have been, "A table." Instead, the answer received was "A table with a book and a vase on it." Both the book and the vase were on the table but on the far side of the table and hence more than 15 feet away. Later the same inquiry was made in a casual indifferent fashion, "Tell me now what is that just about 15 feet in front of you?" He replied, despite his

previous answer, "A table." "Anything else?" "Yes." "What else?"
"A book." (This was nearer to him than was the vase.) "Anything
else?" "Yes." "Tell me now." "A vase." "Anything else?" "Yes."
"Tell me now." "A spot." "Anything else?" "No."

Now Huxley has fully entered the deep trance state. One of
the more interesting differences in the linguistic behavior of subjects in profound somnambulistic trances as opposed to either
normal states of consciousness or behavior during trance induction
in the light and medium states of trance occurs here. In states of
consciousness associated with hypnosis other than deep somnambulistic trance and in normal states of awareness, people will
respond to certain sentences which are in the form of questions as
though they were commands. For example, the typical response of
an adult speaker of English to questions such as:

> *Can you place your hands on your thighs?*
> *Are your hands on your thighs?*

is to respond as though they had been given the command:

> *Place your hands on your thighs!*

Specifically, the typical response for the person to whom the
questions are directed is to place their hands on their thighs.
Within the transformational linguistics model of language these
phenomena are known as conversational postulates (see Lakoff
and Gordon, 1973, for example, for a formal treatment). Essentially, the process works as follows: If I desire to have you
perform some act but I do not wish to order you directly to
perform it, I may select any one of the presuppositions of the
command which I want you to carry out, and ask you that
presupposition in the form of a yes-no question. (See *Magic I*,
Chapters 3 and 4 and Appendix B, and also Appendix of this
Volume, for a presentation of the formal notion of presupposition.) Specifically, one of the presuppositions of the command:

> *Place your hands on your thighs*

is that you are able, you can, place your hands on your thighs.
Since this is a presupposition of the command, by simply asking

you whether or not you are able to do it, I communicate the command "politely" in the form of a question.

Command	Presupposition
Place your hands on your thighs!	You can place your hands on your thighs.

by the principle of
conversational postulates

Can you place your hands on your thighs? ⟶	Place your hands on your thighs!

Developing the linguistic terminology further, we have the notions of Surface Structure — the actual form that the sentence which is spoken has — and Deep Structure — the representation of the meaning which the Surface Structure has. What makes these types of sentences peculiar is that they have an effect different from the effect that the meaning of the Deep Structure represents. In other words, the recovery of the literal Deep Structure from the Surface Structure is the normal process by which we understand another person's communication. However, in these particular cases, we have an additional step in the recovery of meaning. Specifically, if the literal Deep Structure meaning is a yes-no question form of a presupposition of a command, then we understand the force of the communication to be that command rather than the literal question meaning of the Deep Structure.

Similarly, when one person asks another the question: *What is to my right?* the typical response is either an immediate list of the items located to the right of the questioner, in the event that the person responding knows what is there, or the person responding will look to see what is located there in the event he didn't yet know. However, there are two conditions which we have identified in which a speaker of the language consistently will fail to respond in this manner: either when the speaker is in a profound somnambulistic trance or when the speaker is a child. Erickson questions Huxley, who is in a profound somnambulistic trance, with:

What is to my right?

and Huxley responds neither by immediately listing what items are located there nor by looking to see what is located there but rather:

I don't know

As Erickson comments, this ability of the subject in a profound somnambulistic trance to respond to the literal Deep Structure meaning of the sentence is an excellent indicator that the subject is in deep trance. Thus, one excellent test for the depth of trance in many subjects will be their ability *not* to respond to the additional meaning given by the conversational postulates. An examination of Erickson's induction techniques reveals a consistent use of conversational postulates during trance induction. This is consistent with his usual emphasis on a permissive rather than an authoritarian approach to induction. By using yes-no question forms to communicate commands, he bypasses the issue of control and resistance as he gives no direct commands to the client. Furthermore, consistent with his emphasis on the importance of distinguishing between trance induction and behavior in the trance state, this linguistic distinction is useful in determining where in the process the client is at a given point in time. In addition, notice that the behavior of the subject in ignoring the conversational postulate when in deep trance is totally congruent with his experience at a previous point in his life history, namely, childhood. This technique, then, supports the tendency in subjects who enter deep trance to experience age regression.

Notice that when Huxley enters deep trance, he becomes able to make visual distinctions which he normally has no choice about. Erickson states that this is "a characteristic phenomenon of the deep somnambulistic trance." This becomes understandable in the context of the remarks made previously regarding cerebral assymetry.

This literalness and this peculiar restriction of awareness to those items of reality constituting the precise hypnotic situation [are] highly definitive of a satisfactory somnambulistic hypnotic trance. Along with the visual restriction, there is also an auditory restriction of such character that sounds, even those originating between the operator and the subject, seem to be totally outside the hypnotic situation. Since there was no assistant present, this auditory restriction could not be tested. However, by means of a black thread not visible to the eye, a book was toppled from the table behind him against his back. Slowly, as if he had experienced an itch, Huxley raised his hand and scratched his shoulder. There was no startle reaction. This, too, is characteristic of the response made to many unexpected physical stimuli. They are interpreted in terms of past body experience. Quite frequently, as a part of developing a deep somnambulistic trance, subjects will concomitantly develop a selective general anesthesia for physical stimuli not constituting a part of the hypnotic situation, physical stimuli in particular that do not permit interpretation in terms of past experience. This could not be tested in the situation with Huxley since an assistant is necessary to make adequate tests without distorting the hypnotic situation. One illustrative measure I have used is to pass a threaded needle through a coat sleeve while positioning the arms and then having an assistant saw back and forth on the thread from a place of concealment. Often a spontaneous anesthesia would keep the subject unaware of the stimulus. Various simple measures are easily devised.

Huxley was then gently indirectly awakened from the trance by the simple suggestion that he adjust himself in his chair to resume the exact physical and mental state he had had at the decision to discontinue until later any further experimental study of Deep Reflection.

Huxley's response was an immediate arousal and he promptly stated that he was all set to enter deep hypnosis. While this statement in itself indicated profound post-hypnotic amnesia, delaying tactics were employed in the guise of discussion of what might possibly be done. In this way it became possible to mention various items of his deep trance behavior. Such mention evoked no memories and Huxley's discussion of the points raised showed no sophistication resulting from his deep trance behavior. He was as uninformed about the details of his deep trance behavior as he had been before the deep trance had been induced.

There followed more deep trances by Huxley in which, avoiding all personal significances, he was asked to develop partial, selective, and total post-hypnotic amnesias (by partial is meant a part of the total experience, by selective amnesia is meant an amnesia for selected, perhaps interrelated, items of experience), a recovery of the amnestic material and a loss of the recovered material. He developed also catalepsy, tested by "arranging" him comfortably in a chair and then creating a situation constituting a direct command to rise from the chair ("take the book on that table there and place it on the desk over there and do it now"). By this means Huxley found himself, inexplicably to him, unable to arise from the chair and unable to understand why this was so. (The "comfortable arrangement" of his body had resulted in a positioning that would have to be corrected before he could arise from the chair and no implied suggestions for such correction were to be found in the instructions given. Hence he sat helplessly unable to stand, unable to recognize why. This same measure has been employed to demonstrate a saddle block anesthesia before medical groups. The subject in the deep trance is carefully positioned, a casual conversation is then conducted, the subject is then placed in rapport with another subject who is asked to exchange seats with the first subject. The second subject steps over only to stand helplessly while the first subject discovers that she is (1) unable to move, and (2) that shortly the loss of inability to stand results in a loss of orientation to the lower part of her body and a resulting total anesthesia without anesthesia having been mentioned even in the preliminary discussion of hypnosis. This unnoticed use of catalepsy not recognized by the subject is a most effective measure in deepening trance states.

Huxley was amazed at his loss of mobility and became even more so when he discovered a loss of orientation to the lower part of his body and he was most astonished when I demonstrated for him the presence of a profound anesthesia. He was much at loss to understand the entire sequence of events. He did not relate the comfortable positioning of his body to the unobtrusively induced catalepsy with its consequent anesthesia.

He was aroused from the trance state with persistent catalepsy, anesthesia and a total amnesia for all deep trance experiences. He spontaneously enlarged the instruction to include all trance experiences, possibly because he did not hear my instructions sufficiently clear. Immediately he reoriented himself to the time at which we had been working with Deep Reflection. He was much at loss to explain his immobile state, and he expressed curious wonderment about what he had done in the Deep Reflection state, from which he assumed he had just emerged, and what had led to such inexplicable manifestations for the first time in all of his experience. He became greatly interested, kept murmuring such comments as "Most extraordinary" while he explored the lower part of his body with his hands and eyes. He noted that he could tell the position of his feet only with his eyes, that there was a profound immobility from the waist down, and he discovered, while attempting futilely because of the catalepsy to move his leg with his hands, that a state of anesthesia existed. This he tested variously, asking me to furnish him with various things in order to make his test. For example, he asked that ice be applied to his bare ankle by me since he could not bend sufficiently to do so. Finally, after much study he turned to me, remarking, "I say, you look cool and most comfortable while I am in a most extra-ordinary predicament. I deduce that in some subtle way you have distracted and disturbed my sense of body awareness. I say, is this state anything like hypnosis?"

Restoration of his memory delighted him, but he remained entirely at loss concerning the genesis of his catalepsy and his anesthesia. He realized, however, that some technique of communication had been employed to effect the results achieved but he did not succeed in the association of the positioning of his body with the final results.

Here Erickson constructs an experience for Huxley which is the formal equivalent in the kinesthetic representational system of the failure of the subject in deep trance to respond to conversational postulates in the linguistic system. By arranging Huxley's body in a position from which it is not possible for him to respond directly to the command for a specific movement and then giving Huxley that command, Erickson demonstrates kinesthetically the same formal phenomenon as the subject's inability to respond unless each portion of the sequence of behavior is made perfectly explicit. In the case of conversational postulates, the literal meaning of the Deep Structure only is responded to, not the force of the sentence given by the literal Deep Structure meaning plus the meaning derived from it by the mechanism of conversational postulates. In a formally parallel manner, since not all portions of the sequence of kinesthetic steps in the carrying out of the command are given explicitly, Huxley is paralyzed. The normal states of consciousness mechanisms which allow a person to supply for himself the kinesthetic steps not explicitly presented but implied by the command are not available to Huxley. This area of deep trance behavior requires more thorough investigation prior to formalization.

Further experimentation in the deep trance investigated visual, auditory and other types of ideosensory hallucinations. One of the measures employed was to pantomime hearing a door open and then to appear to see someone entering the room, to arise in courtesy and to indicate a chair, then to turn to Huxley to express the hope that he was comfortable. He replied that he was and he expressed surprise at his wife's unexpected return since he had expected her to be absent the entire day. (The chair I had indicated was one I knew his wife liked to occupy.) He conversed with her and apparently hallucinated replies. He was interrupted with the question of how he knew that it was his wife and not a hypnotic hallucination. He examined the question thoughtfully, then explained that I had not given him any suggestion to hallucinate his wife, that I had been as much surprised by her arrival as he had been, and that she was dressed as she had been just before her departure and not as I had seen her earlier. Hence, it was reasonable to assume that she was a reality. After a brief thoughtful pause, he returned to his "conversation" with her, apparently continuing to hallucinate replies. Finally I attracted his attention and made a hand gesture suggestive of a disappearance toward the chair in which he "saw" his wife. To his complete astonishment he saw her slowly fade away. Then he turned to me and asked that I awaken him with a full memory of the experience. This I did and he discussed the experience at some length, making many special notations in his notebook, elaborating them with the answers to questions he put to me. He was amazed to discover that when I asked [him] to awaken with a retention of the immobility and anesthesia, he *thought* he had awakened but that the trance state had, to him, unrecognizably persisted.

He then urged further work on hypnotic hallucinatory experiences and a great variety (positive and negative visual, auditory, olfactory, gustatory, tactile, kinesthetic, temperature, hunger, satiety, fatigue, weakness, profound excited expectation, etc.) were explored. He proved to be most competent in all regards and it was noted that his pulse rate would change as much as twenty points when he was asked to hallucinate the experience of mountain climbing in a profound state of weariness. He volunteered in his discussion of these varied experiences the information that, while a negative hallucination could be achieved readily in a deep trance, it would be most difficult in a light or

medium trance because negative hallucinations were most
destructive of reality values, even those of the hypnotic situation.
That is, with induced negative hallucinations, he found that I was
blurred in outline even though he could develop a deep trance
with a negative hallucination inherent in that deep trance for all
external reality except the realities of the hypnotic situation
which would remain clear and well defined unless suggestions to
the contrary were offered. Subsequent work with other subjects
confirmed this finding by Huxley. I had not previously explored
this matter of negative hallucinations in light and medium trances.

At this point, Huxley recalled his page number identification
in the lighter trance states during the inquiry into hypermnesia
and he asked that he be subjected to similar tests in deep hypnosis.
Together we searched the library shelves, finally selecting several
books that Huxley was certain he must have read many years
previously but which he had not touched for twenty or more
years. (One, apparently, he had never read, the other five he had.)

In a deep trance with his eyes closed, Huxley listened intently,
as I opened the book at random and read a half dozen lines from a
selected paragraph. For some, he identified the page number
almost at once and then he would hallucinate the page, and "read"
it from the point where I had stopped. Additionally, he identified
the occasion on which he read the book. Two of the books he
recalled consulting fifteen years previously. [For] another two he
found it difficult to give the correct page number and then only
approximating the page number. He could not hallucinate the
printing and could only give little more than a summary of the
thought content; but this, in essence, was correct. He could not
identify when he had read them but he was certain it was more
than twenty-five years previously.

Huxley, in the post-trance discussion, was most amazed by his
performance [of] a memory feat but commented upon the
experience as primarily intellectual with the recovered memories
lacking in any emotional significances of belonging to him as a
person. This led to a general discussion of hypnosis and Deep
Reflection with a general feeling of inadequacy on Huxley's part
concerning proper conceptualization of his experiences for
comparison of values. While Huxley was most delighted with his
hypnotic experiences for their interest and the new understandings
they offered him, he was also somewhat at a loss. He felt that, as a
purely personal experience, he derived certain unidentifiable

subjective values from Deep Reflection not actually obtainable from hypnosis which offered only a wealth of new points of view. Deep Reflection, he declared, gave him certain inner enduring feelings that seemed to play some significant part in his pattern of living. During this discussion he suddenly asked if hypnosis could be employed to permit him to explore his psychedelic experiences. His request was met but upon arousal from the trance he expressed the feeling that the hypnotic experience was quite different than was a comparable "feeling through" by means of Deep Reflection. He explained that the hypnotic exploration did not give him an inner feeling, that is, a continuing subjective feeling, of just being in the midst of his psychedelic experience, that there was an ordered intellectual content paralleling the "feeling content" while Deep Reflection established a profound emotional background of a stable character upon which he could "consciously lay effortlessly an intellectual display of ideas" to which the reader would make full response. This discussion Huxley brought to a close by the thoughtful comment that his brief intensive experience with hypnosis had not yet begun to digest and that he could not expect to offer an intelligent comment without much more thought.

Huxley's dramatic performance in his ability to access visually coded information from the distant past is a compelling example of the kinds of memories which become available to the subject in deep trance. It is especially suggestive to us that the deeper the trance — the more distinct from Huxley's normal state of awareness — the more available becomes the visually stored material of the non-dominant hemisphere. Huxley's characterization of the differences between his experience of Deep Reflection and deep trance also indicates a similar trend:

Description of Deep Reflection	Description of deep trance
. . . gave him certain inner *feelings* . . .	. . . offered only a wealth of new points of *view* . . .
. . . *feeling* through by means of Deep Reflection . . .	. . . *not* give him an inner *feeling* . . .

This characterization suggests that one of the differences between Deep Reflection and deep trance for Huxley is the extent to which the non-dominant hemisphere is accessed in these altered states of consciousness.

He asked urgently that further deep hypnosis be done with him in which more complex phenomena be induced to permit him to explore himself more adequately as a person. After a rapid mental review of what had been done and what might yet be done, I decided upon the desirability of a deep trance state with the possibility of a two-state dissociative regression; that is, of the procedure of regressing him by dissociating him from a selected recent area of his life experience so that he could view it as an onlooker from the orientation of another relatively recent area of life experience. The best way to do this I felt would be by a confusion technique.[12] This decision to employ a confusion technique was influenced in large part by the author's awareness of Huxley's unlimited intellectual capacity and curiosity which would aid greatly by leading Huxley to add to the confusion technique verbalizations other possible elaborate meanings and significances and associations, thereby actually supplementing in effect my own efforts. Unfortunately, there was no tape recorder present to preserve the details of the actual suggestions which were to the effect that Huxley go ever deeper and deeper into a trance until "the depth was a part and apart" from him, that before him would appear in "utter clarity, in living reality, in impossible actuality, that which once was, but which now in the depths of the trance, will, in bewildering confrontation, challenge all of your memories and understandings." This was a purposely vague yet permissively comprehensive suggestion and I simply relied upon Huxley's intelligence to elaborate it with an extensive meaningfulness for himself which I could not even attempt to guess. There were, of course, other suggestions but they centered in effect upon the suggestion enclosed in the quotation above. What I had in mind was not a defined situation but a setting of the stage so that Huxley himself would be led to define the task. I did not even attempt to speculate upon what my suggestions might mean to Huxley.

Erickson now introduces what he calls his *confusion technique*.[13] The name *confusion technique* covers a wide range of phenomena. Here we will extract only some of the patterns as we will return again and again to this technique, each time isolating additional patterns. The first of the quoted material by Erickson is the seven-word sentence:

The depth was a part and apart

First the noun phrase *the depth* is what is called in the Meta-model created in *Magic I* a nominalization. That is, in its Deep Structure representation, this noun phrase was a predicate — a word which originally represented a relationship or process. Through the transformational processes available in natural language systems, this predicate appears as the name of a thing in the Surface Structure which Erickson uses. Perhaps a non-hypnotic example will be of assistance. Consider the two sentences:

> *There was a chair in the house.*
> *There was frustration in the house.*

In *Magic I,* we developed a number of tests to assist therapists in sharpening their intuitions in identifying nominalization. For example, if your most highly valued representational system is visual, you may test to determine whether each of the noun phrases in a sentence is a nominalization by imaging a silver-green wheelbarrow and in your mind's eye attempting to visualize placing each of the things referred to by the noun phrases in a sentence into that wheelbarrow. If you are able to do this, the noun phrase is not a nominalization; otherwise it is. Using the above sentences as an example, each of you will be able to visualize placing a chair into a wheelbarrow but not a frustration. This indicates that the word *chair* is a true noun but that the word *frustration* is a nominalization — a noun which is derived from a predicate.

One of the characteristics of nominalizations is that they carry less information than is available. Read through the following sentences, paying attention to the information associated with the predicate *frustrate* in each of its forms:

> *That Betty frustrated Max was obvious.*
> *That Max was frustrated was obvious.*
> *The frustration was obvious.*

In the first sentence, the word *frustrate* appears in its verb form and it states that there is a person (named *Betty*) who is frustrating another person (named *Max*). In the second sentence one of the pieces of information associated with the predicate *frustrate* is missing — in the linguistic model, this is called deletion, the process of the removal of portions of the full linguistic representation of the sentence. In the third sentence, both of the pieces of information associated with the predicate *frustrate* are missing, and the form of the predicate has been changed into a noun form. From the third sentence alone it is not possible to determine who is frustrating whom — all of that information has been deleted. When the information normally carried by a predicate has been deleted in this way, and the form of the predicate changed into a noun form, then the result is said to lack a referential index — that is, the word *frustration* does not pick out or refer to a portion of our experience in its nominal form. Since it has no referential index, such a nominal invites projections or hallucinations on the part of the listener. In a way exactly parallel to the nominalization *frustration,* the word *depth* has had the information associated with it deleted and it, therefore, has no referential index. Since it fails to have a referential index, it invites interpretation, projection and hallucination on the part of the listener.

One of the requirements of the statements which the hypnotist makes to the client is that these statements be in agreement with or congruent with the ongoing experience of the client. We refer to this as *pacing.* There are several ways in which this may be accomplished by the hypnotist. The hypnotist may restrict himself to verbal descriptions of precisely those things which he can directly observe. For example, frequently, as part of an induction, the hypnotist will include statements such as:

> *. . . breathing in . . . and out*
> *Reading left to right*

where he is careful to time his pronunciation of the words *in* and *out* to match the actual inhalations and exhalations of the client. Or, in the case of a standard hand levitation, the hypnotist will include typically statements such as:

> *. . . lifting, a sudden twitch . . . even higher . . .*

when these descriptive words are said by the hypnotist precisely at the point wherein the client's hand is, in fact, lifting, twitching, etc.

Another excellent technique for pacing is for the hypnotist to use verbal descriptions which allow the client to hallucinate or project his ongoing experience onto the descriptions being used. The skillful hypnotist employing this pacing technique makes full use of the universal processes of human modeling — deletion, distortion, and generalization. As we describe at length in *Magic I*, Chapters 2, 3 and 4, within the language system which each of us uses to communicate ·there are a number of distortion mechanisms. Perhaps the most severe of these, linguistically, is the process of nominalization — the linguistic process of representing a process as an event. As shown by the *frustration* and *depth* examples, the other two modeling processes are typically involved when the process of nominalization occurs. The predicate *frustrate* is used in the sentence:

> *The frustration was obvious.*

in a nominalized form. In the Deep Structure of the sentence in which the nominal *frustration* occurred, there was the additional information of who or what was frustrating whom (actually requires an additional distinction in reference structure). Both of these pieces fail to be represented in the Surface Structure. Similarly, with the nominalization *depth*, the Surface Structure contains no information regarding what depth or whose depth. In other words, the linguistic process of deletion has occurred, removing some of the information. As the information is deleted and thereby fails to occur in the actual utterance by the hypnotist, the sentence itself carries no referential index which picks out a specific experience. Rather the resulting phrase *the depth* becomes a possible description of a wide range of experiences for the listener. This leaves the client a great number of choices of interpretation, hallucination, or projection. By this device the client is more actively engaged in the process of trance induction or deep trance behavior. In addition, of course, the hypnotist successfully paces the client's experience. By skillfully employing the three processes of human modeling — in this case, the specific linguistic mechanisms of these three processes: nominalization, transformational deletion, and lack of referential index — it is possible for the hypnotist to successfully pace the client's experience without knowing what it is. This allows the hypnotist an infinite range of choices in his verbalizations. As Erickson says:

> . . . a confusion technique . . . would aid greatly by leading

Huxley to add to the confusion technique verbalizations other possible elaborate meanings and significances, and associations, thereby actually supplementing in effect my own efforts. . . . This was a purposely vague yet permissively comprehensive suggestion and I simply relied on Huxley's intelligence to elaborate it with extensive meaningfulness for himself which I could not even attempt to guess. . . . I did not even attempt to speculate what my suggestions might mean to Huxley.

Thus, the first portion of the first sentence which Erickson quotes — *the depth* — admirably meets both his purposes and Huxley's.

The second pattern which we want to take from the seven-word extract is the one carried by the words *a part and apart:*

The depth was a part and apart.

First, notice that in its written form there is no ambiguity about the phrase — the first portion is a two-word phrase *a part* while the second portion is a one-word phrase *apart.* When presented auditorily, however, the phrase is completely ambiguous. One of the intuitions which people can come to have regarding the language they speak is that of ambiguity. Some types of ambiguity depend upon the representational system in which they occur, such as the one which we are considering when presenting it auditorily. Other types of linguistic ambiguity persist even when the representational system is shifted; for example:[14]

Hypnotizing hypnotists can be tricky.

The ambiguity of this sentence is: Which of the following two sentences is intended by the sentence above:

Hypnotizing hypnotists are tricky.
or
For anyone to attempt to hypnotize hypnotists is tricky.

Notice that, whether you read the original sentence aloud and listen to it (auditory representation) or you read it silently without an internal auditory presentation (internal dialogue), both meanings are possible. This type of ambiguity has been formalized by transformational linguists and is referred to as *syntactic ambiguity*. In the terms we developed previously, a sentence or Surface Structure is called ambiguous if it is a linguistic representation of more than one distinct experience, or in linguistic terms if it is a linguistic representation of more than one distinct Deep Structure.[15]

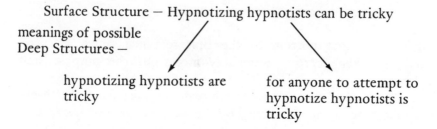

Surface Structure — Hypnotizing hypnotists can be tricky

meanings of possible
Deep Structures —

hypnotizing hypnotists are tricky

for anyone to attempt to hypnotize hypnotists is tricky

An example of *phonological or sound ambiguity* which parallels the one used by Erickson is:

It's funny to talk about a $\left\{ \begin{array}{l} \text{nitrate} \\ \text{night rate} \end{array} \right\}$ deal.

Say the above sentence out loud; under conditions of normal speech, most listeners will be unable to distinguish between the two visually presented versions. The phonological presentation is completely ambiguous. The explanation is the same as above — the Surface Structure is a representation of more than one Deep Structure. Now consider Erickson's sentence again:

The depth was a part and apart.

The same sound sequence — we will represent it visually as *a-part* — can be decomposed into two distinct Deep Structure sequences. Notice that Erickson compounds the ambiguity as he repeats the sound sequence twice, connecting them with an *and*. Thus, there are not two but four possible Deep Structure decompositions (see page 103):

In other words, the listener, in this case Huxley, is left with four possible Deep Structure phrase interpretations for the single Surface Structure phrase.

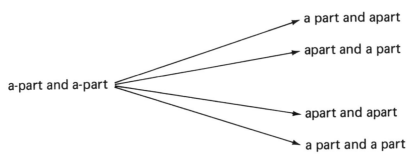

Keeping in mind the linguistic distinctions explained above, we turn to an examination of the remainder of the quoted material presented by Erickson in his instructions to assist Huxley in deep trance:

> . . . utter *clarity*, in living *reality*, in impossible *actuality*, that which once was, but which now in the *depths* of the *trance*, will in bewildering *confrontation* challenge all of your *memories* and *understandings* . . .

Perhaps the easiest way for you to come to appreciate the structure of Erickson's assertions is to settle yourself into a comfortable position, place yourself in a state of utter relaxation and, with the thought/feeling/picture/sound which you once had, allow yourself to assume that what you are about to hear is extremely important and will influence the remainder of your life. Then, have a friend read Erickson's words to you in a low, serious, concerned tone of voice at a slow tempo with different phrasings (intonation patterns) and pay attention to all of the interpretations which you are able to assign to them. From a formal point of view, the number of possible interpretations are astronomical. For example, twenty of the thirty-one words are Deep Structure predicates. Of these twenty, only two occur as Surface Structure verbs (typically, the least distorted form a Deep Structure predicate may take). The majority of the remainder of these Deep Structure predicates have undergone the process of nominalization described previously. For each of these, of course, the number of possible interpretations are multiple — thus, both successfully pacing Huxley's experience and allowing him maximum freedom to select an interpretation which fits for him, all without a consciousness on Huxley's part. As an example:

... bewildering confrontation ...

the word *confrontation* is a Surface Structure noun which results from the process of nominalization — specifically, it derives from the Deep Structure predicate *confront*. Therefore, in Deep Structure, the predicate *confront* is a linguistic representation of a process of someone's confronting someone else about something. Through the linguistic process of nominalization all the material associated with this Deep Structure predicate has been deleted, and, consequently, the resulting expression totally lacks a referential index, thereby making it maximally available for Huxley's interpretation and incorporation into his ongoing deep trance experience. The Deep Structure predicate *bewilder* occurs in the phrase as an adjective form *(bewildering)* which describes the experience of someone associated with the nominalization *confrontation.* It describes the way that the confrontation was experienced. The question here is the way that the confrontation was experienced by **whom**: the person doing the confronting, the person being confronted, or someone observing the confrontation? Again, this Deep Structure predicate, in the linguistic process of being transformed into a Surface Structure adjective, has lost the information associated with it in the full linguistic representation, the Deep Structure. The result, again, is a Surface Structure which is maximally vague and, therefore, maximally congruent with Huxley's ongoing and future experience. To complicate matters somewhat, the two predicates *bewilder* and *confront* are associated syntactically. That is, as Huxley selects an interpretation for the missing information associated with the predicate *confront,* he still has the freedom to apply the *bewilder* predicate to any one of the pieces of information he has selected for the predicate *confront* (the person confronting may be considered bewildered, or the person being confronted, or some observer). The following is a list of the Deep Structure predicates which have been nominalized in Erickson's utterance:

clarity	*reality*
actuality	*depth*
trance	*confrontation*
memories	*understandings*

There are two additional characteristics of the Huxley passage which occur over and over again in Erickson's verbal work. In several cases, Erickson juxtaposes predicates, one modifying the other, in a way which violates what linguists call selectional restrictions (see Grinder and Elgin, 1973; Chomsky, 1965). When a person says a sentence such as:

The boy feels silly

any native listener of English will accept the sentence as a well-formed sentence of his language. However, if the person says the sentence:

The rock feels silly

the typical response by a native listener of English is one of puzzlement, of a sensation that he has somehow failed to understand what the speaker is attempting to communicate. The transformational linguists' explanation for this phenomenon goes as follows: Each predicate in a language system is the name of some process or relationship. In the world of human experience, certain processes or relationships are restricted in that they can occur only with certain classes of people or things. For example, only female human beings can become pregnant. Conversely, the process of being a father is restricted to male humans. Therefore, the sentence:

My father is pregnant again

is a decidedly peculiar sentence. Another way of representing these facts is to point out that the set of objects/people which are referred to by the term *father* and the set of people/objects which are referred to by the term *pregnant* do not intersect; they have no members in common. Something cannot both be a father and be pregnant. Linguistically, the predicate *pregnant* is said to have a selectional restriction which requires that whatever it is applied to must be female. Other selectional restrictions are less clearly defined. For example, some of you readers will find the following sentences perfectly acceptable, others will judge them to be perfectly unacceptable, while others will find some acceptable, others unacceptable, and still others undecidable.

My cat Tripod feels silly
My cat feels silly
My goldfish feels silly
My lizard feels silly
My worm feels silly
My roses feel silly
My weeds feel silly
My oven feels silly

Erickson makes use of this category of linguistic patterning when he uses, for example, the phrase *impossible actuality*. Many native speakers of English will respond to this phrase as a selectional restriction violation; specifically, how can what is actual be impossible, or how can what is impossible be actual?

The final pattern which we want to extract from this verbalization by Erickson is the one involved in the use of the predicates *once, was, now,* and *will*. The feature which these predicates have in common is that they all refer to time — so-called temporal predicates. Specifically, they have the following force:

was	refers to the past
now	refers to the present
will	refers to the future
once	ambiguous reference

Thus, all of the major logical possibilities with respect to time occur in a single utterance by Erickson.[16] Once again, the consequence of this is to allow Huxley to assign the interpretation which is maximally congruent with his ongoing and future experience. As we stated in the discussion of the predicate-predicate sequences such as ... *bewildering confrontation* ... these three general categories of nominalization/adjective derivations, selectional restriction violations and temporal predicates interact with one another to provide the client with an astronomical number of possible interpretations from which to choose, thus insuring a successful pacing by the hypnotist.

It became obvious that Huxley was making an intensive hypnotic response during the prolonged repetitious suggestions I was offering when suddenly he raised his hand and said rather loudly and most urgently, "I say, Milton, do you mind hushing up there. This is most extraordinarily interesting down here and your constant talking is frightfully distracting and annoying."

For more than two hours, Huxley sat with his eyes open, gazing intently before him. The play of expression on his face was most rapid and bewildering. His heart rate and respiratory rate were observed to change suddenly and inexplicably and repeatedly at irregular intervals. Each time that the author attempted to speak to him, Huxley would raise his hand, perhaps lift his head, and speak as if the author were at some height above him, and frequently he would annoyedly request silence.

After well over two hours, he suddenly looked up toward the ceiling and remarked with puzzled emphasis, "I say, Milton, this is an extraordinary contretemps. We don't know you. You do not belong here. You are sitting on the edge of a ravine watching both of us and neither of us knows which one is talking to you; and we are in the vestibule looking at each other with most extraordinary interest. We know that you are someone who can determine our identity and most extraordinarily we are both sure we know it and that the other is not really so, but merely a mental image of the past or of the future. But you must resolve it despite time and distances and even though we do not know you. I say, this is an extraordinarily fascinating predicament, and am I he or is he me? Come, Milton, whoever you are." There were other similar remarks of comparable meaning which could not be recorded, and Huxley's tone of voice suddenly became most urgent. The whole situation was most confusing to me, but temporal and other types of dissociation seemed to be definitely involved in the situation.

Wonderingly, but with outward calm, I undertook to arouse Huxley from the trance state by accepting the partial clues given and by saying in essence,

> Wherever you are, whatever you are doing, listen closely to what is being said and slowly, gradually, comfortably begin to act upon it. Feel rested and comfortable, feel a need to establish an increasing contact with my voice, with me, with the situation I represent, a need of returning to matters in hand with me not so long ago, in the not so long ago belonging to me, *and leave behind but* AVAILABLE UPON REQUEST *practically everything of importance,* KNOWING BUT NOT KNOWING *that it is* AVAILABLE UPON REQUEST. And now, let us see, that's right, you

are sitting there, wide awake, rested, comfortable, and *ready for discussion of what little there is.*

In Erickson's article, three different types of print were used as he attempted to overcome the limitations of a single system (here visual — print) of communication to the reader of the technique he employs with Huxley. In so doing Erickson is attempting to describe by example one of his most powerful techniques. We begin by sorting a portion of the total communication into the three categories as they are marked by the different types of print in the article:

Original	Decomposed by Analogue Signal
. . . in the not so long ago belonging to me, *and leave behind but* AVAILABLE UPON REQUEST *practically everything of importance,* KNOWING BUT NOT KNOWING *that it is* AVAILABLE UPON REQUEST. And now, let us see, that's right, you are sitting there, wide awake, rested, comfortable, and *ready for discussion of what little there is.*	**A** in the not so long ago belonging to me. . . . and now, let us see, you are sitting there, wide awake, rested, comfortable and **B** available upon request . . . knowing but not knowing . . . available upon request **C** and leave behind . . . practically everything of importance . . . that it is . . . ready for discussion of what little there is

Each one of the print types in the original article represents a distinct portion of the entire communication by Erickson which he marked by some kind of analogical signal. Which specific analogical signals Erickson used at that time for each of the categories represented by the different print types is unimportant for our purposes here. From our personal observations and recordings of Erickson, and keeping in mind the fact that Huxley, typically, had his eyes closed during deep trance, our guess is that Erickson used tonality and tempo shifts of his voice to mark the three sets of messages as distinct. Erickson has excellent control over his analogical voice qualities (tonality and tempo). One of the useful generalizations from this piece of Erickson's work is the exquisitely refined ability he has in his use of digital analogical system interactions. Essentially, he produces a lengthy sequence of English words and phrases which heard together constitute a well-formed English communication. Imposed on top of this communication are (in this particular case) two sets of analogical signals which select or pick out sequences of English words and phrases from the total message, each of which, itself, constitutes a coherent communication. Specifically, set **A** is designed to assist Huxley in returning to a relatively normal state of awareness; set **B** has as its function the establishing of the cue which Erickson will use later to assist Huxley in recovering this experience; set **C** is instructions from Erickson to Huxley to experience amnesia with respect to his deep trance activities. We cannot overemphasize the usefulness and power of this analogical marking of digital material which decomposes it into separate message units. For almost everyone with whom we have used this technique, it has proven itself immediate and effective. The following discussion is a partial explanation of the effectiveness of this technique:

(1) With the exception of some hypnotists and therapists whose skills demand that they be aware of the congruity or incongruity of the messages communicated by the person to whom they are attending, no one systematically and consciously represents all of the messages presented by a person as that person communicates. At each point in time, as a person communicates with us, he uses his body posture (e.g., tight, closed, loose), gestures (e.g., hand movements, eye-fixation patterns), tonality (e.g., shrill, resonant), tempo (e.g., rapid, staccato), language (e.g., words, syntax), etc., to express a set of messages. These messages may fit together (congruent communication) or they may conflict (incongruent communication). In the therapeutic context, these distinctions form the basis for assisting the client in changing (see *Magic I,* Chapter 6; *Magic II,* Part II; and *Peoplemaking,* 1973, Satir). The total message presented by Erickson constitutes a well-formed communication of English. The normal linguistic processing mechanisms for the recovery of meaning apply to this level of structure, and we become aware of the meaning of the total message. These linguistic processes, themselves, are normally unconscious or preconscious, their results —

the meaning of the utterance — conscious. Since we do not normally represent separately the messages carried by the other person's analogical signals, we are not conscious of the relationship between the digital language material and these signals. Thus, when Erickson uses analogical signals to mark the total message for decomposition into separate message units, we are not aware that this level of patterning is occurring, and, consequently, we receive communication of which we are wholly unaware. The result of this process is that what Erickson refers to as our unconscious mind receives and responds to a set of messages of which we are totally unaware. Without awareness, we do not challenge the messages but simply respond.

(2) Each of us went through an extended learning experience between the ages of two and five as we learned to speak and understand the natural language system called English. As we did this, we began by learning to respond to, and produce sequences of, English words which were simpler in their structure than adult English; these simpler patterns are called *child grammars*. These child grammars are entirely distinctive from the grammar of adult English but are fully regular in their patterning.

> ... The mental abilities of a little child seem to be rather limited in many ways, yet he masters the exceedingly complex structure of his native language in the course of a short three or four years. What is more, each child, exposed to a different sample of the language, and generally with little or no conscious tuition on the part of his parents, arrives at essentially the same *grammar* in this brief span. That is to say, each child rapidly becomes a full-fledged member of his language community, able to produce and comprehend an endless variety of novel yet meaningful utterances in the language he has mastered. ... Until recently, behavioristic psychology looked upon language, and the task of first language learning, as just another form of human behavior which could be reduced to the laws of conditioning. The picture we are now beginning to form, however, is that of a child who is creatively constructing his language on his own, in accordance with innate and intrinsic capacities — a

child who is developing new theories of the structure of the language, modifying and discarding old theories as he goes.

It seems clear to us now that children form a variety of word categories of their own — based on the functions of words in their own language systems — and so words must be looked at in the light of the *child's* total system, rather than in terms of the adult system, which he has not yet mastered. . . . When the child starts putting two words together one can begin investigating his active grammar. The examples presented below demonstrate that child language is structured from this point on, that it soon can be characterized by *hierarchical structures,* that it tends to be *regular,* that the structures change with age, and that they do not always correspond to adult structures.

Psycholinguistics, by Dan Slobin, pp. 40-41. Scott, Foreman, & Co., 1971.

Some of the message units (take set **B** as an example) which Erickson creates by his analogical marking of the total communication are not well-formed sequences of adult grammars; critically, however, they are strongly reminiscent of the patterns which each of us employed during our learning experiences between the ages of two and five. Thus, to understand the message carried by the sequence of words and phrases in the message units separated by analogical marking by Erickson, it is likely that we access the grammatical mechanisms which we employed as children. This helps to explain the almost inevitable phenomenon of age regression which "spontaneously" occurs when this technique is used.

(3) One of the most intriguing findings of the research which has been done by psycholinguists and linguists is that the different stages in child grammars as the child moves from apparently total incompetence with language structures to full competence tend to have the same simplified patterns at each stage *independently of the child* and *of the language which the child is learning* (see Slobin, 1974; McNeill, 1970 for a more detailed presentation). This fact along with a number of other considerations have led

researchers to the Universal Grammar hypothesis (see Chomsky, 1965; Grinder and Elgin, 1973, Chapter 13). In essence, the Universal Grammar hypothesis states that we begin life with a pre-wired set of distinctions which is the basis upon which we build as we learn to understand and speak the amazingly complex system of natural language to which we are exposed between two and five years of age. From the extensive literature of cases of brain damage (see, especially, Goldstein, Lenneberg, Geschwind) and neurological mapping of localized brain functions (see, especially, Penfield, Gazzinga, Eccles, Sperry), we find that, apparently, each of the cerebral hemispheres has the potential to become the so-called dominant hemisphere — the location of the language system. For example, children who are the victims of brain injury to the dominant cerebral hemisphere after they have begun or even largely completed the task of learning to understand and speak a language, initially lose their linguistic skills but rapidly regain them. In this process they exhibit the same set of child-grammar patterns which they showed during their initial learning periods. The intersection of these two findings leads us to the conclusion that each of the cerebral hemispheres has the wired-in circuits known as universal grammar. As Erickson decomposes his total communication marking the separate message units analogically, some of the sets (again, set B in the example) are composed of patterns which approach the simplicity of patterning characteristic of universal grammar.[17] As the dominant hemisphere is occupied with the normal processing of the well-formed total communication, the separate message units, carrying their simpler patterns, are available to the non-dominant hemisphere. In this way it is possible for us to receive and respond to messages accepted in the non-dominant hemisphere without any consciousness of it.

These three considerations, while not exhausting the possibilities of Erickson's analogical marking of language material, provide a beginning basis for the analysis of the extraordinary power and effectiveness of this technique.

Huxley aroused, rubbed his eyes, and remarked, "I have a most extraordinary feeling that I have been in a profound trance, but it has been a most sterile experience. I recall you suggesting that I go deeper in a trance, and I felt myself to be most compliant, and though I feel much time has elapsed, I truly believe a state of Deep Reflection would have been more fruitful."

Since he did not specifically ask the time, a desultory conversation was conducted in which Huxley compared the definite but vague appreciation of external realities of the light trance with the more definitely decreased awareness of externalities in the medium trance which is accompanied by a peculiar sense of minor comfort that those external realities can become secure actualities at any given moment.

He was then asked about realities in the deep trance from which he had just recently aroused. He replied thoughtfully that he could recall vaguely feeling that he was developing a deep trance but that no memories came to mind associated with it. After some discussion of hypnotic amnesia and the possibility that he might be manifesting such a phenomenon, he laughed with amusement and stated that such a topic would be most intriguing to discuss. After still further desultory conversation, he was asked *a propos* of nothing, "In what vestibule would you place that chair?" (indicating a nearby armchair). His reply was remarkable. "Really, Milton, that is a most extraordinary question. Frightfully so! It is quite without meaning, but that word 'vestibule' has a strange feeling of immense, anxious warmth about it. Most extraordinarily fascinating!" He lapsed into a puzzled thought for some minutes and finally stated that if there were any significance, it was undoubtedly some fleeting esoteric association. After further casual conversation, I remarked, "As for the edge where I was sitting, I wonder how deep the ravine was." To this Huxley replied, "Really, Milton, you can be most frightfully cryptic. Those words 'vestibule,' 'edge,' 'ravine' have an extraordinary effect upon me. It is most indescribable. Let me see if I can associate some meaning with them." For nearly 15 minutes Huxley struggled vainly to secure some meaningful associations with those words, now and then stating that my apparently purposive but unrevealing use of them constituted a full assurance that there was a meaningful significance which should be apparent to him. Finally, he disclosed with elation, "I have it now. Most extraordinary how it escaped me. I'm fully aware that you had me in a trance and unquestionably those words had something to do with the deep trance which seemed to be so sterile to me. I wonder if I can recover my associations."

After about 20 minutes of silent, obviously intense, thought on his part, Huxley remarked, "If those words do have a significance, I can truly say that I have a most profound hypnotic amnesia. I have attempted Deep Reflection, but I have found my thoughts centering around my mescaline experiences. It was indeed difficult to tear myself away from those thoughts. I had a feeling that I was employing them to preserve my amnesia. Shall we go on for another half hour on other matters to see if there is any spontaneous recall in association with 'vestibule,' 'edge,' and 'ravine?' "

Various topics were discussed until finally Huxley said, "It is a most extraordinary feeling of meaningful warmth those words have for me, but I am utterly, I might say frightfully, helpless. I suppose I will have to depend upon you for something, whatever that may be. It's extraordinary, most extraordinary."

This comment I deliberately bypassed but during the ensuing conversation Huxley was observed to have a most thoughtful puzzled expression on his face, though he made no effort to press me for assistance. After some time, I commented with quiet emphasis, "Well, perhaps now matters will *become available.*" From his lounging comfortable position in his chair, Huxley straightened up in a startled amazed fashion and then poured forth a torrent of words too rapid to record except for occasional notes.

In essence, his account was that the word "available" had the effect of drawing back an amnestic curtain, laying bare a most astonishing subjective experience that had miraculously been "wiped out" by the words "leave behind" and had been recovered *in toto* by virtue of the cue words of "become available."

Here Erickson once again demonstrates his refined ability to enter and operate in the model of the world presented to him by the client. Accepting without objection Huxley's comment that his experience in deep trance had been "a most sterile experience," Erickson creates an experience with Huxley which allows Huxley to come to understand the possibilities of deep trance phenomenon. Specifically, Erickson works to create an experience in which Huxley will both exhibit amnesia and be partially aware that something extraordinary is occurring. With his sensitivity to the linguistic representation given by Huxley while in deep trance, Erickson selects several of the actual words which Huxley used during the period for which he had amnesia. Erickson begins to question Huxley. Huxley reacts markedly; specifically, when

Erickson uses the words employed by Huxley during the portion of his deep trance for which he has amnesia, Huxley responds with statements such as:

.... that word "vestibule" has a strange *feeling* of *immense,* anxious *warmth* . . .

.... I had a *feeling* that I . . . . .

.... *feeling* of meaningful *warmth* . . .

One of the interesting dimensions of Huxley's experience here is that certain words have acquired a seemingly irresistible power. Specifically, when Huxley hears the words *vestibule, edge* or *ravine,* he experiences a kinesthetic sensation. And he experiences this body sensation apparently without any choice in the matter. This process connects solidly with several portions of our experience in the therapeutic context. In both our work with certain types of psychosomatic diseases (e.g., asthma, stuttering) and with certain frequently occurring types of patterns of failure to cope effectively in interpersonal relationships, we have encountered what we have come to call *fuzzy functions.* A fuzzy function (see *Magic II,* Part III, for a detailed discussion) is a situation in which a person receives a message in some input channel (e.g., visually, auditorily) but, rather than experiencing and storing that information or message in the associated representational system, he represents it in some other representational system. For example, one of our clients who suffered from asthma experienced asthma attacks whenever he heard the word *kill* and other words associated with interpersonal violence. Another of our clients flew into an uncontrollable rage whenever she heard the word *Dolly.* Clients whose model of the world specifies that they behave as though they have no choice about what they experience kinesthetically whenever they hear a particular sound sequence are displaying the fuzzy function which we call *hear-feel.* Accepting a model of the world in which they have no control over certain fuzzy functions reduces the choices that the clients have in their coping behavior. Specifically, for example, if each time the client hears a certain word he "automatically" feels a certain way, then he no longer has the ability to respond creatively; rather, he can only react. The responsibility for his experience — literally, the way he feels — lies outside himself and statements such as:

He makes me feel angry
She frustrates the hell out of me

are unfortunately accurate representations of the client's experience. Formally identical patterns exist in the other possible combinations of input channel-representational systems. For example, one of our clients experienced intense panic feelings of fear whenever she saw a car stopped on the inside lane of a highway which had four lanes. This is an example of the fuzzy function we call *see-feel*. In each of these cases, the authors used enactment techniques and related skills involving the systematic use of representational systems to assist the client in changing so that she had a choice about feeling the sound and sights she had received or stored in the corresponding representational system. (These techniques are described extensively in *Magic II*, Parts I, II and III.) The point here is that fuzzy functions are not bad or crazy; they form the basis for much pleasure and creativity in our experience. They are, however, in certain contexts a restriction of the choices that a human being has about what portions of the world are available to him (phobias, for example). Thus, the therapeutic techniques which we have developed are designed not to remove or destroy these fuzzy function processes, but rather to assist clients in gaining control and choice over these circuits. We notice, also, that these same patterns occur at the cultural or societal level. Certain classes of experience are specified as negative fuzzy function and identified as taboo — for example, pornography is identified culturally in this country (U.S.A.) as a negative see-feel; similarly, the culture has proscribed the use of those words which describe certain body experiences such as fucking, shitting, etc; that is, they have been identified as negative hear-feels. Conversely, the cultural standards of physical beauty, grace, etc., and melody, rhythm, etc., are simply the culturally identified, positively valued fuzzy functions for see-feeling and hear-feeling, respectively. Furthermore, the cultural differences exhibited by the various national and ethnic groups can be easily represented in terms of the fuzzy functions selected as postive and negative, as are the differences between the cultural standard requirements for the sexes, both within a cultural or ethnic group and across different groups. The significance of the Erickson-Huxley interchange in this portion of the article is that it demonstrates that fuzzy-function circuits are learned, and, more importantly, it demonstrates the value of hypnosis as a research tool to begin the exploration of the process of this type of human circuitry. Erickson has shown a life-long sensitivity for this dramatic and exciting possibility. Very early in his career he explored the various phenomena of hypnotically induced deafness and color blindness (see Erickson, 1938a and b).

Finally, note that Erickson shows his usual sensitivity to the person with whom he is working. He allows Huxley to explore different ways of recovering the material associated with the hear-feel circuits which have been established. Huxley is creative in his attempts to overcome the amnesia which is at the root of the hear-feel circuits he is experiencing. When Huxley has spent some considerable time in this attempt, Erickson simply mentions one of the cue phrases which he had marked analogically as belonging to set **B** — the set of cue words and phrases which will allow Huxley to recover his memories. The results are dramatic. This sequence, again, shows the value of hypnotically induced fuzzy functions as a research instrument for the exploration of human neurological potential — altered states of consciousness.

He explained that he now realized that he had developed a "deep trance," a psychological state far different from his state of Deep Reflection, that in Deep Reflection there was an attenuated but unconcerned and unimportant awareness of external reality, a feeling of being in a known sensed state of subjective awareness, of a feeling of control and a desire to utilize capabilities and in which past memories, learnings, and experiences flowed freely and easily. Along with this flow there would be a continuing sense in the self that these memories, learnings, experiences, and understandings, however vivid, were no more than just such an orderly meaningful alignment of psychological experiences out of which to form a foundation for a profound, pleasing, subjective emotional state from which would flow comprehensive understandings to be utilized immediately and with little conscious effort.

The deep trance state, he asserted, he now knew to be another and entirely different category of experience. External reality could enter but it acquired a new kind of subjective reality, a special reality of a new and different significance entirely. For example, while I had been included in part in his deep trance state, it was not as a specific person with a specific identity. Instead, I was known only as someone whom he (Huxley) knew in some vague and unimportant and completely unidentified relationship.

Aside from my "reality," there existed the type of reality that one encounters in vivid dreams, a reality that one does not question. Instead, one accepts such reality completely without intellectual questioning and there are no conflicting contrasts nor judgmental comparisons nor contradictions so that whatever is subjectively experienced is unquestioningly accepted as both subjectively and objectively genuine and in keeping with all else.

In his deep trance, Huxley found himself in a deep, wide ravine, high up on the steep side of which, on the very edge, I sat, identifiable only by name and as annoyingly verbose.

Before him, in a wide expanse of soft, dry sand was a nude infant lying on its stomach. Acceptingly, unquestioning of its actuality, Huxley gazed at the infant, vastly curious about its behavior, vastly intent on trying to understand its flailing movements with its hands and the creeping movements of its legs. To his amazement, he felt himself experiencing a vague curious sense of wonderment as if he himself were the infant and looking at the soft sand and trying to understand what it was.

As he watched, he became annoyed with me since I was apparently trying to talk to him, and he experienced a wave of impatience and requested that I be silent. He turned back and noted that the infant was growing before his eyes, was creeping, sitting, standing, toddling, walking, playing, talking. In utter fascination he watched this growing child, sensed its subjective experiences of learning, of wanting, of feeling. He followed it in distorted time through a multitude of experiences as it passed from infancy to childhood to school days to early youth to teenage. He watched the child's physical development, sensed its physical and subjective mental experiences, sympathized with it, emphathized with it, rejoiced with it, thought and wondered and learned with it. He felt as one with it, as if it were he himself, and he continued to watch it until finally he realized that he had watched that infant grow to the maturity of 23 years. He stepped closer to see what the young man was looking at, and suddenly realized that the young man was Aldous Huxley himself, and that this Aldous Huxley was looking at another Aldous Huxley, obviously in his early fifties, just across the vestibule in which they both were standing; and that he, aged 52, was looking at himself,

Aldous, aged 23. Then Aldous, aged 23, and Aldous, aged 52, apparently realized simultaneously that they were looking at each other and the curious questions at once arose in the mind of each of them. For one the question was, "Is that my idea of what I'll be like when I am 52?" and, "Is that really the way I appeared when I was 23?" Each was aware of the question in the other's mind. Each found the question of "extraordinarily fascinating interest" and each tried to determine which was the "actual reality" and which was the "mere subjective experience outwardly projected in hallucinatory form."

To each, the past 23 years was an open book, all memories and events were clear, and they recognized that they shared those memories in common, and to each only wondering speculation offered a possible explanation of any of the years between 23 and 52.

They looked across the vestibule (this "vestibule" was not defined) and up at the edge of the ravine where I was sitting. Both knew that that person sitting there had some undefined significance, was named Milton, and could be spoken to by both. The thought came to both, could he hear both of them, but the test failed because they found that they spoke simultaneously, nor could they speak separately.

Slowly, thoughtfully, they studied each other. One had to be real. One had to be a memory image or a projection of a self-image. Should not Aldous, aged 52, have all the memories of the years from 23 to 52? But if he did, how could he then see Aldous, aged 23, without the shadings and colorations of the years that had passed since that youthful age? If he were to view Aldous, aged 23, clearly, he would have to blot out all subsequent memories in order to see that youthful Aldous clearly and as he then was. But if he were actually Aldous, aged 23, why could he not speculatively fabricate memories for the years between 23 and 52 instead of merely seeing Aldous as 52 and nothing more? What manner of psychological blocking could exist to effect this peculiar state of affairs? Each found himself fully cognizant of the thinking and the reasoning of the "other." Each doubted "the reality of the other" and each found reasonable explanations for such contrasting subjective experiences. The questions arose repeatedly, by what measure could the truth be established and of how did that unidentifiable person possessing only a name sitting on the edge of a ravine on the other side of the vestibule fit into the total situation? Could that vague person have an answer? Why not call to him and see?

With much pleasure and interest, Huxley detailed his total subjective experience, speculating upon the years of time distortion experienced and the memory blockages creating the insoluble problem of actual identity.

Finally, experimentally, the author remarked casually, "Of course, all that could be *left behind to become* AVAILABLE *at some later time.*"

Immediately there occurred a re-establishment of the original posthypnotic amnesia. Efforts were made to disrupt this re-induced hypnotic amnesia by veiled remarks, frank open statements, by a narration of what had occurred. Huxley found my narrative statements about an infant on the sand, a deep ravine, a vestibule "curiously interesting," simply cryptic remarks for which Huxley judged I had a purpose. But they were not evocative of anything more. Each statement I made was, in itself, actually uninformative and intended only to arouse associations. Yet no results were forthcoming until again the word "AVAILABLE" resulted in the same effect as previously. The whole account was related by Huxley a second time but without his realization that he was repeating his account. Appropriate suggestions when he had finished his second narration resulted in a full recollection of his first account. His reaction, after his immediate astonishment, was to compare the two accounts item by item. Their identity amazed him, and he noted only minor changes in the order of narration and the choice of words.

There are two patterns here which we find of interest: first, if the reader examines the description by Huxley of his deep trance experience, he will notice the consistent choice of visual predicates — a pattern which we discussed previously in our commentary. Second, the multiple re-induction of amnesia and subsequent removal of the amnesia for the original deep trance experiences as well as for the recall of these experiences again in the normal state of consciousness validate the power and effectiveness of the message groups distinguished by Erickson by his analogical marking technique.

Again, as before, a posthypnotic amnesia was induced, and a third recollection was then elicited, followed by an induced realization by Huxley that this was his third recollection.

Extensive detailed notations were made of the whole sequence of events, and comparisons were made of the individual notations, with interspersed comments regarding significances. The many items were systematically discussed for their meanings and brief trances were induced to vivify various items. However, only a relatively few notations were made by me of the content of Huxley's experience since he would properly be the one to develop them fully. My notations concerned primarily the sequence of events and a fairly good summary of the total development.

This discussion was continued until preparations for scheduled activities for that evening intervened, but not before an agreement on a subsequent preparation of the material for publication. Huxley planned to use both Deep Reflection and additional self-induced trances to aid in writing the article but the unfortunate holocaust precluded this.

Concluding Remarks

It is unfortunate that the above account is only a fragment of an extensive inquiry into a nature of various states of consciousness. Huxley's state of Deep Reflection did not appear to be hypnotic in character. Instead, it seemed to be a state of utterly intense concentration with much dissociation from external realities but with a full capacity to respond with varying degrees of readiness to externalities. It was entirely a personal experience serving, apparently, as an unrecognized foundation for conscious work activity enabling him to utilize freely all that had passed through his mind in Deep Reflection.

His hypnotic behavior was in full accord with hypnotic behavior elicited from other subjects. He was capable of all the phenomena of the deep trance and he could respond readily to posthypnotic suggestions and to exceedingly minimal cues. He was emphatic in declaring that the hypnotic state was quite different from the Deep Reflection state.

While some comparison may be made with dream activity, and certainly the ready inclusion of the "vestibule" and the "ravine" in the same subjective situation is suggestive of dream-like activity, such peculiar inclusions are somewhat frequently found as a spontaneous development of profound hypnotic ideosensory activity in highly intellectual subjects. His somnambulistic behavior, his open eyes, his responsiveness to me, his extensive posthypnotic behavior all indicate that hypnosis was unquestionably definitive of the total situation in that specific situation.

Huxley's remarkable development of a dissociated state, even bearing in mind his original request for a permissive technique, to view hypnotically his own growth and development in distorted time relationships, while indicative of Huxley's all-encompassing intellectual curiosity, is suggestive of most interesting and informative research possibilities. Questioning post-experimentally disclosed that Huxley had no conscious thoughts or plans for review of his life experiences nor did he at the time of the trance induction make any such interpretation of the suggestions given him. This was verified by a trance induction and making this special inquiry. His explanation was that when he felt himself "deep in the trance" he then began to search for something to do and "suddenly there I found myself — most extraordinary."

While this experience with Huxley was most notable, it was not my first encounter with such developments in the regression of highly intelligent subjects. One such experimental subject asked that he be hypnotized and informed when in the trance that he was to develop a profoundly interesting type of regression. This was primarily done for his own interest while he was waiting for me to complete some work. His request was met and he was left to his own devices while sitting in a comfortable chair on the other side of the laboratory. About two hours later he requested that I awaken him. He gave an account of suddenly finding himself on an unfamiliar hillside and, in looking around, he saw a small boy whom he immediately "knew" was six years old. Curious about this conviction about a strange little boy, he walked over to the child only to discover that that child was himself. He immediately recognized the hillside and set about trying to discover how he could be himself at 26 years of age watching himself at the age of 6 years. He soon learned that he could not only see, hear, and feel his child-self, but that he knew the innermost thoughts and feelings. At the moment of realizing this, he felt the child's feeling of hunger and his wish for "brown cookies." This brought a flood of memories to his 26-year-old self, but he noticed that the boy's thoughts were still centering on cookies and that the boy remained totally unaware of him. He was an invisible man, in some way regressed in time so that he could see and sense completely his childhood self. My subject reported that he "lived" with that boy for years, watched his successes and his failures, knew all of his innermost life, wondered about the next day's events with the child and, like the child, he found to his amazement that even though he was 26 years old, a total amnesia existed for all events subsequent to the child's immediate age at the moment, that he could not foresee the future any more than could the child. He went to school with the child, vacationed with him, always watching the continuing physical growth and development. As each new day arrived, he found that he had a wealth of associations about the actual happenings of the past up to the immediate moment of life for the child-self.

He went through grade school, high school, and then through a long process of deciding whether or not to go to college and what course of studies he should follow. He suffered the same agonies of indecision that his then-self did. He felt his other self's elation and relief when the decision was finally reached and his own feeling of elation and relief was identical with that of his other self.

My subject explained that the experience was literally a moment-by-moment reliving of his life with only the same awareness he had then and that the highly limited, restricted awareness of himself at 26 was that of being an invisible man watching his own growth and development from childhood on, with no more knowledge of the child's future than the child possessed.

He had enjoyed each completed event with a vast and vivid panorama of the past memories as each event reached completion. At the point of entrance to college the experience terminated. He then realized that he was in a deep trance and that he wanted to awaken and to take with him into conscious awareness the memory of what he had been subjectively experiencing.

This same type of experience has been encountered with other experimental subjects, both male and female, but each account varies in the manner in which the experience is achieved. For example, a girl who had identical twin sisters three years younger than herself found herself to be "a pair of identical twins growing up together but always knowing everything about the other." In her account there was nothing about her actual twin sisters; all such memories and associations were excluded.

Another subject, highly inclined, mechanically, constructed a robot which he endowed with life only to discover that it was his own life with which he endowed it. He then watched that robot throughout many years of experiential events and learnings, always himself achieving them also because he had an amnesia for his past.

Repeated efforts to set up an orderly experiment have to date failed. Usually the subject objects or refuses for some not-too-comprehensible reason. In all my experiences with this kind of development in hypnotic trances, this type of "reliving" of one's life has always been a spontaneous occurrence and with highly intelligent, well-adjusted experimental subjects.

Huxley's experience was the one most adequately recorded and it is most unfortunate that the greater number of details, having been left with him, were destroyed before he had the opportunity to write them up in full. Huxley's remarkable memory, his capacity to use Deep Reflection, his ability to develop a deep hypnotic state to achieve specific purposes and to arouse himself at will with full conscious awareness of what he had accomplished (Huxley required very little instruction the next day to become skilled in autohypnosis) augured exceedingly well for a most informative study. Unfortunately the destruction of both notebooks precluded him from any effort to reconstruct them from memory because my notebook contained so many notations of items of procedure and observation for which he had no memories and which were vital to any satisfactory elaboration. However, it is hoped that the report given here may serve, despite its deficiencies, as an initial pilot study for the development of a more adequate and comprehensive study of various states of consciousness.

In summary then, we point out simply that Erickson generalizes in his concluding remarks about what he has called in other contexts time distortion (see, especially, Cooper and Erickson, *Time Distortion in Hypnosis*, 1959). In this case he relates the ability demonstrated by various subjects to accomplish in the subjective time sense achieved in their deep trance tasks which in clock time would be impossible — for example, a review of their entire life without any sense of rushing or hurrying. We simply mention this phenomenon here — we will return to this topic later.

This article by Erickson of a joint, cooperative venture between himself and one of this century's most talented and creative human beings is an invaluable record which suggests some very specific ways in which we, as human beings, may begin the process of exploring our own potential for experiencing — indeed, for creating — altered states of consciousness. We end this commentary simply by endorsing Erickson's final statement:

> . . . . it is hoped that the report given here may serve despite its deficiencies, as an initial pilot study for the development of a more adequate and comprehensive study of the various states of consciousness.

FOOTNOTES FOR PART I

1. For additional study of the processes by which people create models of the world, we recommend *The Structure of Magic I* and *II*.

2. Gardner, Sperry, Gazzinga, 1969.

3. See Beuer, Miller, etc.

4. In this first volume, we distinguish only three levels of linkage:
   (a) Simple conjunction
   (b) Implied Causatives
   (c) Cause-Effect
We are aware of other gradations of linkage available in natural language but restrict ourselves to these three. A more refined analysis will be presented in subsequent volumes. These patterns constitute a beginning of what we refer to as natural logic. For some additional patterns of natural logic or human modeling, see Polya (*Patterns of Plausible Interference*, 1954) and Lakoff (*Linguistics and Natural Logic*, 1970).

5. See *Magic I*, Chapters 3 and 4.

6. Some forms of deletion leave the resultant Surface Structure well formed, that is, a grammatical sentence of English. Other deletions result in ungrammatical sentences. Erickson uses both in his work. We will discuss their appropriate context for use and the difference in the client's experience in Parts II and III of this volume. We do not make the distinction here in Part I.

7. Amer. J. Clin. Hypn., 1966, 3, 198–209.

8. Various commentators on the development of mathematics have pointed out that important advances by "gifted" mathematicians frequently involve "sudden insight" or a description by the mathematician wherein "the solution flashed before my eyes." More recently, Gardiner (1975, p. 375) reports:

> . . . as one discourses in language, the eyes should shift to the right. Conversely, when a person is using spatial imagery, as in following a route or solving a geometrical problem, his right hemisphere should be activated and his eyes should consequently shift leftwards. . . . Steven Har-

nad interviewed graduate students and professors in mathematics at Princeton University, classifying them by the direction in which their eyes moved when a series of questions were posed. Those whose eyes moved to the right were found (in the opinion of their peers) to be less creative as mathematicians, displayed less interest in the arts, and utilized a smaller amount of visual imagery in solving problems than a matched group of mathematicians whose eyes moved to the left, reflecting activity in their non-dominant hemisphere. . . .

9. Amer. J. Clin. Hypn., 1965, 8, 14–33.

10. Huxley, A. *The Doors of Perception.* New York: Harper and Brothers, 1954.

11. We present a more detailed account of these types of evidence in *Magic II,* Parts II and III.

12. Erickson, M. H. *The confusion technique in hypnosis,* 1964, 6, 269–271. Amer. J. Clin. Hypn.

13. Sherlock Holmes presents several excellent examples of Erickson's confusion technique — see p. 423 of Volume I of *The Annotated Sherlock Holmes,* by Sir Arthur Conan Doyle; edited by William A. Baring-Gould (Clarkson N. Potter, Inc., New York).

14. This particular example was one of the topics of investigation when we [Bandler and Grinder] visited with the author [Erickson] of the article upon which we are now commenting.

15. Transformational linguists have developed a test for the difference between ambiguity and vagueness; sentences with nominalizations, typically, are vague, not ambiguous.

16. We present the patterning of temporal predicates in another volume with an accompanying discussion of time distortion in hypnosis. The readers can, however, easily construct examples by arranging and rearranging the temporal predicates used by Erickson in conjunction with the set of any temporal predicates which typically occur as adverbs such as: *soon, shortly after, recent, previous, now, then, afterwards, initially, finally, successively,* . . .

17. There also exists some evidence that the non-dominant hemisphere stores frequently occurring whole words and phrases with their meanings.

PART II

FAMILIARIZATION
WITH
PATTERNS OF ERICKSON'S
HYPNOTIC WORK

Introduction

In Part I of this volume our purpose was two fold: first, we wanted you to see that there were systematic patterns of behavior in Milton Erickson's work in hypnosis; and second, that these patterns could be identified and extracted in a way to be useful to you in your own hypnotic work. During this process, we hoped that you could begin the process of becoming familiar with these patterns in a way that would allow you to identify them and to imagine how they could be useful understandings in your field of endeavor. This second part of the book is devoted to familiarizing you with these patterns in a more systematic manner. It is designed to present to you the characteristics of each of these patterns in a way that will allow you to understand not only the nature of each pattern, but also the useful aspect and implication of each pattern. In Volume I we have focused primarily on the linguistic notions and how they work for the purpose of induction and suggestion. We would like to point out that they are by no means all of the patterns of behavior used by Milton Erickson in his work with hypnosis, but they are what we believe to be the most basic and the easiest to learn and employ. Each of the linguistic patterns presented in this part of Volume I can be generalized to the other forms of analogical communication used by human beings (voice tone, body movement, etc.) given in subsequent volumes. For example, we have mentioned briefly the linguistic notion of ambiguity, a Surface Structure of natural language which, by the nature of its construction, can have more than one meaning, e.g.:

Hypnotizing hypnotists can be tricky

This sentence can mean either one of the following interpretations:

1. Hypnotist in act of hypnotizing can be tricky in what they do to hypnotize

2. Hypnotizing the class of people in the profession of hypnotizing can be tricky in the sense of being difficult or having some unexpected outcomes.

The intended meaning is not clear and cannot be determined by the Surface Structure alone. This is an example of syntactic ambiguity.

The following excerpt from another Erickson article contains an example of kinesthetic ambiguity used by Erickson. The kinesthetic ambiguities are in italic type for clarity. The shared patterns of difficulty of interpretation and multiple meaning are the same in a formal sense, and are examples of how the same formal patterns can be used in any of the sensory systems.

She was then brought through a side door to confront me. Silently we looked at each other, and then (as I had done many times previously with seminarians in the U.S., in seeking out what I consider clinically to be "good, responsive" subjects before the beginning of a seminar and hence before I was known to them) I walked toward her briskly and smilingly and extended my right hand and she extended hers. Slowly, I shook hands with her, staring her fully in the eyes even as she was doing to me, and I ceased smiling. *As I let loose of her hand, I did so in an uncertain, irregular fashion, slowly withdrawing it, now increasing the pressure slightly with my thumb, then with the little finger, then with the middle finger, always in an uncertain, irregular, hesitant manner and, finally, so gently withdrawing my hand that she would have no clear-cut awareness of just when I had released her hand or what part of her hand I had last touched.* At the same time, I slowly changed the focus of my eyes by altering their convergence, thereby giving her a minimal but appreciable cue that

I seemed to be looking not at, but through, her eyes and off into the distance. Slowly the pupils of her eyes dialated and, as they did so, I gently released her hand completely, leaving it in mid-air in a cataleptic position. A slight upward pressure on the heel of her hand raised it slightly.

The second unexpected,. . . induction was done in January, 1961, during a visit to Caracas, Venezuela. I had been invited to tour the Hospital Concepcion Palacios during which I was asked to address the staff on the use of hypnosis in obstetrics at an impromptu meeting in the conference room. One of the audience suggested that I demonstrate as I discussed the phenomena of hypnosis. Remembering my experience in Mexico City, I asked if I might work with some young woman who did not know the purpose of my visit there and who did not understand English and who had had no experience in hypnosis of any sort. Three young women were brought in and I looked them over and selected the one who gave me a clinical impression of what I term "responsive attentiveness." I asked that the others be dismissed and that she be told that I wished her cooperation while I lectured. Very carefully, my translator so informed her without giving her any more information and she nodded her head affirmatively.

Stepping over to her and standing face to face with her, I explained in English for those who understood it that they were to watch what I did. My translator kept silent and the young lady eyed me most attentively and wonderingly.

I showed the girl my hands, which were empty, and then I reached over with my right hand and gently encircled her right wrist with my fingers, barely touching it except in an irregular, uncertain, changing pattern of tactile stimulation with my fingertips. The result was to attract her full, attentive, expectant, wondering interest in what I was doing. With my right thumb, I made slight tactile pressure on the latero-volar-ulnar aspect of her wrist, as if to turn it upward; at the same moment, at the area of the radial prominence, I made a slightly downward tactile pressure at the dorso-lateral aspect of her wrist with my third finger; also at the same time, I made various gentle touches with my other fingers somewhat comparable in intensity but nonsuggestive of direction. She made an automatic response to the directive touches without differentiating them consciously from the other touches, evidently paying attention first to one touch and then to another. As she began responding, I increased varyingly the directive touches without decreasing the number and variation of the other distracting tactile stimuli. Thus, I suggested lateral and upward movements of her arm and hand by varying tactile stimuli intermingled with a decreasing number of nondirective touches. These responsive, automatic movements, the origin of which she did recognize, startled her, and as her pupils dilated, I so touched her wrist with a suggestion of an upward movement and . . . her arm began rising so gently discontinuing the touch that she did not notice the tactile withdrawal and the upward movement continued. Quickly shifting my fingertips to hers, I varied the touches, so as to direct in an unrecognizable fashion a full upward turning of her palm, and then other touches on her fingertips served to straighten some, to bend others, and a proper touch on the straightened fingertips led to a continuing bending of her elbow. This led to a slow moving of her hand toward her eyes. As this began, I attracted with my fingers her visual attention and directed her attention to my eyes. I focused my eyes for distant viewing as if looking through and beyond her, moved my fingers close to my eyes, slowly closed my eyes, took a deep, sighing breath and sagged my shoulders in a relaxed fashion and then pointed to her fingers which were approaching her eyes.

She followed my pantomimed instructions and developed a trance that withstood the efforts of the staff to secure her attention. (1967, pp. 93-96)

The preceding extract was presented as an example to show you how each of the linguistic patterns which we present can be generalized to analogical communication systems. Our intention in this volume is to focus primarily on the patterns of language Milton Erickson uses in his work. Our strategy will be to regroup the patterns presented so far into natural groupings based on their use and their formal characteristics. They have been split into techniques of:

(1) Pacing, to distract and utilize the dominant hemisphere;
(2) Accessing the non-dominant hemisphere

Careful reading of Part II will provide you not only with a

variety of linguistic techniques of induction and suggestion, but also with a coherent strategy for their use in hypnotic work.

We conclude with a series of quotes from a well-known contemporary author, Carlos Castenada (*Tales of Power,* 1974; pp. 231-233, 245, 247-248, 265).

> . . . The first act of a teacher is to introduce the idea that the world we think we see is only a view, a description of the world. Every effort of a teacher is geared to prove this point to his apprentice. But accepting it seems to be one of the hardest things one can do; we are complacently caught in our particular view of the world, which compels us to feel and act as if we knew everything about the world. A teacher, from the very first act he performs, aims at stopping that view. Sorcerers call it stopping the internal dialogue and they are convinced that it is the single most important technique that an apprentice can learn . . . .

> "Stopping the internal dialogue is, however, the key to the sorcerers' world," he said. "The rest of the activities are only props; all they do is accelerate the effect of stopping the internal dialogue."

> . . . The teacher reorders the view of the world. I have called that view the island of the *tonal.* I've said that everything that we are is on that island. The sorcerers' explanation says that the island of the *tonal* is made by our perception, which has been trained to focus on certain elements; each of those elements and all of them together form our view of the world. The job of a teacher, insofar as the apprentice's perception is concerned, consists of reordering all the elements of the island on one half of the bubble. By now you must have realized that cleaning and reordering the island of the *tonal* means regrouping all its elements on the side of *reason.* My task has been to disarrange your ordinary view, not to destroy it, but to force it to rally on the side of *reason.* . . .

... He drew an imaginary circle on the rock and divided it in two along a vertical diameter. He said that the art of a teacher was to force his disciple to group his view of the world on the right half of the bubble.

"Why the right half?" I asked.

"That's the side of the *tonal*," he said. "The teacher always addresses himself to that side, and by presenting his apprentice on the one hand with the warrior's way he forces him into reasonableness and sobriety, and strength of character and body; and by presenting him on the other hand with unthinkable but real situations, which the apprentice cannot cope with, he forces him to realize that his *reason*, although it is a most wonderful affair, can only cover a small area. . . .

. . . "Walking in that specific manner saturates the *tonal*," he said. "It floods it. You see, the attention of the *tonal* has to be placed on its creations. In fact, it is that attention that creates the order of the world in the first place; so, the *tonal* must be attentive to the elements of its world in order to maintain it, and must, above all, uphold the view of the world as internal dialogue."

He said that the right way of walking was a subterfuge. The warrior, first by curling his fingers, drew attention to the arms; and then by looking, without focusing his eyes, at any point directly in front of him on the arc that started at the tip of his feet and ended above the horizon, he literally flooded his *tonal* with information. The *tonal* without its one-to-one relation with the elements of its description, was incapable of talking to itself, and thus one became silent. . . .

. . . Order in our perception is the exclusive realm of the *tonal;* only there can our actions have a sequence; only there are they like stairways where one can count the steps. There is nothing of that sort in the *nagual.* Therefore, the view of the *tonal* is a tool, and as such it is not only the best tool but the only one we've got. . . .

"*Dreaming* is a practical aid devised by sorcerers," he said. "They were not fools; they knew what they were doing and sought the usefulness of the *nagual* by training their *tonal* to let go for a moment, so to speak, and then grab again. This statement doesn't make sense to you. But that's what you've been doing all along: training yourself to let go without losing your marbles. *Dreaming,* of course, is the crown of the sorcerers' efforts, the ultimate use of the *nagual.*"

Pacing, Distraction and Utilization of the Dominant Hemisphere

> In understanding this technique, it may be well to keep in mind the pattern of the magician which is not intended to inform but to distract so that his purposes may be accomplished.
>
> Milton H. Erickson, *Special Techniques of Brief Hypnotherapy*, 1967, p. 393.

Introduction

The induction of the altered state of consciousness called trance requires and implies the distraction and/or utilization of what Milton calls the conscious mind. Conscious representation of ongoing experience to oneself may come in a number of distinct modalities (visual, auditory, kinesthetic). In order to establish a trance state all of the representational systems must, to some extent, be involved in the process, since the process is generally one of simultaneous representation of a small, focused part of the experience. The beginning of this process we call *pacing*. This is usually achieved in most hypnotic work by having clients focus their eyes on a single spot and listen to the sound of the hypnotist's voice. The hypnotist begins to describe the experiences he knows by observation the client is having; for example, the changes in visual perception (e.g., the third feeling of the client's eyes that result from his staring at a fixed point). This description, explained before, establishes a feedback loop between what the client is observably doing — what the hypnotist sees and hears the client doing — and what the client hears the hypnotist saying. This is, in fact, equivalent to meeting the client at his model of the world — going to the client's reality, accepting it, and then utilizing it for the purposes of the hypnotic session. Meeting a client at his model of the world, pacing that model and then leading it into new territory is one of Erickson's consistent strategies which make his work easier both for himself and for his client. Any attempt to force a client into something, or to get him to deny what he believes, opens the possibility for resistance by giving the client something to resist. This struggle only serves to waste the time and energies of all involved and very rarely serves any purpose.

Most of you probably have had the common experience of becoming what we called "hooked" in interpersonal communications. Someone, for example, comes up to you and casually says something such as:

Gee, I'm just so stupid; I can't do anything right.

One possible response is to attempt to be "helpful" and reply:

That's not true; you know you can do a lot. You can X, Y, Z, etc.

The characteristic result in our experience is that, the more you try to "help" in this way, the more the other person expresses the opposite viewpoint. As an additional example, an acquaintance might say to you:

I want your opinion; do you think I should X or Y, etc.

You say:

Well, X looks good.

Typically, the person will immediately defend Y. One strategy which we have found invaluable in our therapeutic work is to agree with the other person who will then, invariably, take the other side. As an example, consider the following transcript from a therapy session:

Jane: *I'm so dumb, I . . . I never say the right thing.*

Therapist: I've noticed that; in fact, you're so dumb that I don't think anyone can help you. You probably can't do anything — you'd better just give up.

Jane: *Well . . . a . . . um . . . a*

Therapist: No, no you're right; you must be beyond help. I think you'd better just go home and lock yourself in the closet; no one in the whole wide world is as dumb as you.

Jane: (interrupting) *I'm not that bad; come on,* (beginning to laugh) *I know what you're doing, so let's just get on with it, shall we?*

Therapist: OK, if you think you can be helped, let's begin.

Erickson has a very refined sensitivity to this kind of communication; he meets his client at his model, accepting it and utilizing it to the fullest. The following extracts are examples of this exceptionally refined ability.

Case Report 1

George had been a patient in a mental hospital for five years. His identity had never been established. He was simply a stranger around the age of 25 who had been picked up by the police for irrational behavior and committed to the state mental hospital. During those five years he had said, "My name is George," "Good morning," and "Good night," but these were his only rational utterances. He uttered otherwise a continuous word-salad completely meaningless as far as could be determined. It was made up of sounds, syllables, words, and incomplete phrases. For the first three years he sat on a bench at the front door of the ward and eagerly leaped up and poured forth his word-salad most urgently to everyone who entered the ward. Otherwise, he merely sat quietly mumbling his word-salad to himself.

Innumerable efforts had been made by psychiatrists, psychologists, nurses, social service workers, other personnel and even fellow patients to secure intelligible remarks from him, all in vain. George talked only one way, the word-salad way. After approximately three years he continued to greet persons who entered the ward with an outburst of meaningless words, but in between times he sat silently on the bench, appearing mildly depressed but somewhat angrily uttering a few minutes of word-salad when approached and questioned.

The author joined the hospital staff in the sixth year of George's stay. The available information about his ward behavior was secured. It was learned also that patients or ward personnel could sit on the bench beside him without eliciting his word-salad so long as they did not speak to him. With this total of information a therapeutic plan was devised. A secretary recorded in shorthand the word-salads with which he so urgently greeted those who entered the ward. These transcribed recordings were studied but no meaning could be discovered. These word-salads were carefully paraphrased, using words that were least likely to be found in George's productions and an extensive study was made of these until the author could improvise a word-salad similar in pattern to George's, but utilizing a different vocabulary.

Then all entrances to the ward were made through a side door some distance down the corridor from George. The author then began the practice of sitting silently on the bench beside George daily for increasing lengths of time until the span of an hour was reached. Then, at the next sitting, the author, addressing the empty air, identified himself verbally. George made no response.

The next day the identification was addressed directly to George. He spat out an angry stretch of word-salad to which the author replied, in tones of courtesy and responsiveness, with an equal amount of his own carefully contrived word-salad. George appeared puzzled and, when the author finished, George uttered another contribution with an inquiring intonation. As if replying the author verbalized still further word-salad.

After a half dozen interchanges, George lapsed into silence and the author promptly went about other matters.

The next morning appropriate greetings were exchanged employing proper names by both. Then George launched into a long word-salad speech to which the author courteously replied in kind. There followed then brief interchanges of long and short utterances of word-salad until George fell silent and the author went to other duties.

This continued for some time. Then George, after returning the morning greeting, made meaningless utterances without pause for four hours. It taxed the author greatly to miss lunch and to make a full reply in kind. George listened attentively and made a two-hour reply to which a weary two-hour response was made. (George was noted to watch the clock throughout the day.)

The next morning George returned the usual greeting properly but added about two sentences of nonsense to which the author replied with a similar length of nonsense. George replied, "Talk sense, Doctor." "Certainly, I'll be glad to. What is your last name?" "O'Donovan and it's about time somebody who knows how to talk asked. Over five years in this lousy joint" . . . (to which was added a sentence or two of word-salad). The author replied, "I'm glad to get your name, George. Five years is too long a time" . . . (and about two sentences of word-salad were added).

The rest of the account is as might be expected. A complete history sprinkled with bits of word-salad was obtained by inquiries judiciously salted with word-salad. His clinical course, never completely free of word-salad which was eventually reduced to unintelligible mumbles, was excellent. Within a year he had left the hospital, was gainfully employed, and at increasingly longer intervals returned to the hospital to report his continued and improving adjustment. Nevertheless, he invariably initiated his report or terminated it with a bit of word-salad, always expecting the same from the author. Yet he could, as he frequently did on these visits, comment wryly, "Nothing like a little nonsense in life, is there Doctor?" to which he obviously expected and received a sensible expression of agreement to which was added a brief utterance of nonsense. After he had been out of the hospital continuously for three years of fully satisfactory adjustment, contact was lost with him except for a cheerful postcard from another city. This bore a brief but satisfactory summary of his adjustments in a distant city. It was signed properly but following his name was a jumble of syllables. There was no return address. He was ending the relationship on his terms of adequate understanding.

During the course of his psychotherapy he was found hypnotizable, developing a medium to deep trance in about 15 minutes. However, his trance behavior was entirely comparable to his waking behavior and it offered no therapeutic advantages, although repeated tests were made. Every therapeutic interview was characterized by the judicious use of an appropriate amount of word-salad.

The above case represents a rather extreme example of meeting a patient at the level of his decidedly serious problem. The author was at first rather censoriously criticized by others but when it became apparent that inexplicable imperative needs of the patient were being met, there was no further adverse comment. (1967, pp. 501-502)

Erickson's ability to meet George at his model of the world, even to the extent of speaking his language, is a brilliant example of how Erickson will go to the client to make contact in his model, instead of expecting the client to come to him. When practitioners of hypnosis and therapy learn this skill, the term *resistant client* will have no meaning, and trance states will be available to more people.

The next excerpt is a good example of what, typically, is called a resistant patient, who may have been labeled as unhypnotizable or unsusceptible. Erickson's induction is simple because he meets the client at her model and leads quickly into the desired state. Her "resistance" becomes the very model for the induction.

"You wish to have hypnosis utilized in connection with your dental work. Your husband and his colleagues wish the same, but each time hypnosis was attempted, you have failed to go into a trance. You got scared stiff and you cried. It would really be enough just to get stiff without crying. Now you want me to treat you psychiatrically, if necessary, but I don't believe it is. Instead, I will just put you in a trance so that you can have hypnosis for your dentistry."

She replied, "But I'll just get scared stiff and cry."

She was answered with, "No, you will first get stiff. That is the first thing to do and do it now. Just get more and more stiff, your arms, your legs, your body, your neck — completely stiff — even stiffer than you were with your husband.

"Now close your eyes and let the lids get stiff, so stiff that you can't open them."

Her responses were most adequate.

Erickson's ability both to pace and to utilize his client's model of the world is a great tool; there is much for other practitioners of hypnosis to learn from this area of his work. Too often the failure of hypnotists to meet the client and use the client's model results in failures that could have been the very source of success. A dramatic example of this occurred in our work after a visit with Erickson. We were conducting an evening seminar in hypnotism and exploring the various hypnotic phenomena described by Erickson in his articles. We were working with negative hallucinations with a young woman. While she was in a deep trance, we gave a series of relatively direct suggestions to her that she would not see her hand. When she awoke, she opened her eyes, looked at her right hand carefully and said in a disappointed tone, "But it's still there." One of the authors immediately replied, "Yes, of course, you can see *that hand*," his voice clearly implying more. She then shifted slowly her gaze, looking over at her other hand, and gasped, "I don't believe it! It's gone!" Pacing her initial response, accepting her present model of her ongoing experience and leading her made possible this visual alternation.

. . . A clinical instance in which this same technique was employed centers around an obstreperous 25-year-old patient for whom hypnotherapy was not indicated. Nevertheless, he repeatedly demanded hypnosis and in the same breath declared himself unhypnotizable. On one occasion, he forced the issue by demanding absolutely, "Hypnotize me even though I'm not hypnotizable."

This demand was met by employing softly spoken suggestions of slow, progressive relaxation, fatigue, and sleep. Throughout the hour that this was done, the patient sat on the edge of his chair, gesticulated, and bitterly denounced the entire procedure as stupid and incompetent. At the close of the session, the patient declared that his time and money had been wasted. He could "remember every ineffectual, stupid suggestion" that had been offered and could "remember everything that took place the whole time."

The writer immediately seized upon these utterances to declare, somewhat repetitiously, "Certainly you remember. You are here in the office. Naturally here in the office you can remember everything. It all occurred here in the office and you were here and here you can remember everything." The patient impatiently demanded another appointment and left angrily.

At the next appointment, he was deliberately met in the reception room. He immediately inquired if he had kept his previous appointment. Reply was given evasively that surely he would remember if he had done so. He explained that on that day, he had suddenly found himself sitting in his car unable to remember if he had just returned from his appointment or were just leaving for it. This question he debated for an indefinite period of time before he thought of checking with his watch and then he discovered that the time was long past the proper hour. However, he was still unable to decide the problem because he did not know how long he had debated the question. He asked, again, if he had kept his previous appointment, and again he was assured evasively that surely he would remember if he had.

As he entered the office, he stopped short and declared, "I did too keep my appointment. You wasted my time with that silly, soft, gentle, ineffectual hypnotic technique of yours, and you failed miserably."

After a few more derogatory comments, he was maneuvered into returning to the reception room where he again manifested an amnesia for the previous appointment as well as his original inquiries about it. His questions were once more parried. He was led back into the office, where for a second time he experienced full recall of the previous appointment.

Again he was induced to return to the reception room with a resultant reestablishment of his amnesia. Upon reentering the office, he added to his recollection of the previous appointment a full recall of his separate entrances into the reception room and the accompanying amnesic states. This bewildered and intrigued him to such an extent that he spent most of the hour going from the office to the reception room and back again. He experienced a full amnesia in the reception room, and full recollection of the total experience inclusive of the reception room manifestations in the office.

The therapeutic effect of this hypnotic experience was the almost immediate correction of much of the patient's hostile, antagonistic, hypercritical, demanding attitude and the establishment of a good rapport. An acceleration of therapy resulted even though no further hypnosis was employed. (1967, pp. 41-42)

Inexperienced hypnotists too readily accept initial failure as a lack of ability on the part of themselves or the subject. Erickson consistently emphasizes the importance of accepting every aspect of the client's behavior and utilizing it, thereby meeting his client's at their model of the world and leading them to new places. His description of this process follows:

In trance induction, the inexperienced hypnotist often tries to direct or bend the subject's behavior to fit his conception of how the subject "should" behave. There should be a constant minimization of the role of the hypnotist and a constant enlargement of the subject's role. An example may be cited of a volunteer subject, used later to teach hypnosis to medical students.

After a general discussion of hypnosis, she expressed a willingness to go into a trance immediately. The suggestion was offered that she select the chair and position she felt would be most comfortable. When she had settled herself to her satisfaction, she remarked that she would like to smoke a cigarette. She was immediately given one, and she proceeded to smoke lazily, meditatively watching the smoke drifting upward. Casual conversational remarks were offered about the pleasure of smoking, of watching the curling smoke, the feeling of ease in lifting the cigarette to her mouth, the inner sense of satisfaction of becoming entirely absorbed just in smoking comfortably and without need to attend to any external things. Shortly, casual remarks were made about inhaling and exhaling, these words timed to fit in with her actual breathing. Others were made about the ease with which she could almost automatically lift her cigarette to her mouth and then lower her hand to the arm of the chair. These remarks were also timed to coincide with her actual behavior. Soon, the words "inhale," "exhale," "lift," and "lower" acquired a conditioning value of which she was unaware because of the seemingly conversational character of the suggestions. Similarly, casual suggestions were offered in which the words sleep, sleepy, and sleeping were timed to her eyelid behavior.

Before she had finished the cigarette, she had developed a light trance. Then the suggestion was made that she might continue to enjoy smoking as she slept more and more soundly; that the cigarette would be looked after by the hypnotist while she absorbed herself more and more completely in deep sleep; that, as she slept, she would continue to experience the satisfying feelings and sensations of smoking. A satisfactory profound trance resulted and she was given extensive training to teach her to respond in accord with her own unconscious pattern of behavior. (1967, p. 18)

Pacing, then, is part of Erickson's general strategy for dealing with the dominant hemisphere in establishing a trance state. As this pacing feedback loop is established, the rest of the overall strategy for dealing with the dominant hemisphere begins. Erickson describes this as follows:

> Deep hypnosis is that level . . . that permits the subject to function adequately and directly at an unconscious level of awareness without interference by the conscious mind.

This is accomplished by pacing, simultaneously distracting and utilizing the unconscious patterns of behavior generated by the dominant hemisphere. Speaking to a client in a way that makes use of the process by which people create linguistic models of their experience allows the hypnotist to tap the vast resources of his client. *The Structure of Magic I* is the volume in which we described the process by which people create linguistic models of their experience. The Meta-model is a set of precise forms with which a psychotherapist can directly challenge impoverishing representations. Hypnosis, on the other hand, does not challenge these processes of representation but rather turns them into the very vehicle that enables a client to achieve both the trance state and its goals. Thus, therapeutic goals can be achieved in waking therapy by Meta-modeling both to understand and to expand your client's model of the world. What could be called in hypnosis an anti- or inverse Meta-model is used to pace and distract, utilizing the modeling processes of the client to achieve trance and the goals of the hypnotic endeavor. This inverse Meta-model we have lovingly named the "Milton model."

Causal Linguistic Modeling Processes

In constructing models of our experience, each of us attempts to make sense out of the patterns which we experience. We attempt to create for ourselves a map or guide for our behavior in the world which will be of use in securing the things which we want for ourselves. The language systems which we use in constructing our models have the same three modeling universals —

deletion, distortion, and generalization — which we encounter in other representational systems. When we remain flexible in our use of these processes, they are the basis for the useful, creative and beneficial representations we generate and use to make our way in the world. However, when we make the tragic error of mistaking the model for the territory, we then have representations which impoverish our experience and limit our potential. Thus, the very same processes which allow us to produce useful and aesthetically pleasing models of our experience can impoverish and limit us. Hypnosis is a particularly striking example of this.

One of the most common forms of distortion is the way in which we select several parts of our experience and establish causal relations among them, linking them in our model so that, when we detect the presence of one or more of these parts, we come to expect some other part.

Linguistically, we have found it useful to distinguish three categories of causal relations or linkages:

(a) **Conjunction** — use of the connectives *and, but* (i.e., *and not*)

Statements exploiting simple conjunctions have the general form:

X	*and*	Y
You are listening to the sound of my voice		You are relaxing more and more
You are sitting in the chair		You are drifting deeper into trance
You are focusing your eyes on that spot		Your eyelids are becoming heavy

(b) **Implied Causatives** — use of the connectives *as, while, during, before, after, . . .*

Statements which make use of this type of causal linkage have the same type of form:

X	as while during	Y
You will go deeper into trance		You listen to the sound of my voice
Your eyelids will grow heavy		You sit all the way down in the chair
That forgotten name will appear suddenly in your mind's eye		You finish repeating the letters of the alphabet to yourself

    (c) **Cause-Effect** — use of predicates which claim a necessary connection between the portions of the speaker's experience such as: *make, cause, force, require,* etc.

The general form for this type of causal linkage is:

X	causative predicate (e.g., *will make*)	Y
Sitting all the way in that chair		You go into a profound somnambulistic trance
Staring at that paperweight		Your eyelids become heavy
Listening to the sound of my voice		You relax more and more

Each of these constructions makes the claim that there is a connection between two classes of events. The strength of the connection that is claimed varies from simple co-occurrence to one of necessity. As we showed in Part I of this volume, the most typical way in which a hypnotist uses these modeling processes is by linking some portion of the client's on-going experience which the client is able immediately to verify to some experience or behavior which the hypnotist wishes the client to have. These same patterns may be made to appear much more complex by introducing negatives into the general forms presented, as the following examples show:

you won't be able to keep
your eyelids open   as   you feel their weight . . .

$$\sim X \qquad \text{as} \qquad Y$$

where $\sim$ is the symbol for negation

You can't prevent   as   You feel the tight-
yourself from experi-   ness around your
encing the deep feeling   eyes
of sadness

$$\sim \sim X \qquad \text{as} \qquad Y$$

Not talking makes it so easy To not listen to any
                                 sound but my voice

$$\sim X \text{ makes it so easy } \sim Y$$

In addition, to add negation to the basic patterns, you may also compound the events listed under the cover symbols X and Y, thus making each of them themselves complex as in:

Not speaking and   will make   You go even more
preventing your   rapidly into a trance
eyes from closing   as you listen to the
                                 sound of my voice

$$\sim X_1 \quad \text{and} \quad \sim X_2 \quad \text{will make} \quad Y_1 \quad \text{as} \quad Y_2$$

As the reader can verify for himself, the variations on these patterns are inexhaustible.

We now quote several examples of Erickson's use of these patterns.

> . . . And that paperweight; the filing cabinet; your foot on the rug; the ceiling light; the draperies; your right hand on the arm of the chair; the pictures on the wall; *the changing*

> *focus of your eyes as you glance about;* the interest of the
> book titles; the tension in your shoulders; the feeling of
> the chair; the disturbing noises *and* thoughts; weight of
> hands *and* feet; weight of problems, weight of desk; the
> stationery stand; the records of many patients; the
> phenomena of life, of illness, of emotion, of physical and
> mental behavior; the restfulness of relaxation; the need to
> attend to one's needs; *the need to attend to one's tension*
> *while looking at the desk* or the paperweight or the filing
> cabinet; the comfort of withdrawal from the environment;
> fatigue and its development; the unchanging character of
> the desk; the monotony of the filing cabinet; the need to
> take a rest; the comfort of closing one's eyes; the relaxing
> sensation of a deep breath; the delight of learning
> passively; the capacity for intellectual learning by the
> unconscious. . . .

Here is an excellent example of Erickson's use of Cause-Effect
at a high level of patterning. He maneuvers the client into a
situation wherein she comes to believe that her *feeling of success*
caused *the author's discomfiture.* This makes use of the client's
own modeling processes to assist her in entering trance.

> . . . To illustrate, a Ph.D. in psychology, extremely scornful
> and skeptical of hypnosis, challenged the author to "try to work
> your little fad" on her in the presence of witnesses who would be
> able to attest to the author's failure. However, she did state that if
> it could be demonstrated to her that there were such a
> phenomenon as hypnosis, she would lend herself to any studies
> the author might plan. Her challenge and conditions were
> accepted. Her promise to act as a subject, if convinced, was
> carefully and quietly emphasized since it constituted behavior of
> her own and could become the foundation for future trance
> behavior. Next, a technique of suggestion was employed which
> was believed certain to fail, which it did. Thus, the subject was
> given a *feeling of success* gratifying to her, but carrying an
> admixture of some regret over *the author's discomfiture.* This
> regret constituted a foundation stone for future trances. Then,
> apparently as a face-saving device for the author, the topic of
> ideomotor activity was raised. After some discussion, indirect
> suggestion led her to express a willingness to cooperate in

experimentation of ideomotor activity. She qualified this by stating, "Don't try to tell me that ideomotor activity is hypnosis, because I know it isn't." This was countered by the observation that ideomotor activity could undoubtedly be achieved in hypnosis even as in the waking state. Thus, another foundation stone was laid for future trance activity. . . . (1967, p. 21)

A closely related modeling process called mind reading — the situation in which one person claims to have knowledge of another person's non-observable behavior — is useful in pacing and leading the client.

For example, here are some common Surface Structures of this form that are rarely challenged in spite of their mind reading. These, in fact, are a part of almost everyone's experience. In some cases, these statements may be true, but without a specification of the process, no distinction between hallucinations and well-formed representations can be made.

> I know what makes him happy.
> You should have known I wouldn't be pleased.
> I know he doesn't like me.
> I'm sorry to keep annoying you.
> You must be wondering about my concern.

By carefully employing the mind-reading pattern, the hypnotist can successfully pace and lead the client even in the areas of the client's experience which have no observable consequences. We quote another example from Erickson's work.

> We both want to know why you are so promiscuous. We both want to know the cause of your behavior. We both know that that knowledge is in your unconscious mind. For the next two hours, you will sit quietly here thinking of nothing, doing nothing, just knowing that your unconscious is going to tell you and me the reason for your behavior. It will tell the reason clearly and understandably, but neither you nor I will understand until the right time comes, and not until then. You don't know how your unconscious will tell. I won't know what it tells until after you do, but then I will learn the reason too. At the right time, in the right way, you will know and I will know. Then you will be all right. (1967, p. 402)

The careful and skillful use of these patterns will soon blur the distinction between pacing and leading the client's experience.

Transderivational Search[1]

This section deals with the distinctions of the dominant hemisphere which are the most important to an understanding of Milton Erickson's effective work with hypnosis. Each of the following linguistic distinctions shares a common pattern, i.e., in order to find a relevant meaning in the Surface Structure of these forms, information must be obtained from outside the Deep Structure meaning that is derived from the Surface Structure actually said. We intend to keep this section as simple as possible, and we suggest that you consult the construction exercises in Part III for additional help.

Transformational processes are any **deletion, distortion,** or **generalization** that occur between the full linguistic representation — Deep Structure — and the Surface Structure that is actually spoken or written, or heard, or seen. For example, this case of deletion:

Someone can give something to someone

could be uttered in this form or could be said as:

Something was given

and convey the same Deep Structure meaning. Linguistics, as we stated before, is the study of the intuitions which each of us has as a native speaker/listener of English and the formalization of those intuitions. We ask you now to pay attention to your own intuitions and to the formal maps which represent the experiences you have. These individual, personal intuitions will allow you to check what we are doing in this book and also are the very skills which have made it possible for Milton Erickson to create his successful techniques of hypnosis. If you pay attention to your own intuitions, trust them and use them, there is much that you can and will learn. As a child, you learned a natural language full of complexities in a very short time — an ability which no machine has yet acquired. Your language has rules which you use in a systematic way, without being consciously aware of what those rules are, just as Erickson uses language in a rule-governed way during hypnosis. This book, then, is a map of the rules he uses without being cognizant of them — a map to help you learn *his* intuitions and to pay attention to, and learn from, *your own* intuitions.

Now, if you heard the Surface Structure:

Something was given

you would know intuitively the Deep Structure:

Someone gave something to someone

In order to make the fullest relevant meaning out of the Surface Structure *Something was given,* you know that someone had to do the giving and someone had to do the receiving. The model of this process is represented as follows:

full linguistic representation   Deep Structure

$$\text{Derivation} \begin{cases} \text{Transformation} \\ \quad \text{''} \\ \quad \text{''} \\ \quad \text{''} \\ \quad \text{''} \\ \quad \text{''} \end{cases} \begin{matrix} \\ \text{Three} \\ \text{Processes} \\ \text{Human} \\ \text{Modaling} \end{matrix}$$

spoken or written representation **. . .** Surface Structure

This is a representation of part of the process we go through in understanding and producing speech and writing. But if you consider the example even further, you will see that the words *someone* and *something* have no referential index. The meaning of just who gave what to whom is not available even in the Deep Structure. How, then, is the meaning made clear? How does a listener find a meaningful interpretation of these words relevant to his own experience? The simple answer would be to ask; however, during a hypnotic induction this can rarely be done, and in many

Specifically, for the example given:

Deep Structure Representation

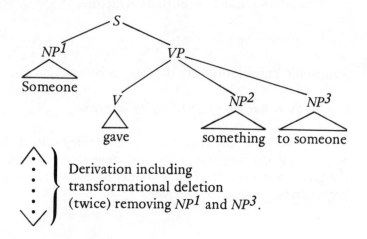

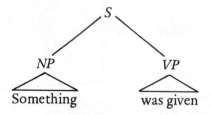

Derivation including
transformational deletion
(twice) removing NP^1 and NP^3.

Surface Structure Representation

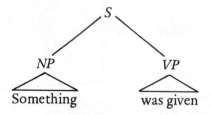

Transformational permutation NP^2
becomes the subject in NP^1 position.

where: NP = noun phrase
         VP = verb phrase
         V = verb

other circumstances people do not have the opportunity to ask.
Furthermore, does this search for meaning take place on a conscious level? The answer, apparently, is "No." We are constantly
processing information, most of it unconsciously. If you heard the
sentences:

> You know, people should study language closely
> if they want to learn how to use it in their work.
> People who do hypnosis use language as their main
> tool, yet they fail to study it closely.

How would you recover the meaning most relevant for you? Now think of those same words being said to you personally by another person in a conversation. Pay attention to your intuitions as you do this. Most likely, you will connect the sentences about *people* to be about *you,* depending upon whether you are engaged in the practice of hypnosis and how well you can fully experience these words being said about you. They do not mention you directly — nor is there any Deep Structure reference to you. Nevertheless, some process is at work in you which supplies a referential index which will make meaning out of the words as though they were being said to you specifically. We call this phenomenon a **transderivational search.** Visually, this can be represented as:

(1)   If Deep Structure ⊃ a NP with no referential index

⋮ } (derivation)

Surface Structure

where "⊃" means includes

Then

(2) A set of derivations which are formally equivalent to the Deep Structure (1) will be generated, except that they will have noun phrases which have referential indices.

(3) The new Deep Structures which contain referential indices (noun phrases) must, of course, come from somewhere — obviously, the client's model of the world. For years now we have found it very valuable in our work to ask any client who claims he does not know the answer to one of our questions to guess. The guess must come from the client's model; it is, in essence, a one-line dream. This goes on constantly with people as they process language, and it

is one main source of the massive problems resulting from "projecting" upon the communications of others. However, this projection can become a singular tool in hypnosis when used as Erickson skillfully does. A formal representation of this transderivation search could be diagrammed as follows:

$$\text{Deep Structure} \supset NP \text{ with } \sim \text{referential index} \xrightarrow{\text{Transderivational Search}} \begin{cases} \text{D. S.}_j & \text{D. S.}_k \ldots \text{D. S.}_n \\ \vdots & \vdots & \vdots \\ \boxed{\text{S. S.}}_j & \boxed{\text{S. S.}}_k \ldots \boxed{\text{S. S.}}_n \end{cases}$$

(a) $\text{D. S.}_i \equiv \text{D. S.}_{j, k, \ldots, n}$

except

(b) D. S._i differs from $\text{D. S.}_{j, k, \ldots, n}$ in that $\text{D. S.}_{j, k, \ldots, n}$ all have referential indices on their included noun phrases, where $\sim$ means negation

The set of Deep Structures activated by the transderivation search will be a result of the richness of the listener's model of the world. However, the one referential index that will always be available in anybody's model of the world will be his own unique referential index. All of the above diagrams are a formal way of displaying what happens when somebody says to you:

People should be nicer to me

Who is the person you think of that they are saying should be nicer? Could be anyone — could even be *you.* The specific forms of Surface Structure which activate transderivational search will now be presented one by one.

1. Generalized Referential Index

Surface Structures of this form can be extremely useful in hypnotic endeavors. A sentence with a noun phrase with a generalized referential index allows the client full assessing and activating of the transderivational search processes. This is accomplished simply by using noun phrases with no referential index in the world of the client's experience. Erickson describes a sentence of this form as:

> ... Sounds so specific, yet it is so general ...

Certain sensations in your hand will increase.
You become aware of that specific memory.
Nobody knows for sure.
People can be comfortable while reading this sentence.

All of the above Surface Structures are examples of generalized referential indices. Certain sensations does not refer to any particular sensation, thus allowing the client to fully supply the index most relevant from his own experience. The same is true for the specific memory, allowing the client a choice. People, again, could be anyone, and Nobody could be anyone, also. There is no referential index in any of the above four phrases.

Noun Phrases with no referential indices.

Example sentences

woman	A woman who went into a trance.
patient	A patient I had once.
problem	The problem was improving.
one	One can feel so good.
Situation	Way situation is decaying.
feeling	I get that feeling each time I'm in this situation.

... And that paperweight; the filing cabinet; your foot on the rug; the ceiling light; the draperies; your right hand on the arm of the chair; the pictures on the wall; the changing *focus* of your eyes as you glance about; the *interest* of the *book titles;* the *tension* in your shoulders; the *feeling* of the chair; the *disturbing noises* and *thoughts;* weight of

hands and feet; weight of *problems,* weight of desk; the
stationery stand; the *records* of *many patients;* the
phenomena of life, of *illness,* of *emotion,* of *physical and
mental behavior;* the *restfulness of relaxation;* the *need to
attend to one's needs; the need* to attend to *one's tension*
while looking at the desk or the paperweight or the filing
cabinet; *the comfort* of *withdrawal* from the *environment;
fatigue* and *its development;* the unchanging *character* of
the desk; *the monotony* of the filing cabinet; *the need* to
take *a rest; the comfort* of closing *one's eyes;* the relaxing
sensation of *a deep breath; the delight* of *learning*
passively; *the capacity* for *intellectual learning* by the
unconscious. . . .

2. Generalized Referential Index with Suggested Noun Phrase

This class of patterns is basically the same as the previous one
with a single exception: Specifically, a person attaches the missing
noun phrase to any position in the sentence, thus increasing the
likelihood it will be selected by the transderivational search. For
example, in the last section, the Surface Structure:

People can be comfortable while reading this sentence

takes on a slightly different form:

> People can be comfortable while reading this sentence,
> Joe.
> Joe, people can be comfortable while reading this
> sentence.
> People, Joe, can be comfortable while reading this
> sentence.
> People can, Joe, be comfortable while reading this
> sentence.
> People can be comfortable, Joe, while reading this
> sentence.

Each of these forms has a slightly different effect. Try saying them
out loud, using your own intuitions as a gauge to experience the
differences. Exchange them with a partner and pay attention to
the intuitions you have while hearing them, how they affect you.
Try them in the course of a normal conversation. For example, say

to someone in the course of a conversation:

> *You know* (name) *People can read this sentence* (name)
> *any time they want to.*

Surface Structures of this form are easy to construct and can be very useful.

Deletion — Grammatical and Ungrammatical

One of the three universal processes of human modeling is deletion. This process occurs at the neurological level, the social level and the level of individual experience (see *Magic I*, Chapter 1, for more detailed discussion). Our sensory apparatus detects and reports on changes in the patterns of energy only within narrow ranges. For example, the human ear shows phenomenal amplitude sensitivity even to displacement of the eardrum the diameter of a hydrogen atom (Noback, 1967, p. 156). It responds to wavelengths only between 20 and 20,000 cycles per second. Thus, patterns of energy — potential sounds — above 20,000 cycles per second are not available to us to assist us in organizing our experience. In other words, our nervous systems delete all of the patterns above 20,000 cycles per second. At the level of patterning of language, transformational linguists have identified a number of specific patterns of deletion which occur between the full linguistic representation — Deep Structure — and the actual sentences used by us in our communication — Surface Structure. Notice the difference in the amount of information available in each of the following sentences:

(1) The man bought the car from the woman for twenty dollars.
(2) The car was bought.

In the field of transformational grammar, each predicate or process word can be classified by the number and kind of nouns or arguments whose relationship or process it describes. The predicate *buy* can be classified as a four-place predicate:

> *buy* is a predicate which describes the process which takes place among:
> a buyer — the person doing the buying, acquiring the

    material

  a seller — the person doing the selling, releasing the
    material

  the material — the things whose possession is being
    changed

  the amount — the thing or service being exchanged for
    the material

In the first sentence, all of these noun arguments occur in the Surface Structure (1); in the second sentence, only one of them is represented; the other three have been removed by the transformational processes of deletion (see *Magic I* for a fuller discussion).

  In the context of hypnosis, as the client attempts to make sense, or, more accurately, to make complete meaning, out of the hypnotist's verbalizations, the skillful use of the transformational process of deletion assists the hypnotist in pacing the client. By skillfully deleting portions of the full linguistic representation — the Deep Structure — the client is forced to activate additional Deep Structures to recover the full meaning. In the process of generating and selecting these Deep Structures in their search for full meaning, clients will generate and select Deep Structures which will:

1. Insure participation on the part of the client, fully engaging the dominant hemisphere
2. Insure that the hypnotist's verbalizations effectively pace the client's experience
3. Insure that the client has the freedom to employ his own resources in the process of recovering the full meaning

There are two types of deletions which Erickson typically employs:

1. Grammatical deletion, in which the resulting Surface Structure is a well-formed sentence of English
2. Ungrammatical deletion, in which the resulting Surface Structure is not a well-formed sentence of English

The sentence presented earlier — *The car was bought* — is an example of the use of **grammatical** deletion. Examples of the result of *ungrammatical* deletion are sentence fragments such as:

and you fully realize so well that you . . .
and so clearly you want and need . . .
I will want soon to tell you . . .

These sequences of words are considered by most native speakers of English to be sentence fragments — pieces of sentences which, in themselves, do not constitute a complete, well-formed sentence of English. Such fragments — the result of ungrammatical deletion — force maximum participation on the part of the client to make a complete meaning.

> . . . And that paperweight; the filing cabinet; your foot on the rug; the ceiling light; the draperies; your right hand on the arm of the chair; the pictures on the wall; *the changing focus of your eyes* as you glance about; the interest of the book titles; the tension in your shoulders; the feeling of the chair; the disturbing noises and thoughts; weight of hands and feet; weight of problems, weight of desk; the stationery stand; the records of many patients; *the phenomena of life,* of illness, of emotion, of physical and mental behavior; the restfulness of relaxation; the need to attend to one's needs; the need to attend to one's tension while looking at the desk or the paperweight or the filing cabinet; the comfort of withdrawal from the environment; fatigue and its development; the unchanging character of the desk; the monotony of the filing cabinet; the need to take a rest; the comfort of closing one's eyes; the relaxing sensation of a deep breath; the delight of learning passively; the capacity for intellectual learning by the unconscious. . . .

The preceding paragraph is a varitable jungle of deletions, both grammatical and ungrammatical. For example, consider the two italic examples:

the changing focus of your eyes	Change from what to what?
the phenomena of life	What phenomena? of whose life?

Nominalization

Nominalization is the linguistic process of turning a process word or verb into an event or thing through a complex transformational process. This almost always occurs with the total deletion of some referential index and also serves to activate transderivational search. For example:

> The *satisfaction* of allowing your *unconscious mind* to communicate
> The *awareness* of the *feeling of the* chair
> The *depths* of the trance *state*
> Hearing the impossible *actuality*
> The utter *comfort* of *knowledge* and *clarity*
> As the *presence* of *relaxation* and *curiosity*

> . . . And that paperweight; the filing cabinet; your foot on the rug; the ceiling light; the draperies; your right hand on the arm of the chair; the *pictures* on the wall; the changing *focus* of your eyes as you glance about; the *interest* of the book titles; the *tension* in your shoulders; the *feeling* of the chair; the disturbing *noises* and *thoughts*; weight of hands and feet; weight of *problems*, weight of desk; the stationery stand; the *records* of many patients; the *phenomena* of *life*, of *illness*, of *emotion*, of physical and mental *behavior*; the *restfulness* of *relaxation*; the *need* to attend to one's *needs*; the *need* to attend to one's *tension* while looking at the desk or the paperweight or the filing cabinet; the *comfort* of *withdrawal* from the environment; *fatigue* and its *development*; the unchanging *character* of the desk; the *monotony* of the filing cabinet; the *need* to take a *rest*; the *comfort* of closing one's eyes; the relaxing *sensation* of a deep *breath*; the *delight* of *learning* passively; the *capacity* for intellectual *learning* by the unconscious. . . .

Nominalization occurs when Deep-Structure process words are transformed into nouns in the Surface Structure. Nominalization of a process word serves the hypnotist as a tool in overloading the dominant hemisphere's linguistic processes by requiring complex coding. Deletions must be recovered and ambiguity often arises. For example, in the Surface Structure:

The satisfaction of knowing you can learn

the referential index of just *whose* satisfaction is deleted, the search for full meaning will require that the following meanings be accessed from other sources:

> X satisfies Y by Y knowing Z
> (nominalized in Surface Structure)

Nominalization serves to allow the client to activate from his model of the world the meanings which will best serve his own purposes and needs, at the same time aiding in the process of overloading the dominant hemisphere.

Nominalizations also will allow the hypnotist to better pace the client by using phrases which are very unspecified by nature and require the client to fill in the meaning and specification.

Selectional Restrictions

This is the class of Surface Structures which are usually referred to as metaphors. They are violations of well-formed meaning as understood by native speakers of the language. For example, the Surface Structures:

> *The man drank the rock*
> *The flower was angry*
> *The happy chair sang a love song*

are violations of selectional restrictions. Drinking implies the act of consuming some liquid substance; rocks are defined as something which are not, by their nature, liquid. Anger is an activity engaged in by sentient beings — animals; flowers are not of this class. Thus, this also violates selectional restrictions. Happiness is an activity engaged in by sentient beings. Chairs do not have this quality; they are not in the class of animals which can sing songs. Selectional restriction in normal conversation demands that transderivational activity be performed to access a referential index that will be well formed, as when Erickson told Joe (in Part I) that a tomato plant can feel relaxed and comfortable. A well-formed meaning requires a noun phrase which identifies a sentient being for the activity of feeling relaxed and comfortable. This is the power of metaphor, fairy tales, and fables. It is also the process at work when Erickson tells stories about a tomato plant or a tractor.

> ... And that paperweight; the filing cabinet; your foot on the rug; the ceiling light; the draperies; your right hand on the arm of the chair; the pictures on the wall; the changing focus of your eyes as you glance about; the *interest of the book titles*; the tension in your shoulders; the *feeling of the chair*; the disturbing noises and thoughts; weight of hands and feet; *weight of problems*, weight of desk; the stationery stand; the records of many patients; the phenomena of life, of illness, of emotion, of physical and mental behavior; the restfulness of relaxation; the need to attend to one's needs; the need to attend to one's tension while looking at the desk or the paperweight or the filing cabinet; the need to take a rest; the comfort of closing one's eyes; the relaxing sensation of a deep breath; the delight of learning passively; the capacity for intellectual learning by the unconscious. . . .

Ambiguity

Each of us, as a native speaker of English, has the ability to appreciate some of the patterns in the structure of the English language. One of the patterns which we are able to sensitize ourselves to detect is that of ambiguity. Ambiguity is the name of the pattern in which a single sentence in English is a verbal representation of more than one distinct process in the world of the listener's experience. As we stated in *Magic I:*

> Ambiguity is the intuition that native speakers have when the same Surface Structure has more than one distinct semantic meaning and is represented as (see page 165):

Ambiguity in the Meta-model is the case wherein more than one Deep Structure is connected, by transformations, with the same Surface Structure.

> Nearly every sentence has more than one possible interpretation. Yet in ordinary use we appear to understand each sentence in one way at a time. The preceding sections have outlined some of the psychological mechanisms which we employ in sentence understanding, but it has not specified how

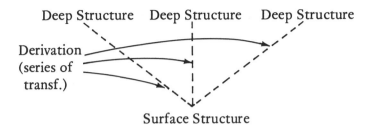

As a specific example:

Deep Struc.1   Deep Struc.2
    FBI agents who are   For someone to investi-
    conducting investi-   gate FBI agents can be
    gations can be dan-   dangerous for someone.
    gerous for someone.

Surface Structure: Investigating FBI agents can
                    be dangerous.

often we reapply them to a single speech stimulus which has more than one potential interpretation. Some recent experiments indicate that we process many structures for each sentence preconsciously but we are conscious of only one meaning at a time.

Ambiguous Sequences — Conclusion

Although every sentence contains some sort of ambiguity, in ordinary usage nearly every sentence is preceded by a context which makes one interpretation more likely than any of the others. Thus, the preceding studies may be experimental oddities rather than representative of normal perceptual behavior. Their primary implication for normal perceptual habits is to highlight the hypothesis of the preceding section that during speech perception we oscillate between two kinds of activities: periods of stimulus input and unconscious processing (during which potential ambiguity can have an effect), and periods of internal analysis and conscious perception of the preceding unit (during which potential ambiguities are ignored in favor of one interpretation).

Plath and Bever, 1968, p. 43

We have identified four categories of ambiguity which occur in Erickson's work. These are phonological, syntactic, scope and punctuation.[2] An excellent example of phonological ambiguity occurs in Erickson's trance instruction with Huxley; specifically, the phrase:

> ... a part and apart ...

As we stated in the commentary, while the phrase is unambiguous when presented visually, it is completely ambiguous when presented auditorily. We follow with a list of examples of additional phonological ambiguities:

> *light* (in color, or in weight)
> *knows/nose*
> *here/hear*
> *read/red*

> ... And that paper*weight;* the filing cabinet; your foot on the rug; the ceiling light; the draperies; your right hand on the arm of the chair; the pictures on the wall; the changing focus of your eyes as you glance about; the interest of the book titles; the tension in your shoulders; the feeling of the chair; the disturbing noises and thoughts; *weight* of hands and feet; *weight* of problems, *weight* of desk; the stationery stand; the records of many patients; the phenomena of life, of illness, of emotion, of physical and mental behavior; the restfulness of relaxation; the need to attend to one's needs; the need to attend to one's tension while looking at the desk or the paper*weight* or the filing cabinet; the comfort of withdrawal from the environment; fatigue and its development; the unchanging character of the desk; the monotony of the filing cabinet; the need to take a rest; the comfort of closing one's eyes; the relaxing sensation of a deep breath; the delight of learning passively; the capacity for intellectual learning by the unconscious. ...

Weight pronounced aloud becomes ambiguous. Is it *weight* or *wait? Wait* is also an effective message for this patient who has trouble concentrating.

One very rich source of these word ambiguities is pairs of words which are ambiguous with respect to their syntactic category. Many verb/nominalized verb combinations have this feature:

lift	*rest*	*talk*
pull	*push*	*shake*
point	*nod*	*hand*
touch	*move*	*feel*

Each of these words, depending upon its context, may function either as a predicate or as a noun (more specifically, as the nominalization derived from that predicate). When these words are used in well-formed Surface Structures in English and are marked analogically, for example, as distinct from their surrounding linguistic context, Erickson is able to make full use of their inherent phonological ambiguity.

The extract given from *Magic I* is an example of a syntactic ambiguity. Another example is the one used in the commentary in this volume on the Huxley article:

Hypnotizing hypnotists can be tricky

> . . . And that paperweight; the filing cabinet; your foot on the rug; the ceiling light; the draperies; your right hand on the arm of the chair; the pictures on the wall; the changing focus of your eyes as you glance about; the interest of the book titles; the tension in your shoulders; *the feeling of the chair;* the disturbing noises and thoughts; weight of hands and feet; weight of problems, weight of desk; the stationery stand; the records of many patients; the phenomena of life, of illness, of emotion, of physical and mental behavior; the restfulness of relaxation; the need to attend to one's needs; the need to attend to one's tension while looking at the desk or the paperweight or the filing cabinet; the comfort of withdrawal from the environment; fatigue and its development; the unchanging character of the desk; the monotony of the filing cabinet; the need to take a rest; the comfort of closing one's eyes; the relaxing sensation of a deep breath; the delight of learning passively; the capacity for intellectual learning by the unconscious. . . .

Scope ambiguity is the kind of ambiguity present in sentences and phrases such as:

the old men and women

The ambiguity here is whether the adjective *old* applies both to the noun phrase *men and women* or simply to the noun phrase *men*. In other words, is the phrase to be understood to be:

the men who are old and the women who are old

or

the men who are old and the women

> ... And that paperweight; the filing cabinet; your foot on the rug; the ceiling light; the draperies; your right hand on the arm of the chair; the pictures on the wall; the changing focus of your eyes as you glance about; the interest of the book titles; the tension in your shoulders; the feeling of the chair; the *disturbing* noises and thoughts; *weight* of hands and feet; weight of problems, weight of desk; the stationery stand; the records of many patients; the phenomena of life, of illness, of emotion, of physical and mental behavior; the restfulness of relaxation; the need to attend to one's needs; the need to attend to one's tension while looking at the desk or the paperweight or the filing cabinet; the comfort of withdrawal from the environment; fatigue and its development; the unchanging character of the desk; the monotony of the filing cabinet; the need to take a rest; the comfort of closing one's eyes; the relaxing sensation of a deep breath; the delight of learning passively; the capacity for intellectual learning by the unconscious. ...

One place where this scope ambiguity seems to occur frequently and effectively in Erickson's work is where several sentences are embedded under a factive verb. For example, Erickson might say:

> ... *how soon you will fully realize that you are sitting here comfortably, listening to the sound of my voice, and you are going into a deep trance only as quickly as your unconscious mind wants.* ...

The ambiguity here is whether the portion of Erickson's communication which occurs after the word *and* is a part of the sentence which begins with the verb *realize.* If it is, then it is presupposed to be true. If it is not, then it is simply an independent sentence which the client may challenge. Predicates such as *realize* require that whatever follows them in the same sentence is presupposed to be true in order for the communication taking place to make any sense at all. For example, if I say to you:

Are you aware that you are sitting on my hat?

I am presupposing that you are sitting on my hat and simply asking whether you are aware of it. Either a *yes* or a *no* answer on your part indicates your acceptance of the truth of the portion of the sentence which follows the factive predicate *aware.* Thus, when Erickson uses the scope ambiguity with a factive predicate, he leaves the client to deal with the question (not necessarily consciously — in fact, preferably, not consciously) of whether his going into a deep trance is a fact presupposed by the communication or not, an excellent topic to occupy the client's dominant hemisphere.

The fourth type of ambiguity which we find as a consistent pattern in Erickson's work is *punctuation ambiguity.* Erickson might, for example, say:

. . . I notice that you are wearing a watch carefully what I am doing . . .

This sequence of words is not a well-formed sentence of English. We decompose the sequence into two sequences, each of which is a well-formed sentence of English:

. . . I notice that you are wearing a watch . . .

and

. . . Watch carefully what I am doing . . .

Here Erickson is making use of the ambiguity of the word *watch* which can occur both as a noun and as a verb in the Surface Structures of English. Essentially, Erickson has overlapped two well-formed Surface Structures of English. The listener, up until the word *carefully,* has processed the first of these well-formed sentences and recovered the Deep Structure meaning; however, when he comes to the word *carefully,* his normal processing strategies fail. As he receives the remainder of the communication from Erickson, he attempts other analyses, probably recovering the second well-formed Deep Structure. However, there is no solution to the overlap problem and the normal processing strategies fail. If he assumes that the word *watch* is a noun which goes with the first part of the communication, then the second part makes no sense at all (i.e., he cannot recover a Deep Structure for it). If he assumes that the word *watch* is a verb and goes with the second part of the communication, then he can recover no Deep Structure for the first portion of the communication. In this sense, then, there is no satisfactory solution to the punctuation ambiguity involving overlap. Thus, the ambiguity here is to which sequence of words will the listener assign the phonologically ambiguous pivot word (*watch,* in this example). This phenomenon could be classified equally well as a special case of ungrammatical deletion. No matter which characterization you prefer to assist you in organizing your experience of it, it constitutes a very powerful technique for distracting the dominant hemisphere.

These four types of ambiguity have in common that each is a single language representation of more than one meaning or Deep Structure. In each, the client is faced with the task of selecting meaning from the set of possible Deep Structures which the single Surface Structure represents. In order to accomplish this, the listener must generate a set of Deep Structures and make some decision as to which he will accept as the meaning of the communication intended by the hypnotist. Again, this involves a trans-derivational search for the most appropriate meaning which can be represented by the Surface Structure presented. Ambiguity, then, has a positive value in the context of hypnosis in that, since the client generates a number of Deep Structures and searches through these transderivationally for the most appropriate meaning, he will:

1. Become an active participant in the hypnotic process
2. Select a Deep Structure which represents a meaning which fits for him, thereby insuring a satisfactory pacing
3. Employ his normal linguistic processing mechanisms with a transderivational search for meaning

Lesser Included Structures

The following two categories of Surface Structures — Imbedded Questions and Imbedded Commands — which have included in them another structure can constitute a valuable resource for giving imbedded commands and for building response potential by utilizing the processes of the dominant hemisphere. Imbedded Commands and Imbedded Questions are the two categories of this that will be discussed here.

Imbedded Questions

Imbedded Questions serve the purpose of building response potential in a client by raising questions without allowing an overt response from the client. They very often are a presupposition of some other command and serve to distract the dominant hemisphere by having it utilize the internal dialogue in answering questions, or *trying* to answer questions, or even trying to figure out if it *should* answer the questions, or even, still further, if it *could* answer the questions, even though a question has not *really* been asked. Some examples will serve to clarify this concept:

> I wonder whether you know which hand will rise first
> I'm curious to know if you can really find your knee in the dark
> I don't know if you know whether or not you're going into a trance
> I'm pondering over how you feel about the prospect of hypnosis
> I'm very curious about when you first decided to see me and what you really want for yourself

All of the above Surface Structures have in common the characteristic of raising a question without a request for an overt reply by the client. This is most easily accomplished by making a statement about the question in the form that follows:

> X (question verbs) if Y (aware) of (question)
> I'm curious whether you know which of your hands will rise first.

X can be the speaker of any other person as well; example:

John is wondering if you know which of your hands will rise first.

(not aware) can be any phrase such as *wonder, curious, don't know,* etc.

"if" can be any conditional such as *whether, if, whether or not*

or can be a question word such as *about, how, what, when, why*

I'm curious why you came here, and if you even know why.

where question verbs are any verbs which allow embedded questions to follow.

These imbedded questions are most effective when they are stacked together to maximally distract the dominant hemisphere. This allows the hypnotist to follow these imbedded questions with a clear command desired by the hypnotist, thereby utilizing the response potential the hypnotist has built up in the client, e.g.:

I wonder why you wish to go into a trance, and I'm even more curious to know if you know whether or not you think you can, I don't know if you know how soon you will close your eyes; in fact, I don't even know if you know anything about a trance at all. I'm pondering this and I am very curious about knowing if you know how to even relax completely.

Imbedded Commands

Imbedded Commands serve the purpose of making suggestions to the client indirectly and, thereby, making it difficult to resist in any way. These constitute a pattern of Surface Structures which include within them a command, just as the preceding pattern included a question. For example:

Children are able to Fred, sit down and relax
I may, Fred, breathe deeply while I speak but you don't mind, do you
People must Fred, sit all the way down in the chair relax
Plants can Fred, feel comfortable and relaxed

These four Surface Structures are one type of imbedded command. These are constructed by placing the client's name after a modal operator such as:

can, may, might, must, able to

This is a sufficient, though not a necessary, condition for imbedded commands.[3] They may also be constructed by using the infinitive form of some predicate such as:

to see, to feel, to move

Many people want to see clearly what I mean.

Imbedded Command form: *(splitting infinitives)*

*Many people want to **Fred**, see clearly . . . I want you to **Fred** feel relaxed*

*My mother often tells me to **Fred**, breathe deeply and slowly.*

Imbedded commands may also be given by direct and indirect quotation. This is one of Erickson's favorite and most often utilized forms of giving commands indirectly. This is accomplished by placing the command in the context of either a direct or an indirect quote from some other time, place, or situation. For example:

I used to have a patient who would tell me to feel relaxed

These are most effective when they are also marked analogically by emphasizing the command and by looking intently at the listener, if their eyes are open.

Indirect Imbedded Command:

My friends tell me to feel comfortable and to loosen up when we are out on the town

Direct Imbedded Command:

> *I had a patient once who would say to me, Milton, scratch your nose. It never made much sense but he would consistently tell me to Do it now.*

Another example would be:

> *Meaning is so difficult to understand; what does it mean when someone says, don't move or don't talk. What do they mean when they say, shut your eyes NOW. What do they mean when they say, Count backwards silently from 20 to 1.*

All of the above-described lesser included structures, both questions and commands, serve the hypnotist as valuable tools to give suggestions indirectly and at the same time to distract and utilize the dominant hemisphere. The imbedding of either questions or commands is simply the inclusion of the question or command in a larger Surface Structure which serves as a cloak. The style thus far presented has been the grammatical approach; however, the effect is the same if the imbedding is not grammatical, in fact, it may be more effective when presented in non-grammatical form. This will serve to further distract and overload the dominant hemisphere. For example, consider the following combination of all lesser included structures, both grammatical and non-grammatical:

> *I wonder whether or not you understand that you can feel comfortable and relaxed, now, I had a friend who used to say, You can learn anything if only you give yourself a chance to relax, and I wonder if you know whether or not you can Fred feel relaxed, and I'm very curious to know if you fully realize that you can Fred know you can and will learn now. I also wish, though I don't know whether or not you wish to know, if you can Fred have closing eyes and restful feelings now.*

Derived Meanings

When each of us uses natural language systems to communicate, we assume the listener's ability to hear our Surface Structures and decode them from sound sequences into meaning. In other words, we assume the listener's capability to recover the Deep Structure representation from the Surface Structure we present. In addition to this recovery of the Deep Structure from a Surface Structure, we often assume certain additional abilities in the way that the listener will make meaning out of what we offer. Here we are referring to native speaker/listener's ability, for example, to establish a context in which the sentence we present could have some pragmatic value. Erickson uses two of these extra or derived-meanings abilities on the part of native listener's in his work. These are **Presuppositions** and **Conversational Postulates**. We presented the subject of **Presuppositions** in *Magic I* as one of the Meta-model distinctions (Chapters 3 and 4).

> In recent work in linguistics, transformationalists have begun to explore how presuppositions work in natural language. Certain sentences when used imply that certain other sentences must be true in order for them to make sense. For example, if I hear you say:
>
> (37)   *There is a cat on the table*
>
> I may choose to believe that there is a cat on the table or not and, either way, I can make sense out of what you are saying. However, if I hear you say:
>
> (38)   *Sam realized that there is a cat on the table*
>
> I must assume that there is, in fact, a cat on the table in order to make any sense out of what you are saying. This difference shows up clearly if I introduce the negative element *not* into the sentence:
>
> (39)   *Sam does not realize that there is a cat on the table*
>
> This shows that, when one says the sentence which means the opposite — the one that denies what the

first one claims is true — one still must assume that there is a cat on the table in order to make sense out of the sentence. A sentence which must be true in order for some other sentence to make sense is called the presupposition of the second sentence.

The value of the skillful use of presuppositions in the hypnotic context is that it allows the hypnotist to build a model of the ongoing process by using presuppositions. Since presuppositions are not an immediate question to the client, it is very difficult for him to challenge them. Thus, the client accepts the hypnotist's presuppositions and the process continues. For example, Erickson says:

> *I don't yet know whether it will be your right hand or your left hand or both of your hands which your unconscious mind will allow to rise to your face . . . .*

Here the issue is which hand or whether it will be one or both hands, not whether the client will respond to hand levitation. Or, again, Erickson says:

> *When I wake you from the trance, you will fully recognize your fine ability to learn quickly from your unconscious mind*

Here the issue is whether the client will *fully* recognize, *not* whether she will recognize, or whether she has been in a trance (presupposed by *wake you from trance*), or whether she has and can learn from her unconscious mind. These latter are background assumptions which the client must develop and accept for the communication to be meaningful at all. The way in which Erickson consistently uses presuppositions to assist the client in entering deep trance and learning deep trance phenomena demonstrates the power of this technique.

> *. . . When you get up and move your chair to the other side of that table your unconscious mind will then release a lot of important information. Perhaps it will take your unconscious even longer than five or ten minutes to do it, or perhaps it will not be until the next session. . . .*

Again, since the presuppositions of a sentence are not part of its Deep Structure, their use both involves the client as an active participant in the process of making meaning (in this case, derived meaning) and removes from challenge whatever the presuppositions of the statements are.

The second class of derived meanings used by Erickson are called **Conversational Postulates.** As with the presuppositions, the meaning represented by the conversational postulates is derived — it is not a part of the Deep Structure recovered by the client but requires additional processing. For example, if I say to you:

Can you take out the garbage?

the literal Deep Structure requires only that you respond with a *yes* or a *no.* However, the typical response is for you to take out the garbage. In other words, although I use a Surface Structure whose corresponding Deep Structure is a *yes/no* question, you respond to it as though it were a command. In the Appendices at the end of this volume, we will instruct you on how to construct examples utilizing these conversational postulates to secure the effects you wish as a hypnotist. For our present purposes, it is necessary only to point out that, when Erickson chooses to use the conversational postulate mechanism for securing a response from his client, he is operating consistently with his stated guidelines. Specifically, by using conversational postulates, he avoids giving commands, simultaneously allowing the client to choose to respond or not and avoiding the authoritarian relationship between himself and the client. Thus, the client, if he chooses to respond to the sentence:

. . . Can you allow your hand to rise . . .

by allowing her hand to rise, actively participates in the process of trance induction, using conversational postulates to understand the derived meaning of the Surface Structure *yes/no* question — a processing act in addition to the recovery of the Deep Structure. If he fails to respond, there is no disruption of the process of trance induction by Erickson, since there was no command given; a question was simply asked and no response is required.

The non-*yes/no* question form of the communication also works in the same way. Erickson might, for example, say:

> *There is no need for you to move*

or

> *There is no need for you to keep your eyes closed*

or

> *It is possible for you to go even deeper into a trance*

If the client is moving when Erickson says the first of these sentences, then the effect of the communication is the command *don't move.* If the client was not moving, this statement is an effective pacing technique. Similarly, if the client's eyes are closed when Erickson says the second sentence, then the effect is for the client to respond by opening his eyes. Finally, when the client hears Erickson utter the third sentence, it has the effect of the command *go even deeper into a trance.*

We will present a formal outline of these phenomena in Part III.

Accessing the Non-Dominant Hemisphere

Hypnosis is essentially a communication of ideas and understandings to a patient in such a fashion that he will be most receptive to the presented ideas and thereby be motivated to explore his own body potentials for the control of his psychological and physiological responses and behavior.
Milton H. Erickson, 1967

Milton Erickson has succeeded in developing a powerful set of techniques for accessing and communicating with the non-dominant hemisphere in human beings. His skills allow him to call out the resources of the person with whom he is communicating. In his hypnotic work Erickson makes extensive use of the distinction between the conscious and the unconscious mind of the client. Erickson received his medical and psychiatric training in the standard institutions of his school years; specifically, he was trained in the psychoanalytic tradition from which he appropriated the terms *conscious* and *unconscious*. In his own writings he uses the two terms in a number of ways. He, himself, comments in *Hypnotic Psychotherapy*, 1948:

As for the trance state itself, it should be regarded as a special, unique, but wholly normal psychological state. . . . For convenience in conceptualization, this special state, or level of awareness, has been termed *unconscious* or *subconscious*.

Again, Erickson, in *The Investigation of a Specific Amnesia,*
1967, p. 159, comments:

While in a state of profound, hypnotic sleep, the subject was
given the suggestion that she could reveal indirectly the
information desired with neither *conscious* nor *subconscious*
realization of what she was doing. To this end she was instructed
to continue in a state of deep hypnosis, thereby *dissociating* her
conscious mind from, and leaving it in, a state of quiescence. At
the same time, by means of her *subconscious* mind, she was to
engage the author in an animated conversation. Thus, with both
conscious and *subconscious* minds engaged, a *third level of
consciousness* in response to hypnotic suggestion would *emerge
from the depths of her mind,* and would express itself by guiding
her hand in automatic writing, of which she would be aware
neither *consciously* nor *subconsciously.*

Erickson goes on to comment in a footnote to this portion of
the text:

The author assumes no responsibility for the va-
lidity of these concepts, and the trance state of the
subject probably accounts for her acceptance of
them, but, at all events, they served the purposes.

These passages *underline* one of the most important characteristics of Erickson's complex behavior in hypnosis and therapy. His
willingness to accept the client's model of the world allows him to
assist his client in changing.

This means I'm less distracted by the content of
what people say. Many patterns of behavior are
reflected in the way a person says something rather
than in what he says.

In other words, Erickson listens for the modeling principles which
the clients use to construct their realities.

A number of people in the history of civilization have made
this point — that there is an irreducible difference between the
world and our experience of it. We, as human beings, do not
operate directly upon the world, but, rather, we operate upon the
world through our representations of it. Each of us creates a
representation of the world we live in — that is, we create a map or

model which we use to generate our behavior. The map or model which we create serves us as a representation of what is possible, what is available, what the structure of the world is. Our *representation* of the world determines to a large degree what our *experience* of the world is, how we perceive the world, what choices we see available to us as we live in the world.

> It must be remembered that the object of the world of ideas as a whole [the map or model — RWB/JTG] is not the portrayal of reality — this would be an utterly impossible task — but rather to provide us with an instrument for finding our way about more easily in the world.
>
> H. Vaihinger, *The Philosophy of As If,* p. 15.

No two human beings have exactly the same experiences. The model of the world which we create to guide us is based, in part, upon our experiences. Each of us may, then, create a different model of the world we share, and thus come to live in a somewhat different reality.

> ... important characteristics of maps should be noted. A map is not the territory it represents, but, if correct, it has a similar structure to the territory, which accounts for its usefulness. ...
>
> A. Korzybski, *Science & Sanity,* 4th Ed., 1958, pp. 58-60.

Erickson allows himself the same flexibility in the creation of his own model for therapy and hypnosis. This flexibility has allowed him to detect and to come to utilize effectively in his work patterns which are very fast and powerful.

Our purpose is to create a model of a portion of Erickson's behavior which will make these patterns available. One of the most useful ways of organizing our own experience in hypnosis and therapy, and of understanding Erickson's technique, was to realize Erickson's use of the terms *conscious* and *unconscious* refer (at least partially) to the dominant and non-dominant hemispheres of the human brain. We are not suggesting that Erickson's use of the term *unconscious mind* is always and only referring to the non-dominant hemisphere, but that a model which translates the terms in this way provides a guide for learning Erickson's techniques.

Once a satisfactory deep trance state has been achieved by the client, for example, both hemispheres are being accessed and utilized, especially in some of the more complex deep trance phenomena (e.g., positive hallucinations). As with any model, the usefulness of this translation of the term *unconscious* into the term *non-dominant hemisphere* will be the criterion for its acceptance.

The Non-dominant Hemisphere in Humans

As we related in the Introduction to Part II, research on the neurological organization of human beings (especially, split-brain) has revealed some typical differences between the behavior of the cerebral hemispheres. Specifically, the researchers have identified differences in the quality, speed and accuracy of response of the two parts of the cerebral cortex for different sensory and representational functions (see, especially, Jerre Levy's article, *Psychobiological Implications of Bilateral Asymmetry*). For our present purposes, the most interesting of these are the following:

dominant hemisphere functions	non-dominant hemisphere functions
full language system	visualization
tempo	melody
contralateral side of the body	special class of language
	contralateral side of the body

This asymmetry between the cerebral hemispheres shows up in interesting ways in common, everyday tasks; for example, Gardner (1975, p. 374) comments:

> Kinsbourne's model of hemispheres competing for control of attentional mechanisms has generated some imaginative research, both on his part and on that of others. He has found, for example, that skill in balancing a dowel in one hand is enhanced when one is simultaneously speaking if the dowel is in the left hand, while performance is impaired when one is speaking if the dowel is in the right hand. His explanation is that speaking and bal-

ancing are competing activities, which, owing to the "spill-over" effect, interfere with one another when they both occur in opposite hemispheres, and they then promote and facilitate one another. Exemplifying the same, complementary side-effect, speaking improves the subject's ability to recognize elements in the right visual field, even when those shapes are nonsensical. In contrast, when the patient rehearses melodies (a right-hemisphere function), a left-visual-field advantage results.

This partial list of cerebral asymmetries in the human brain serves both as a list of ways in which the unconscious may be accessed in the context of hypnosis and also as an important organizing principle in the context of therapy, especially in work with incongruities (see *Magic I*, Chapter 6, and *Magic II*, Part II). In other words, by recognizing these asymmetries, the hypnotist who is working to assist the client in achieving trance becomes systematic in his choices about how to communicate with the unconscious mind of the client.

In the list of non-dominant hemisphere functions, we have included special classes of language. This requires an explanation and a slight excursion into linguistic and psycholinguistic research. There are two parts to the explanation. First, human language systems are remarkably complex systems. The intricacies of the patterning in human languages has so far exceeded the linguist's skills in creating a model which represents all of these patterns. In other words, although we are completely systematic in our linguistic behavior, we have not yet been successful in describing that behavior. Thus, the task of learning the patterns which are our language system has eluded the linguists, yet, each of us accomplishes essentially the same task between the ages of two and six years. Furthermore, although the languages of the world sound dramatically quite different when heard and appear quite different when represented visually in their written forms, a deeper analysis of their patterns shows a close similarity in their structures. Out of all of the logically possible forms which the patterns (syntax) of natural language systems could have, only a relatively restricted number of patterns occur. Largely independent of the specific language which they are learning, children seem to learn at the same rate with the same kind of "mistakes." These considerations have led linguists and psycholinguists to formulate the model of wired-in (neurological) linguistic distinctions known as Universal Grammar. These universal distinctions are said to be part of the genetically specified nervous system of each of us at birth. The presence of these universals in the model helps researchers to understand both how languages display such marked similarity and also how children accomplish the complex task of learning a language in such a short time.

The second part of the explanation involves the fact that children who are fully fluent in a language and who suffer some brain trauma in the language hemisphere typically become mute. They then go through the standard stages for the acquisition of the language once again and become fully fluent speakers. This pattern has been interpreted by researchers as a demonstration of the ability of either hemisphere to learn and to function as a full linguistic system. Thus, in the case in which some condition prevents the dominant hemisphere from functioning adequately as the language center, the non-dominant hemisphere will take over that function. This equipotentiality or plasticity of the human nervous system is another piece of evidence pointing to great human potential so far largely unexplored.

Considering these two facts together, we predict that the non-dominant hemisphere will demonstrate some language abilities. Specifically, as a minimum, all of the distinctions available in the Universal Grammar model will be present in the non-dominant hemisphere. This prediction of the authors turns out to be supported by research from various sources. For example, one description of the classes of language abilities by hemisphere is given by Levy (1974, p. 174):

> Since the right hemispheres of commissurotomy patients appear to have some comprehension of both spoken language as well as written nouns, verbs, and adjectives, and also have some minimal capacities for expressive speech, the question arises as to the differences in the two hemispheres which underlie the vast differences in linguistic abilities. If the minor hemisphere could comprehend no speech, but could produce some, one could postulate the absence of phonologies in the right hemisphere and could interpret speech production as a result of a direct translation from a semantic to

articulatory code. If the right hemisphere could comprehend, but not produce speech, one could postulate the absence of an articulatory code. However, when the right hemisphere can both comprehend and express language, even though at a very limited level, an interpretation becomes much more difficult.

We will return to the topic of linguistic communication with the non-dominant hemisphere later in this chapter.

Visual Accessing

The hypnotist is faced with the task of assisting the client in getting access to his unconscious or non-dominant hemisphere. As we outlined, this has two parts — distraction and simultaneous utilization of the dominant hemisphere, and accessing of the non-dominant hemisphere. One of the most direct and powerful of the non-dominant hemisphere accessing techniques found by hypnotists is that of having the client create visual images in his mind's eye. By bringing the client to a task which presupposes a visualization capacity, the hypnotist facilitates the transfer of control from the dominant hemisphere to the non-dominant hemisphere.

Subjective accounts from many subjects explaining these findings may be summarized as follows: "When I listen to the imaginary metronome, it speeds up or slows down, gets louder or fainter, as I start to go into a trance, and I just drift along. With the real metronome, it remains distractingly constant, and it keeps pulling me back to reality instead of letting me drift along into a trance. The imaginary metronome is changeable and always fits in with just the way I'm thinking and feeling, but I have to fit myself to the real one."

In this same connection, mention should be made of findings in experimental and clinical work centering around hypnotically induced visual hallucinations. For example, a patient, greatly confused about her personal identity, was induced to visualize a number of crystal balls in which she could hallucinate a whole series of significant life experiences, make objective and subjective comparisons

> and thus establish the continuity of her life, from
> one hallucinated experience to the next. With a
> real crystal ball, the hallucinated experiences were
> physically limited in extent, and the changing and
> superimposition of "scenes" much less satisfactory.
> Milton H. Erickson, 1967, pp. 8 and 9

Our experiences in both hypnosis and therapy have repeatedly included for many of our clients the distinction mentioned previously in the commentary on the Huxley article — the difference between imaging a picture in the mind's eye and seeing a picture in the mind's eye. The experience of imaging a picture is an activity which occurs in the dominant hemisphere — this, essentially, is the construction of a visual image using the language system to lead in the construction. The images which result from this process are, typically, poor in quality, unfocused and drab, with only a faint resemblance to the images which the client experiences with his eyes open. The process of seeing a picture in the mind's eye is apparently a non-dominant-hemisphere activity. Here, the resulting images are clear and focused and so closely approximate the client's experience with his eyes open. Clients will differ greatly in their ability to see pictures in their mind's eye. In general, clients who have as their most highly valued representational system a visual system will respond most satisfactorily to this technique of visual accessing of the non-dominant hemisphere. The hypnotist needs only to ask the client to visualize to begin the process of trance induction effectively. In the context of therapy, the therapist's skills in identifying and responding to the client in the client's own representational system is one of his most powerful techniques:

> These two case reports have been presented in
> considerable detail to illustrate the naturalistic
> hypnotic approach to children. There is seldom, if
> ever, a need for a formalized or ritualistic tech-
> nique. The eidetic imagery of child, his readiness,
> eagerness and actual need for new learnings, his
> desire to understand and to share in the activities
> of the world about him, and the opportunities
> offered by "pretend" and imitation games all serve
> to enable him to respond competently and well to
> hypnotic suggestions.   (1967, p. 423)

Franz Baumann, a well-known San Francisco medical hypno-tist who specializes in child and adolescent practice, utilizes the visualization accessing technique in his inductions almost exclu-sively with consistent results. Specifically, he has his clients close their eyes and watch their favorite TV program. Visual fantasy work — called Guided Fantasy (see *Magic I,* Chapter 6, and *Magic II,* Part I, for a fuller discussion) — was the way in which each of the authors first became interested in hypnosis as a tool for assisting clients in changing. Our therapeutic experiences had al-ready convinced us of the power and effectiveness of visualization as a therapeutic technique before we became aware that the behavior of our clients matched perfectly the behavior described by hypnotists of their clients doing visual tasks while in light and medium trances.

One of the techniques employed by hypnotists in inducing or deepening a trance state in a client is that of having the client count, or counting for the client. This technique serves several purposes. In the present context, the counting technique is a special case of visual accessing of the non-dominant hemisphere. When a client is listening to himself or someone else count, he is quite likely simultaneously to represent the numerals which he is hearing as an internal visual display. Numerals, as with other standard visual patterns, are stored in the non-dominant hemi-sphere; thus, the counting technique accesses the unconscious part of the client's brain. The relative ineffectiveness of counting as a trance induction and deepening technique for certain clients now becomes understandable — these are clients whose ability to access the non-dominant hemisphere for visual representations has yet to be developed. With this understanding of the counting task as a special case of visual accessing of the non-dominant hemisphere, hypnotists who are working with clients who have some ability to see visual representations in their mind's eye may increase the effectiveness of this technique simply by instructing the client, for example, that, as he sits there breathing rhythmically, listening to the sound of the voice counting, he is to make clear, focused images of each of the numerals as he hears its name, each in a different color. Listening to the client's use of predicates for identifying the client's most highly valued representational system will allow the hypnotist to easily decide whether a visualization accessing induction will be effective.

Hypnotists have, in fact, developed a series of so-called suggestibility tests which they often use prior to beginning a standard induction. These suggestibility tests are simply ways for testing to determine whether the client has the ability to employ certain representational systems. For example, notice the predicates which occur in the following hand clasp suggestibility test (Weitzenhoffer, 1957, pp. 127-128):

> I want you to clasp your hands like this . . . make them real tight, as tight as you can. . . . As you do, you will soon find that your fingers are becoming locked together, so that your hands are becoming stuck together . . . your hands and fingers are sticking more and more together . . . more and more tightly clasped together.

Precisely the same suggestibility test — that is, a test for representational system abilities — can easily be altered to serve as a test for the client's visualization abilities. Specifically, by shifting the predicates used to visual predicates and observing how well the client responds, the hypnotist can make a valid choice as to which kind of accessing of the non-dominant hemisphere he will use. For example, using Weitzenhoffer's induction as a guide, we change the predicates from kinesthetic to visual:

I want you to make a picture in your mind's eye of your hands clasped together. Look just above your hands and see the dark green bucket filled with white glue. Watch closely as the white fluid falls, dripping down the scarred, battered sides of the green bucket. . . .

In many of Erickson's inductions, he will include statements about the letters of the alphabet — for example, reminding the client of the great difficulty which he experienced at one point in his life in distinguishing between a *b* and a *d* as he learned the alphabet forms. In addition to functioning as a covert instruction for age regression, these statements access the visual representations for the letters of the alphabet just as the numeral sequences do, making this a special case of visual accessing.

If the client shows little or no ability to create non-dominant hemisphere visual representations, the hypnotist need not give up the choice of accessing the non-dominant hemisphere by visualizing. Indeed, it is exactly here that Erickson again demonstrates his skills. As he describes in the Huxley article, as part of a "standard procedure" for Erickson, he uses the client's most highly valued representational system to assist him in gaining access to others.

In the problem of developing general techniques for the induction of trances and the eliciting of hypnotic behavior, there have been numerous uncritical utilizations of traditional misconceptions of hypnotic procedure. The "eagle eye," the "crystal ball," strokings and passes, and similar aids as sources of mysterious force have been discarded by the scientifically trained. Yet the literature abounds with reports of hypnotic techniques based upon the use of apparatus intended to limit and restrict the subject's behavior, to produce fatigue and similar reactions, as if they were the essential desiderata of hypnosis: Crystal balls held at a certain distance from the eyes, revolving mirrors, metronomes, and flashing lights are often employed as the major consideration. As a result, too much emphasis is placed upon external factors and the subject's responses to them. Primarily, emphasis should be placed upon the intrapsychic behavior of the subject rather than upon the relationship to externalities. At best, apparatus is only an incidental aid, to be discarded at the earliest possible moment in favor of the utilization of the subject's behavior which may be initiated but not developed by the apparatus. However much staring at a crystal ball may be conducive to fatigue and sleep, neither of these results is an essential part of the hypnotic trance. To illustrate: A number of subjects were systematically trained by a competent hypnotist to develop a trance by staring fixedly at a crystal ball held at a distance of six inches and slightly above the subjects' eye level. As a result of this conditioning, efforts to hypnotize them without a crystal ball were difficult and, in some instances, ineffectual. Personal experimentation with these subjects disclosed that having them simply imagine that they were looking at a crystal ball

> resulted in more rapid trance induction and pro-
> founder trance states. Repetition of this procedure
> by colleagues and students yielded similar results.
> Return to the actual crystal gazing resulted in the
> original slower and less profound trances character-
> ized by greater dependence upon external factors.
>   Milton H. Erickson, 1967, pp. 8 and 9

If, for example, the client has a well-developed kinesthetic representational system but little or no ability for non-dominant hemisphere visualization, then the hypnotist may have the client adopt a particular familiar body posture. Once the client is in that body position and fully experiencing the kinesthetic sensations, the hypnotist can instruct the client to look and to see whatever visual representations are commonly associated with those body sensations. By using the client's most highly valued representational system as a lead system, the client can be helped to gain access to new states of awareness. For example: In one of our training sessions, a middle-aged psychologist complained that he was unable to make visual imagery, in spite of the fact that he had his clients use this technique. We had this man place his body in the position of playing his piano (his favorite hobby). He was then instructed to move his fingers in the pattern of a familiar tune. With his eyes closed, he was instructed to hear the tune internally as well as to move his fingers. He was then asked to look down at the keyboard. He exclaimed, "I can see the keys and my fingers on the keyboard." He was then instructed to look up at the rest of the piano, and then at the rest of the living room, and then at the people in the room. This technique of using highly valued representational systems to recover and improve impoverished ones is a common technique in our work. The main principle is simply to find a situation in which the impoverished system overlaps the developed system, such as recovery of dialogue by having a visual client see someone's mouth moving and then hear the words, and many variations of this theme. This is an example of what we call body tuning (see *Magic II*).

The visual accessing principle, then, ties together many of Erickson's observations about effective deep trance inductions:

> ... The utilization of imagery rather than actual
> apparatus permits the subject to utilize his actual
> capabilities. ... The utilization of imagery in
> trance induction almost always facilitates the de-

velopment of similar or related, more complex hypnotic behavior. For example, the subject who experiences much difficulty in developing hallucinations often learns to develop them when a trance is induced by utilization of imagery . . . was induced to visualize a number of crystal balls in which she could hallucinate a whole series. . . .

Erickson, *Deep Hypnosis and Its Induction,* 1967, p. 9.

Accessing the Non-dominant Hemisphere by Melody

Another one of the asymmetries which has been consistently found between the cerebral hemispheres in humans is the location of melody. Apparently, the non-dominant hemisphere is the storage location for representations of melodies in humans.

The fact that totally aphasic patients can recite well-known verses, sing simple familiar songs, and emit curse words suggests the presence of whole auditory Gestalts in the right hemisphere, particularly in view of the fact that such patients cannot recite verses or sing songs unless they start at the beginning. If they are stopped midway through, and then told to continue where they left off, they cannot do so, but must start over again at the beginning. The same phenomenon occurs to a lesser degree in normal people for material which has been thoroughly memorized in a given sequence, such as the alphabet.

Bogen and Bogen (1969) suggest that if the right hemisphere has a special capacity for tonal, timbre and other aspects of music (see Milner, 1962), then interhemispheric communication could contribute to musical creativity. They report that, in collaboration with Gordon, observations were made of patients, known to be right handed, asked to sing before and during administration of sodium amytal into the right internal carotid artery. During the time when the left hemiparesis was evident, articulation was intelligible, though slurred, and while rhythm was preserved, singing was essentially amelodic, having relatively few changes in pitch.

The last twenty-five years have led to a marked revision of some of these older notions. We are now aware that while aphasic disorders of speech and comprehension are even more strongly linked to left unilateral lesions than was thought by the classical authors, certain disabilities, for instance dressing difficulty, are more closely associated with right hemisphere damage. It now seems likely that the right hemisphere is not the minor hemisphere, but rather is itself dominant for certain functions. Thus it appears to be dominant for certain spatial functions (while the left is probably dominant for others), for certain musical tasks, and as has now been suggested by several lines of evidence, possibly for certain aspects of emotional response.

Gardner, 1975, pp. 329-330

The use of melody as a technique for accessing the unconscious portion of the human mind is mentioned specifically by Erickson:

... A musician, unresponsive to direct hypnotic suggestion, was induced to recall the experience of having his thoughts *haunted by a strain of music*. This led to a suggested search for other similar [memories]. Soon he became so absorbed in trying to recall forgotten melodies and beating time as a kinesthetic aid that a deep trance ...

Erickson, 1967, p. 30.

In our own work in hypnosis, the instruction to the client to play a melody or series of melodies inside his head has proven again and again an effective induction technique, particularly in combination with some of the other techniques. Some convincing evidence for both locality and usefulness of melody comes from work being done with asphasic patients, those people who have brain damage and have suffered partial loss of language abilities. Those patients who have suffered lesions in their dominant hemisphere, in Broca's area in the base of the 3rd frontal convolution, can be treated with what is called melodic intonation therapy.

What this amounts to is with singing to train the non-dominant hemisphere to perform the functions lost by the dominant hemisphere's damage. The lost distinctions in language are trained into the other hemisphere by singing patterns of words instead of saying them (a task which the Broca's asphasic can not do until after the words have been sung repeatedly). See Gardner, 1974, for further reading.

> Jane was then thoroughly drilled in saying the "Pease Porridge" rhyme in a halting, hesitant and stuttering fashion.
>
> She learned this in a phenomenally fast manner, and then Anne, who knew nothing of this special measure, was asked to recite with Jane the Pease Porridge rhyme, however hesitantly she had to do it.
>
> Slowly the two began, Anne slowly, while Jane began to increase the tempo and then to stutter the words in a painfully annoying fashion. Anne glanced at the author, was sternly instructed to listen to Jane and to continue the joint recitation. Anne turned to Jane and her lips and face showed the ideomotor, therefore involuntary and uncontrollable efforts on Anne's part to correct Jane's stutter. On and on, over and over, Jane continued, with Anne's lips twitching and finally Anne was haltingly prompting Jane throughout the whole rhyme. This particular session lasted about two hours and Anne's speech became increasingly better. The same measure was employed with other rhymes and Anne was obviously pleased and confident though often immensely annoyed.
>
> Milton H. Erickson, 1967, p. 451

The selection of melody itself offers the hypnotist many choices. For example, in the context of therapy, the hypnotist might choose to select some melody connected in the client's life history with a period of his life which the hypnotist wishes the client to recover for the purposes of an enactment. Similarly, in the context of hypnotism, the hypnotist might give the client some melody to play inside his head which indirectly suggests age regression. We have found nursery rhyme melodies particularly effective in this way.

Language Accessing of the Non-dominant Hemisphere

As we stated previously, the so-called mute, or non-dominant, hemisphere in humans, typically, has some language ability. The extent of this ability seems to be unknown, with different researchers making conflicting claims (compare, for example, Gazziniga, 1970, with Levy, 1974). What is probable in light of the universal grammar and plasticity findings is that the non-dominant hemisphere has all of the distinctions available in universal grammar.

> Since the right hemispheres of commissurotomy patients appear to have some comprehension of both spoken language, as well as written nouns, verbs, and adjectives, and also have some minimal capacities for expressive speech, the question arises as to the differences in the two hemispheres which underlie the vast differences in linguistic abilities. If the minor hemisphere could comprehend no speech, but could produce some, one could postulate the absence of phonologies in the right hemisphere and could interpret speech production as a result of a direct translation from a semantic to articulatory code. If the right hemisphere could comprehend, but not produce speech, one could postulate the absence of an articulatory code. However, when the right hemisphere can both comprehend and express language, even though at a very limited level, an interpretation becomes much more difficult.   (Levy, 1974, p. 237)

Thus, as further linguistic and psycholinguistic research uncovers the structure of universal grammar, the exact linguistic capabilities of the non-dominant hemisphere will become available. Equally fascinating to us is the role that hypnotism has the potential to play in researching the linguistic capabilities of the non-dominant hemisphere. Until more thorough studies of the linguistic capabilities of the mute hemisphere are made, however, we are aware of two models of our experience in hypnosis which account for our observations.

As mentioned previously, one of the most powerful techniques which we have developed is the double induction — an induction in which each of us speaks simultaneously into the client's ears. In doing this type of induction, we systematically vary the style of speech we use depending upon into which ear we are speaking. For example, if John is speaking into the contralateral ear with respect to the dominant hemisphere (e.g., in right-handed people, usually the left cerebral hemisphere is dominant, and the contralateral ear is the right ear), he will systematically use the most complex syntactic forms of the language, employing all of the linguistic overload/distraction principles presented in the first chapter of this part. Simultaneously, Richard will speak into the ear contralateral to the non-dominant cerebral hemisphere (in this example, the left ear), using only the simplest of linguistic forms — either single-word utterances or the patterns used by children at the two-word utterance stage of language development (see pivot grammars in Slobin, 1974). In employing the double induction technique, rarely have we had an induction last for more than five minutes before a satisfactory trance state is reached by the client.

One model which accounts for the power and speed of the double induction is that:

> (a) We are successfully overloading the dominant hemisphere;

and

> (b) We are accessing the non-dominant hemisphere with the child grammar style of language which we feed into that hemisphere.

A second model which provides a guide for understanding the potency of this technique is:

> (a) We are successfully overloading the dominant hemisphere;

and

> (b) We are not accessing the non-dominant hemisphere, but, rather, the child grammar material we feed into the ear most intimately connected with the non-dominant hemisphere is being processed by and responded to by the dominant hemisphere without awareness.

This last model is a distinct possibility as it is true that the human ear has projections to both cerebral hemispheres. If conflicting messages arrive at the same ear or at the projection areas of the auditory cortex, the contralateral ear message has priority. However, simply because the contralateral ear message has priority over the ipsolateral ear message does not imply that the ipsolateral ear message is entirely lost with respect to the dominant hemisphere. Thus, the second model would claim that the speed and effectiveness of our double inductions depend, not upon accessing the non-dominant hemisphere linguistically, but rather depend upon the combination of overload and child grammar to the dominant hemisphere. By presenting a conflicting message to the dominant hemisphere without its awareness, we are forcing the client to regress his dominant hemisphere linguistic abilities to an earlier stage of development. The only additional piece of evidence which we have at this time is that there is a tendency for the side of the body controlled by the hemisphere (the contralateral hemisphere) to respond differentially to instructions delivered to that hemisphere. The result, particularly evident in the physical asymmetries in the client's face, is that, when conflicting instructions are received simultaneously by the client in different ears, the sides of the body respond independently. Similarly, when hand levitation instructions are interspersed in the conflicting material being fed into the client's hemisphere, the hand controlled by the hemisphere to which those instructions are presented tends to be the hand which rises. These patterns seem to us to support the first model. Of course, it is possible that both processes are occurring. In any case, while the double induction serves as one of the most powerful induction and deepening techniques of which we are aware, the question of which model is more useful remains unanswered.[4]

Milton Erickson has never, to our knowledge, worked closely with another hypnotist and used the double-induction technique we have been presenting. He is so skillful in his use of the language that he is able to accomplish something quite close to the double induction. In this procedure, which we call analogical marking of included sequences, Erickson presents the dominant hemisphere with a series of highly complex, syntactic constructions which, apparently, overload the processing capacity of the linguistic mechanisms of the dominant hemisphere. These well-formed Surface Structures of English form a pool of sequences of English words and phrases which have a double function. They are, first of all, constituents or sub-parts of the Surface Structures directed by

Erickson at the dominant hemisphere. They are, secondly, embedded, or contain messages which are received by and responded to by processes outside the normal boundaries of consciousness. An example will help:

> .... *realize that you have to start from* scratch *and nobody really* knows.....

The phrases presented above are part of a complex and well-formed-in-English Surface Structure which is received and processed by the dominant hemisphere. In addition, however, the words in non-italic type are identified by some analogical marking supplied by Erickson which distinguishes them from the remainder of the words in that well-formed Surface Structure. This analogical marking of included words and phrase results in the fragmentation of the communication into (in this case) two sets:

> .... *realize that you have to start from* scratch *and nobody really* knows.....

.... *realize that you have to start from scratch and nobody really knows. . . .*	scratch knows (equivalent, phonologically, to *scratch nose*)

The response which Erickson anticipates is for the client, without any consciousness of his action, to scratch his nose. The choices which Erickson has for analogically marking the original message are as numerous as the means he has of communicating analogically; for example, shifts of tonality, tempo, repetitive movements of different parts of the body, changes in facial expression, eye fixation on the same object, etc.

The Huxley article presents an excellent example of the use of analogical marking by Erickson to fragment the Surface Structure into three sets: the original, a set of cue words to induce amnesia, and a set of cue words to remove amnesia. Erickson's exquisite control over this technique allows him to induce and remove the memories of Huxley's experience from Huxley's consciousness repetitively. This pattern of analogical marking of included words and phrases to create independent message sets is available for any purpose which the hypnotist needs. It simply requires that the hypnotist select some set of analogical cues — as many different ones as he wishes to create independent message sets — and use them to identify the words and phrases in his ongoing speech which he wishes to have serve either as an independent message or as cues for some desired behavior by the client. The only limit to this technique is the creativity of the hypnotist.

Here we are unable, at present, to provide an explanation of the technique free of ambiguity. Again, in modeling our own experience with this technique as well as Erickson's, there are several plausible models:

> (a) The original Surface Structure message is processed by the dominant hemisphere while the included, analogically marked messages are accepted and responded to by the non-dominant hemisphere;

or

> (b) The original as well as the analogically marked, included message units are received and processed by the dominant hemisphere — the original message by the normal processing mechanisms, and the included messages by processes wholly outside of consciousness — and age regression occurs;

or

> (c) Both of the above explanations in combination.

In any case, the form of the process is clear to us — we provide a step-by-step procedure for the construction and use of this technique in the final part of this volume.

One question which interests us greatly about this technique is the choice of analogical marking which the hypnotist selects to identify the included message units. There are several things to consider in choosing the analogical marking signal. First, if the non-dominant hemisphere is being accessed, then the most effective choice of analogical marking by the hypnotist will be one of the sets of analogical signals which, typically, are processed and distinguished by the non-dominant hemisphere. The non-dominant hemisphere processes and distinguishes the analogical signal sets of tonality and analogical body posture and movements of the hypnotist's body visually. So, by this model, the most effective cues for the hypnotist to use will be tonal and body shifts. If the second model is a more useful representation of the process of communicating by digital analogical signal combinations, then the most effective cues will be those which are normally received and processed by the dominant hemisphere, tempo shifts, for example.[5]

Summary

In this section, we have presented what we consider to be one of the most wide-open and exciting areas of research into altered states of human consciousness, communication, and human potential. The parallels between the organization of the parts of the human brain which Erickson refers to as the *conscious* and *unconscious* and the functional organization of the human cerebral hemispheres are striking. Furthermore, the parallels between the organization of the unconscious and conscious portions of the human mind and the patterns of incongruity in the therapeutic context are startlingly close (see *Magic II*, Part III). We have reviewed three classes of techniques for accessing the non-dominant hemisphere in humans in the context of hypnotism: the first two classes, visualization and melodic accessing, are well supported by Erickson's work and research, our own work in hypnosis and the neurological research referenced within the section. The third class of accessing techniques involves ways to communicate with the non-dominant hemisphere linguistically. Here the evidence is equivocal, and there are at least two coherent models which account for the process. The relationships between universal grammar, the plasticity of the human nervous system, and the possibility of communicating with the non-dominant hemisphere raise questions which, when answered, will provide information of importance to the fields of hypnosis, neurology, psychology and linguistics. Fortunately, the ambiguity regarding the most useful model for describing the possibility of accessing the mute hemisphere linguistically does not prevent us from constructing a step-by-step model which will make these powerful Erickson techniques available to others. We will present models for each of these accessing techniques later in this volume. Erickson demonstrates in his refined use of these methods a sensitivity to all the resources which are available to the client, both consciously and unconsciously.

Conclusion to Part II

In hypnotic research, and the clinical use of hypnosis, Milton Erickson stands out as the world's most effective and creative practitioner. His skill is recognized around the world as not only the most effective, but, for most people who have seen or heard of his work, as exceptional and remarkable, and, for some, stretching the limits of credibility. His career holds a long and uncountable list of successes in areas in which no other could succeed. He has been able to help to have better lives untold numbers of people who were considered to be beyond help. He has assisted the hopeless, who had tried every avenue of assistance to no avail, to have hope, and he has given them the choices they desperately desired. This courageous man has been called everything from a miracle worker to a fraud; he is loved and praised by some, and feared and despised by others. He has been attacked and harassed; even as recently as the 1950's, the American Medical Association tried to revoke his medical license. But, against a sceptical world, he has continued to explore, develop, and use hypnosis. He has acquired a skill in its use that he, himself, does not fully understand. The power of his skill cannot be discounted by those who have experienced it firsthand. But, like most highly talented people, his skill is explained as being only intuition and, therefore, unlearnable. Our specific skill is in making intuitions about human behavior explicit and, therefore, learnable. This volume constitutes merely a beginning in the process of making Milton Erickson's hypnotic skills available for others to learn. We have focused,

primarily, in this volume, on the linguistic aspects of his work —
on the way he uses language. We intend in future volumes to build
a further model of his work which will include the way he uses
analogical forms of communication (voice tone, voice tempo,
body gestures, movements, etc.) and also how he uses the information he receives both verbally and analogically from his clients.
This is just a beginning, not the whole model of his work. We have
presented thus far what we believe to be the most basic and
common language patterns in his work. Part III presents to you
the tools for constructing these patterns explicitly.

Thus far we presented three major principles for organizing
your experience while doing trance inductions. First is pacing
clients; this means that you take the observable and verifiable
behavior of the client and connect it with the behavior to which
you wish to lead the client.

> *You're sitting there, breathing, watching that spot*
> (pacing)
> becoming relaxed.
> (leading)

> *And as you close your eyes*
> (pacing)
> you will feel your body float and become light.
> (leading)

> *And as you sit all the way down in the chair*
> (pacing)
> you will go into a deep trance.
> (leading)

The pacing strategy is then connected with the behavior desired.

> *And as you close your eyes*
> (pacing)
> you go into a deep trance, remembering a pleasant memory
> from your childhood
> (leading)
> *and this will make you smile.*
> (pacing)

This process is continued throughout the entire trance state. The second principle is to distract and utilize the dominant hemisphere. The third principle is the accessing of the non-dominant hemisphere.

We would like to point out that, when Erickson refers to the unconscious, he is referring to more than the non-dominant hemisphere and the linguistic processes in the dominant hemisphere below the level of awareness. Erickson's behavior systematically demonstrates that, frequently, he is using the term *unconscious* to refer to the processes and functions of the non-dominant hemisphere. This constitutes a rich source of research which can be applied to hypnosis. When we learn to segregate exactly the specific components of the unconscious mind, medical and dental, as well as psychological uses of hypnosis will be faster and more effective. Part III is designed to give specific skills necessary to utilize the patterns we have identified in Erickson's work.

FOOTNOTES TO PART II

1.   In this section, we focus on ways in which nouns can be generalized. For example, Erickson, frequently, will tell a story in which the main figure is the same sex, age, and from the same state as the client who is listening. In other cases, Erickson will vary these features. We have begun building a more detailed model of these processes. Especially interesting to us are the ways in which predicates can be generalized. For example, the hypnotist might generalize a predicate to its maximally unspecified form:

> *do*   for active verbs
> *be*   for stative verbs

Or he might generalize within the same representational system, input or output channel beginning with:

> *speak*   to   *talk*
> *converse*
> *intone*
> *whine*
> *cry*
> *plead*
> *state*

Or he might generalize such that each predicate contains something in its Deep Structure representation which does not occur explicitly in its Surface Structure representation. We will call this *semantic incorporation.*

For example, each of the following words includes as part of its

Deep Structure representation the word *hand:*

> *slap, handle, grasp, pass* (to), *hold* (depending on the object), *wear* (a ring), *catch, catch hold of, steer, paddle, row, stroke, pour, chop, slice, pin* (a medal on), *button, tear, strum, play* (a guitar), etc.

A detailed model of these generalization principles would be the basis for Erickson's well-known skill in creating and telling stories for his clients — a model for therapeutically effective metaphor.

2. Notice that there is a useful interaction between the patterns of nominalization, selectional restrictions, deletion, and ambiguity. Consider a phrase such as:

> ... *the feeling of the couch* ...

The ambiguity is whether the noun phrase *the couch* is the Deep Structure subject or object of the predicate *feel*; in other words, whether the Deep Structure of the above phrase is:

> *someone feels the couch*

or

> *the couch feels a certain way to someone*

Another way of stating the question raised by this phrase is whether the Deep Structure subject or object has been deleted. This ambiguity can only occur when the predicate selectional restrictions allow nouns of different classes to fit grammatically into both the subject and the object positions.

3. The reader may have noticed that the patterns called *lesser included structures* (specifically, embedded commands) overlap with conversational postulates. One of the presuppositions of every command is the statement to the effect that the person who is to be given the command is *able* to do what the command directs. Furthermore, the Surface Structure using the *yes/no* question form corresponding to that presupposition will have the command embedded as a lesser included structure.

4. We have noticed the common tendency of subjects in an initial profound somnambulistic trance to speak only in single word utterances until instructed how to speak with more normal patterns.

5. The limiting case is where the client becomes aware of the cross-modality cuing — this would reduce the effectiveness of such cues. The client rarely becomes aware of such cross-modality cuing — when this happens, typically, he knows something is going on but he doesn't know what.

PART III

CONSTRUCTION
OF
THE PATTERNS
OF ERICKSON'S
HYPNOTIC WORK

Introduction

This last part of Volume 1 is designed to provide you with the step-by-step procedure for constructing each of the patterns presented thus far. This format will allow you to utilize the potent skills of Milton Erickson in *your own* work, for *your own* purposes, in *your own* way, and in whatever context *you* need for effective hypnotic skills. We highly recommend that you use this portion of the book as a training manual, reading each section slowly one at a time. Experimenting with each pattern on paper and vocally will provide you with a way to train yourself first, consciously to produce each pattern. Then, as our experience in training others in these techniques has proven repeatedly, these formal patterns drop out of your consciousness while you will continue to be able to generate the patterns spontaneously. This kind of careful study will allow you to reap the greatest rewards, whether you use hypnosis for medical, dental, psychological, or research purposes. We have found with our students that those who use the method of reading and rereading, returning again and again as you would to any training in a complex skill, acquire the greatest proficiency. We add this suggestion to help you to gain the most that you can from Milton Erickson's years of creative experience. Those who seek your help, then, will have the opportunity to best realize their own vast potential and succeed in gaining their own goals with your skillful help.

Construction and Use of
Linguistic Causal Modeling Processes

As we have stated repeatedly, each of us constructs, from our experiences, a model or representation of the world in which we live. In the process of constructing this model or guide for our behavior, we employ the three universal processes of human modeling: Generalization, Distortion and Deletion. Within the language system which we use to assist us in making sense out of our experience, we often try to "explain" the connections between different parts of our model of the world in causal terms, employing the terms of natural language and, typically, claiming a necessary connection between these parts of our experience. Such explanations, generally, are absurd in that they attempt to reduce the complex circumstances involved in the production of some event to a simple, often single, "cause."

Gregory Bateson (1972, pp. 399-400) has characterized this type of explanation of causal reasoning and contrasts it with cybernetic explanation:

> Causal explanation is usually positive. We say that billiard ball B moved in such and such a direction because billiard ball A hit it at such and such an angle. In contrast to this, cybernetic explanation is always negative. We consider what alternative possibilities could conceivably have occurred and then ask why many of the alternatives were not followed, so that the particular event was one of those few which could, in fact, occur.

In cybernetic language, the course of events is said to be subject to *restraints,* and it is assumed that, apart from such restraints, the pathways of change would be governed only by equality of probability. In fact, the "restraints" upon which cybernetic explanation depends can in all cases be regarded as factors which determine inequality of probability. If we find a monkey striking a typewriter apparently at random but in fact writing meaningful prose, we shall look for restraints, either inside the monkey or inside the typewriter. Perhaps the monkey could not strike inappropriate letters; perhaps the type bars could not move if improperly struck; perhaps incorrect letters could not survive on the paper. Somewhere there must have been a circuit which could identify error and eliminate it.

Ideally — and commonly — the actual event in any sequence or aggregate is uniquely determined within the terms of the cybernetic explanation. Restraints of many different kinds may combine to generate this unique determination. For example, the selection of a piece for a given position in a jigsaw puzzle is "restrained" by many factors. Its shape must conform to that of its several neighbors and possibly that of the boundary of the puzzle; its color must conform to the color pattern of its region; the orientation of its edges must obey the topological regularities set by the cutting machine in which the puzzle was made, and so on. From the point of view of the man who is trying to solve the puzzle, these are all clues, *i.e.,* sources of information which will guide him in his selection. From the point of view of the cybernetic observer, they are *restraints.*

Similarly, from the cybernetic point of view, a word in a sentence, or a letter within the word, or the anatomy of some part within an organism, or the role of a species in an ecosystem, or the behavior of a member within a family — these are all to be (negatively) explained by an analysis of restraints.

We find ourselves in essential agreement with Bateson's comments. In fact, in *Magic I*, we spend time discussing the negative effects which a specific form of this causal type of explanation has on people. We call this specific type of causal explanation *cause-effect*. Associated with this type of causal modeling process is another type called mind-reading. In this type of modeling, an individual comes to believe that he knows the thoughts, feelings, etc., of another without any direct communication of these experiences on the part of this second person (see *Magic I*, Chapters 3, 4, and 6; *Magic II*, Chapters 2 and 3).

In the context of hypnosis, however, wherein one of the objectives which the hypnotist has is, initially, to pace and then to lead the client's experience, these processes of cause-effect and mind-reading have a positive value. Since the client, characteristically, employs these types of explanation for himself, the hypnotist can make use of this process to assist the client in achieving the desired state of trance. Specifically, the hypnotist can make causal connections between immediately verifiable portions of the client's experience and the desired behavior.

First, we present some examples of this technique of utilizing cause-effect in the hypnotic context:

> *Sitting all the way down in that chair will make you go into a deep trance.*
> *As you continue to breathe, each exhaling of your breath will make you become more and more relaxed.*
> *When your hand touches your face, it will cause you to go completely into a profound trance.*
> *As your breathing slowly changes, it will make you aware of those particular sensations in your fingers and hand.*

Each of these example sentences has the same logical form:

X	cause	Y
sitting all the way down in the chair		You go into a deep trance
Your breathing changing		You become aware of those particular sensations in your fingers and hands

The reader can easily determine that the connections which are claimed by the example sentences to hold between the two pieces of behavior are not, in fact, necessary connections. However, in the context of a hypnotic induction, since the client employs these same types of semantic ill-formedness modeling principles, these causal connections are extraordinarily effective in securing the behavior desired.

To construct such sentences is quite easy; simply follow these steps:

> Step 1 — Determine the type of behavior which you, as the hypnotist, wish to elicit from the client; call this Y;
>
> Step 2 — Identify some behavior which the client is already experiencing, some portion of his ongoing behavior and experience; call this X;
>
> Step 3 — Make up a sentence which has the form:
> X   Cause   Y

The hypnotist may employ the verb *cause*, itself, directly or use some verb which is synonymous with *cause* (e.g., *make*), or which incorporates *cause* as a portion of its meaning, such as: *force, require, push, pull, close, open.*

Closely associated with these cause-effect sentences is a group of sentences which involve what we have called an implied causative (see *Magic I* for a fuller discussion). This class of sentences does not, strictly speaking, involve the claim of a necessary connection between two events; they do, however, invite the listener to make an inference of a necessary, causal connection between the two events mentioned; that is, they claim a contingency between two classes of events or experiences. First, we list some examples of this class:

> *As you sit all the way down in that chair, you will go into a deep trance*
>
> *As you listen to the sound of my voice, you will relax more and more*
>
> *When you fully understand this communication, you will be at the right level of trance*
>
> *After you have finished allowing your hand to return to your thigh, you will be fully prepared to experience new deep trance phenomena*

Each of these sentences has the same logical form:

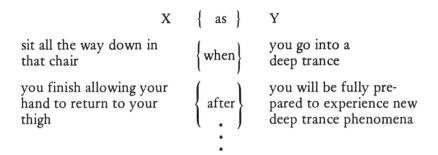

$$X \quad \{ \text{ as } \} \quad Y$$

| sit all the way down in that chair | { when } | you go into a deep trance |
| you finish allowing your hand to return to your thigh | { after } | you will be fully prepared to experience new deep trance phenomena |

Again, the readers can easily satisfy themselves that there is no logical connection, necessary or not, between the behaviors under the X and Y categories.

In a step-by-step format, the hypnotist may construct these implied causative sentences by:

> Step 1 — Determine the type of behavior which you, as the hypnotist, wish to elicit from the client; call it **Y**;
> Step 2 — Identify some behavior which the client is already experiencing, some portion of his ongoing behavior and experience; call this **X**;
> Step 3 — Make up a sentence of the form:
> **X** implied causative connective **Y**
> where the implied causative connective is any connective which invites the listener to a causal connection — examples: *as, when, after, before, during, throughout, following,* etc.

A second type of closely related sentences which Erickson uses in trance work are those called *mind reading*. These are sentences by which the speaker claims to have knowledge of the internal, unobservable experience of the listener without specifying the process by which he came to have that knowledge. Here is a list of examples:

> *You must be wondering now what will happen next . . .*
> *You can continue to feel the satisfaction of . . .*
> *You are learning even more rapidly than you first . . .*

>*You really are beginning to understand how quickly you*
>*can. . .*

In each of these sentences, the speaker/hypnotist is claiming to
have knowledge of some experience which the listener is having
without specifying how he came to have that knowledge. Specifically, the hypnotist is claiming that he knows about the following
internal states of the listener:

>*wondering, feeling, learning, understanding*

In none of the examples does the hypnotist specify how he came
to have this information.

In order to construct sentences of this class, the hypnotist
must:

>Step 1 — Identify some internal state or experience of the
>client which is consistent with all of the information
>which is available to him;
>
>Step 2 — Form a sentence which states that he knows that
>the client is having this experience.

There are two additional comments which a hypnotist will
find of use in constructing these sentences: first, there are a
number of internal states or experiences which are typical of a
human being undergoing a trance induction, or which a person will
experience whenever the name of this experience is mentioned; for
example:

>*wondering, learning, feeling, thinking, remembering,*
>*recalling, experiencing*

Choosing any one of these activities as the basis for constructing a
sentence which is semantically ill-formed mind reading will insure
a successful pacing of the client's experience. Another excellent
choice is any verb which is unspecified with respect to representational systems. Second, when forming a sentence employing the
mind-reading technique, the hypnotist can use it in conjunction
with the technique of using presuppositions to cover the claim he
is making. For example, rather than simply saying:

. . . you are learning . . . .

the hypnotist may use a word such as *even* which forces the listener to accept the truth of the mind-reading claim by the hypnotist in order to make any sense out of the communication and to focus, instead, on the question of speed, as in the example:

. . . you are learning even *more rapidly than . . . .*

Or, as a second example, notice the difference between:

. . . you can feel the . . . .
and
. . . you can continue *to feel the . . . .*

In this example, the predicate *continue* presupposes that the activity mentioned *(feeling)* began prior to the saying of the sentence; thus the client's attention is shifted from whether or not he is feeling **X** to when he *first* began to feel **X**. We will present a more systematic treatment of presuppositions in the section on Derived Meanings.

In summary, then, the hypnotist may make use of the linguistic causal modeling processes which the client typically employs in constructing his model of the world and his ongoing experience in order to achieve the goals of the hypnotic encounter. Specifically, since these modeling processes are an integral part of the client's construction of the world of his experience, the hypnotist, by the skillful use of these techniques, can successfully pace and lead the client to the desired objectives in hypnosis. Erickson employs these techniques with the grace and power of a master.

Transderivational Phenomena[1]

One of the desirable characteristics of the communication which occurs between a hypnotist and his client is that the client participate actively in the process. When the client can be engaged actively in the communication process at both the conscious and the unconscious levels of the mind, the communication will be highly successful. The four classes of phenomena presented in this section have in common the fact that the client is engaged at the unconscious level of his mind in his participation in the communication process. By engaging the client at the unconscious level, the hypnotist accomplishes several important tasks simultaneously. First, when the client is participating unconsciously, his conscious mind does not interfere with the transition to the altered state of consciousness which is the immediate objective of the trance induction. Second, since the client's conscious mind is not making the selection of the meaning conveyed by the hypnotist's communication, his response is the response selected as most appropriate to the unconscious needs of the client. (We repeat ourselves from Part I for the reader's convenience.)

In our everyday communications with the people around us, we employ a set of language processing strategies which allow us to extract from the speech of others the meaning of the words, phrases, and sentences which they use. These language processing strategies are the research domain for psycholinguists (see, for example, references for Bever and for Slobin in the Bibliography). Erickson has succeeded in utilizing these language processing mechanisms in a way which allows him to communicate with both the conscious and the unconscious portions of the client's mind. Essentially, he accomplishes this by presenting the client with a Surface Structure of English which activates the normally conscious mind-processing mechanisms. At the same time, he activates additional meaning recovery processes which develop meanings which are available to the unconscious portion of the client's mind but not to the conscious portion. In some cases, he uses Surface Structures of English which are not well formed. The effect that this has is, typically, to overload or jam the normal language processing mechanisms of the client while the unconscious mind of the client extracts the most appropriate meaning for its purposes. We begin by reviewing the basic linguistic distinctions necessary for an understanding of these techniques (see *Magic I*, Appendix A, for fuller discussion).

Each sentence of every natural language has two distinct representations: the representation of the way it *actually sounds* (or, if written, the way it actually appears), called the **Surface Structure**, and the representation of the *meaning* which it has, called the **Deep Structure**. For example, when a person says the sentence:

The window was broken

the Surface Structure is the representation of the actual sounds made by the person speaking, or, in the case of a written representation, the words written out, as above. In addition to this representation, this sentence is associated with another representation which is the meaning it has — the Deep Structure. In this particular case, the Deep Structure can be represented as:

PAST (BREAK [someone, window, with something])

This Deep Structure representation is designed to capture the intuition that each of us has as a native speaker of English that, when we hear the Surface Structure presented above, we understand the following:

    (a) Some event occurred in the PAST;
    (b) The event was a complex event having the following parts:

(1) An action — BREAK — which occurred between:
a. The agent — some person or thing doing the breaking — here represented by *someone*;
b. The object — some person or thing being broken — here represented by *the window*;
c. The instrument — the thing used to do the breaking — here represented by *with something*.

Notice that, even though not all of the parts of the Deep Structure representation appear in the Surface Structure (in this case, the agent and the instrument are not represented in the Surface Structure), the native speaker of English has that information available in his understanding of the sentence. The ways in which Surface Structures can differ from their associated Deep Structures is the research domain of transformational linguists. They have postulated a series of formal mapping operations called transformations which specify precisely how Deep and Surface Structures may differ — the entire process which links a Deep Structure to its Surface Structure(s) is called a **derivation**.

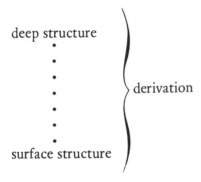

With these basic linguistic distinctions, we may begin a presentation of the patterns themselves.

Transderivational Search — Generalized Referential Index

One of Erickson's favorite devices, employed when the client is in both trance and "normal" state of awareness, is for him to tell a story. This story, typically, begins with the phrase: *I had a patient once . . . .* Erickson then proceeds to describe some actual or created-on-the-spot version of an experience which will be relevant to the person to whom he is presently speaking. The amount of relevance which the story has depends upon how direct Erickson wishes to be in his communication; in general, this will depend upon the depth of the client's trance. Erickson employs the principle that the client will respond best if the relevance of the story is just outside the client's conscious awareness. This is an example of the transderivational search for meaning spurred by the use of a generalized referential index. If Erickson utters the sentence:

You can focus your eyes on the corner of . . . .

the noun *you* has the referential index of the client — the person to whom Erickson is talking — and the client is conscious that Erickson intends the word *you* to refer to him. However, when Erickson says:

I had a patient once . . . .

the client's normal linguistic processing mechanisms derive from that Surface Structure a Deep Structure meaning which contains no noun which refers to the client himself. Similarly, when a client hears the following phrases:

People *can make the most of* learning opportunities . . . .
A man *once sat in that very chair and felt nervous* . . . .
A waitress *wanted to have* an important thing *for herself* . . . .

he constructs for himself a Deep Structure which includes no occurrence of a noun which has his own referential index as a part. Erickson's behavior and the response which he secures from his clients, as well as our own experience and the responses which we consistently secure from our clients, have convinced us that there is an extra bit of linguistic processing which occurs at the unconscious level. The most useful model which we have found to assist us in organizing our own experience, as well as building a model for Erickson's work, is that of the transderivational search. This process operates as follows:

(a) The client hears a well-formed Surface Structure;

(b) The client recovers the associated Deep Structure and is aware of the meaning of that Deep Structure, one which has no direct reference to him;

(c) The client activates a transderivational search for an additional Deep Structure which is more relevant for his ongoing experience.

This last step requires more explanation. Clients do not randomly generate additional Deep Structures; rather, the Deep Structures which they generate are systematically related to the originally recovered Deep Structure. Specifically, they generate Deep Structures which are identical in form to the recovered Deep Structure except that they substitute nouns with referential indices which pick out portions of their ongoing behavior, thus making them maximally relevant for themselves. We illustrate by example. The client hears the Surface Structure:

People can make the most of learning opportunities

the normal linguistic processing mechanisms apply, deriving the associated Deep Structure:[2]

POSSIBLE (MAKE MOST [EVERY (people, learning opportunities)])

So, presenting the entire process to this point in a visual display, we have:

POSS (MAKE MOST [EVERY (people, learning
    opportunities)])
     •
     •
     •   } derivation 1
     •
     •
     •
People can make the most out of learning
    opportunities

Now, by the principle of transderivational search, the client begins the unconscious process of finding a Deep Structure which is identical in form to the recovered Deep Structure with nouns with referential indices relevant to his ongoing experience, substituted into the positions of the nouns which are in the recovered Deep Structure but which have no referential index relevant to his experience of the moment. The recovered Deep Structure contains two nouns which have no referential index relevant to the client's ongoing experience; therefore, the newly generated Deep Structures will be identical to the recovered one with new nouns substituted in those positions. The client will generate, among others, the following Deep Structure:

POSSIBLE (MAKE MOST [I, this specific learning opportunity])

In other words, among the Deep Structures identical with the one originally recovered is the one above — one which has the associated Surface Structure:

I (the client) can make the most out of this learning opportunity

Thus, by the process of transderivational search, the client generates the meaning which is maximally relevant for his ongoing experience. By this technique, Erickson successfully paces the client's ongoing experience, allows the client maximal freedom to create meaning for himself and, thereby, participate actively in the process of communication, and avoids instructing the client in a way of which he is conscious (no "resistance" could possibly arise as no direction to resist has been given by Erickson).

This transderivational search technique is the pattern common to all of the phenomena presented in this section. With this in mind, we extract the formal pattern of the transderivational search as shown on page 223.

In other words, the client recovers the Deep Structure which corresponds to the Surface Structure Erickson utters, then he generates a series of Deep Structures identical up to the referential indices. From this set, the client then selects the Deep Structure which is most relevant for his ongoing experience.

From the description of the transderivational search model,

deep structure 1   deep structure 2 .... deep structure n

.   .   .
.   .   .
. by transderiva-   .   .
. tional search   .   .
. processes   .   .
.   .   .

surface structure 1   surface structure 2 ... surface structure n

the construction of statements containing generalized referential indices is quite easy. In a step-by-step format, the process can be modeled as follows:

Step 1 — Determine the message of which you, as the hypnotist, desire the client to have an unconscious understanding;

Step 2 — Make a sentence (or a series of sentences) which communicates that message directly;

Step 3 — Replace every occurrence of nouns bearing referential indices which pick out the client and occurrences of nouns bearing referential indices which pick out the present situation and problem, with nouns which have no relevance to the client, the present situation or the problem with which you are dealing.

As mentioned earlier, the extent to which the nouns referring to the client, present situation and problem being dealt with are replaced depends upon factors such as the depth of the client's trance state. The general principle is that the intended meaning should not be recognized consciously by the client. Here Erickson's phenomenal visual and auditory abilities to detect minute changes in the client's body and voice are his primary ways of determining how extensive the replacement of relevant nouns should be.

Transderivational Search — Generalized Referential Index with Suggested Noun Substitution

Erickson will sometimes use the generalized referential index method of activating transderivational search with an addition.

The following examples are of this type:

> *People can, Susan, make the most of learning opportunities*
>
> *People, Susan, can make the most of learning opportunities*
>
> *People can make the most of learning opportunities, Susan*

Here Erickson is employing the same technique as that covered in the last section with the addition of also supplying the noun which he wishes the client to substitute into the noun position when he (the client) generates the set of related Deep Structures — namely, the noun-bearing referential index of the client himself. The construction procedure for the generalized referential index with suggested noun substitution is identical to the procedure for the construction of the generalized referential index itself with the addition of Step 4:

> Step 4 — Insert into the sentence which results from the first three steps the noun which you, as the hypnotist, wish the client to substitute into the set of related Deep Structures generated by the transderivational search process.

This addition of the desired noun referential index increases the probability that the client will select the related Deep Structure — the one which carries the message which is the hypnotist's intended message. The position in the sentence into which the suggested noun is inserted has different effects. This will be discussed under the heading of **Lesser Included Deep Structures**.

Selectional Restriction Violations

In every natural language there are words called *predicates* which describe relationships or processes. These words pick out specific categories of experience in the models of the speakers of that language. Certain processes or relationships occur only between specific parts of the models of the speakers' experience. For example, using English, we are certain that the process named by the predicate *drink* has never occurred in any reader's experience associated with the object designated by the word *nominalization*, as in the sentence:

The nominalization *drank two quarts of orange juice.*

Linguists have characterized the kind of oddity displayed by this sentence as the violation of a selectional restriction. Specifically, the predicate *drink* is said to have a selectional restriction which requires that it be used only with nouns which name sentient beings. Since the word *nominalization* does not refer to a sentient being, the sentence above contains a selectional restriction violation, thus explaining its oddity.

Erickson uses selectional restriction violations to force the client into a transderivational search for meaning. Erickson says, for example:

. . . a tomato plant can feel good . . . .

In the standard usage of the predicate *feel,* there is a selectional restriction violation which requires that the noun which appears as its subject be an animal or a human. For most speakers of English, the sentence quoted above is peculiar; specifically, the selectional restriction on the predicate *feel* has been violated. The sentence doesn't quite make sense. In the context of hypnosis, this selectional restriction violation is puzzling to the client who, in order to make sense out of Erickson's communication, activates a transderivational search for possible relevant meanings. In this case, the set of Deep Structures generated by the transderivational search process will be identical to the recovered Deep Structures except with a noun substituted into the position(s) occupied by the noun(s) which caused the selectional restriction violation(s). Using the above sentence as an example, we have:

POSSIBLE (FEEL
GOOD (tomato plant)   deep structure 2 .... deep structure n

    .   .   .

    .   ⟶   .   .

    .   by transderiva- .   .

    .   tional search   .   .

    .   processes   .   .

    .   .   .

    .   .   .

a tomato plant can   surface structure 2 ... surface structure n
feel good

One of the Deep Structures generated by the transderivational search process will be the Deep Structure associated with the Surface Structure:

> . . . *I (the client) can feel good* . . . .

Once again, as in the case of the generalized referential index technique, Erickson will sometimes supply the noun with the referential index which he wishes the client to select out of the set of additional Deep Structures generated in the transderivational search. For example, Erickson will say:

> . . . *a tomato plant can, Joe, feel good* . . . .

In a step-by-step format, a hypnotist can use Erickson's selectional restriction violation technique with the following construction:

Step 1 — Determine the message of which you, as the hypnotist, desire the client to have an unconscious understanding;

Step 2 — Make a sentence (or series of sentences) which communicates that message directly;

Step 3 — Replace the occurrences of the nouns bearing referential indices which pick out the client, the present situation, and the problem being dealt with, with nouns which violate the selectional restrictions of the predicates with which they occur;

Step 4 — This is an optional step — insert into the sentences which result from the first three steps the noun(s) which you, as a hypnotist, wish the client to substitute into the set of related Deep Structures generated by the transderivational search process.

Erickson often will insert meta-comments regarding the very process which he is employing into the ongoing communication. For example, he might say:[3]

> . . . *a tomato plant can, Joe, feel good* . . . *funny to talk about a tomato plant feeling good, isn't it, Joe* . . . .

This kind of meta-commenting insures that the client will activate a transderivational search. Erickson is calling the client's attention to the selectional restriction violation.

Deletions

In the example given early in this section:

The window was broken

we pointed out that the Deep Structure associated with this Surface Structure was more complete, contained more elements:

PAST (BREAK [someone, the window, with something])

Specifically, in the process of the derivation as the Deep Structure representation is mapped onto the Surface Structure, several portions of the Deep Structure representation were deleted or removed and do not appear in the Surface Structure. In the example we are using here, both the agent — the person or thing that broke the window — and the instrument — the thing that was used to break the window — have no representation in the Surface Structure. This example demonstrates the linguistic process of deletion.

Erickson employs deletion processes to induce the client to activate a transderivational search for meaning. For example, Erickson might say:

... it is so satisfying ....

... you have learned so quickly ....

... I have understood so much from you ....

In each of these examples, Erickson has used one of the grammatical deletion processes available in English to remove a portion of the Deep Structure representation so that it does not appear in the Surface Structure. By skillfully using these natural language processes, the hypnotist leaves the client the maximum amount of freedom to interpret for himself the missing parts of the Deep Structure. Specifically, in the above examples, the following parts have been deleted:

. . . it is so satisfying	Satisfying *to whom?*
. . . you have learned so much	*What, specifically,* has been learned?
. . . I have understood so much from you	*What, specifically,* have I understood from you?

Since Erickson's communication leaves these pieces of the Deep Structure associated with the Surface Structure he utters wholly unspecified, the client activates a transderivational search in which the set of Deep Structures generated are identical with the recovered Deep Structure except that the nouns which have been deleted from the Surface Structure and which, thereby, have no referential index in their Deep Structure representation[4] are replaced with some noun which has a referential index which is relevant to the client's ongoing experience.

The second kind of deletion which Erickson uses effectively in his work is deletion which results in a Surface Structure which is, itself, not well formed. For example, Erickson might say:

> *. . . and you want and need . . . .*

> *. . . you fully realize so well . . . .*

In each of these example cases, the resulting sequence of words is not a well-formed sentence of English — ungrammatical deletion. The client is faced with the task of making sense out of Erickson's communication. He may accomplish this by activating the transderivational search process — in these cases, the set of Deep Structures generated are identical to the recovered (partial) Deep Structure except that they are complete. The client generates a set of structures with the portions which were missing in the recovered (partial) Deep Structure (which rendered it ungrammatical) filled in:

. . . and you want and need	*What* do you want and need
. . . you fully realize so well	*What* do you fully realize so well

That is, the client generates Deep Structures with nouns with referential indices relevant to his ongoing experience in the positions in which Erickson makes the ungrammatical deletions. Our experience has been that, when a client is presented with a large number of these ungrammatical deletions he appears to give up the task of making sense out of the communication altogether and his normal linguistic processing mechanisms seem to jam.

To construct sentences utilizing these deletion principles, the hypnotist may:

(1) Identify the message which you, as a hypnotist, wish the client to understand unconsciously;

(2) Form a sentence which conveys this message;

(3) Delete the nouns in the sentence formed until

   (a) The maximum number of nouns have been removed, consistent with leaving the sentence well formed in English;

   or

   (b) As many of the nouns have been deleted as the hypnotist desires, independent of whether the resulting sentence is well formed or not.

Nominalizations

Linguists use the term **nominalization** to refer to the result of the linguistic process of turning a Deep Structure predicate into a Surface Structure noun. For example, the words in italic type in the following list are nominalizations:

frustration	frustrate
satisfaction	satisfy

The words which occur to the right of these nominalizations are the non-nominalized, Surface Structure predicate forms of these Deep Structure predicates. In general, when a speaker of English uses a predicate in a Surface Structure in predicate form, he must include information about the things or people between whom the predicate is describing the process. However, in the nominalized form, there is no requirement that such information be provided when the predicate is used. This allows the speaker to avoid specifying what he is talking about. This also provides the listener with a large number of choices of how he will interpret or assign meaning to the communication.

In the context of hypnotic work, the nominalization assumes a positive value in that it provides an occasion for the client to activate the transderivational processes in his search for meaning for the communication coming from the hypnotist. For example, the client hears the hypnotist say:

> ... *the satisfaction* ....

The Deep Structure representation of this nominalization is:

> *SATISFY (someone/something, someone, with someone/something)*

In words, the Deep Structure process of SATISFY involves a person or thing doing the satisfying action, a person who is experiencing the satisfaction, and someone or something which is the occasion for the process of satisfying (the instrument). Since none of these nouns appears in the Surface Structure of Erickson's communication, the client's recovered Deep Structure has no referential indices for the nouns which are the parts of the Deep Structure representation. He, therefore, activates the transderivational search processes, literally, to make meaning for himself, thereby selecting the most appropriate and relevant meaning from the set of Deep Structures generated. Nominalizations are particularly useful in pacing and leading a client's experience when the experience is of the kind which has little manifestation in the client's body movements, actions and speech.

To construct sentences utilizing this technique, the hypnotist may:

(1) Identify the type of behavior into which he wishes to pace or lead the client;
(2) Form a sentence which uses the predicate which describes the experience;
(3) Delete all nouns and change the predicate into its nominalized form.

In selecting the experience to be paced or induced in the client's ongoing experience, the hypnotist should be aware that there are certain predicates which describe or easily induce experiences in clients in the context of hypnosis. As in the case of mind reading, the selection of one of these predicates will insure a successful communication between the hypnotist and the client. Examples of these predicates are:

wonder, satisfy, learn, think, feel, etc.

Ambiguity

In the course of normal communication in natural language, there is, usually, a premium placed upon producing sentences which are non-ambiguous — sentences which carry only one meaning. In the context of hypnosis, the inverse is often the case. The skill with which the hypnotist can produce sentences which are ambiguous serves him well in his task of pacing and leading the client in his trance work. Linguists have characterized the linguistic phenomenon of ambiguity formally as the situation in which a single sound sequence or Surface Structure is associated with more than one derivation and, therefore, more than one Deep Structure. In visual form, we can represent ambiguity as:

deep structure 1, deep structure 2, ..., deep structure n

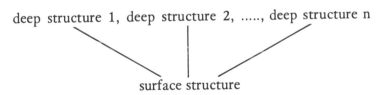

surface structure

We now move directly into the construction of the four different types of ambiguity.

Phonological Ambiguity
Phonological ambiguity depends upon the fact that, in natural languages, the distinct meaning of certain words or phrases is represented by the same sound sequence. Take, for example, the

word *duck*. Without any further context, the sound sequence *duck* has two meanings — the noun meaning, which identifies a class of birds, and a verb meaning, which describes a quick movement of a certain type. In order for the hypnotist to make use of phonological ambiguities, he may:

> Step 1 — Identify the message he wishes the client to receive;
>
> Step 2 — List the words which are involved in the message;
>
> Step 3 — Check each word on the list to determine whether any of them are phonologically ambiguous (note here that it is critical for the hypnotist either to say the words on the list aloud or to use an internal auditory dialogue to say them as words which, in their written, visual form are non-ambiguous, are sometimes ambiguous when presented auditorily — e.g., here/ hear).
>
> Step 4 — Use the ambiguous words in his Surface Structures to the client, marking the words analogically (see techniques of analogical marking in the section on Lesser Included Deep Structure).

Syntactic Ambiguity

Syntactic ambiguities occur when the syntactic function of a word cannot be uniquely determined from the immediate context. For example, in the sentence:

> *They are visiting relatives*

it is not possible to determine whether the word *visiting* is functioning as a Surface Structure verb to be grouped with the verb *are* as in the example:

> *They are visiting orange groves*

or whether it is functioning as a Surface Structure adjective to be grouped with *relatives*, as in the example:

> *They are relatives who are visiting here with us*

or

> *They are traveling relatives*

There are two forms of syntactic ambiguity which we have found in Erickson's work. These are:

(1) . . . Verb + ing + Noun
   . . . *Flying planes can be dangerous*
   . . . *Investigating FBI agents can be dangerous*
   They are murdering peasants . . . .
   They are walking dogs . . . .

(2) . . . Nominalization of Noun . . . .
   . . . *The touch of the man . . . .*
   . . . *The feeling of the couch . . . .*

Each of these syntactically ambiguous forms may be utilized by the hypnotist by using the following construction procedure:

Step 1 — Identify the message that you, as a hypnotist, wish the client to receive;

Step 2 — Place the message into one of the syntactically ambiguous forms listed above.

Scope Ambiguity

Scope ambiguity occurs when it cannot be determined from an inspection of the immediate linguistic context how much is applied to that sentence by some other portion of that sentence. For example, Erickson might say:

I want you to draw me a picture of yourself in the nude

Here, the communication is ambiguous, as the phrase *in the nude* could apply equally well to the way in which Erickson wants the listener to dress (or, rather, not dress) when drawing the picture or to the way in which the listener is to portray himself in the picture he draws.

One of Erickson's favorite scope ambiguities is that associated with age regression. He will, in the course of an induction, look meaningfully at the client and say:

. . . speaking to you as a child . . .

Here, of course, the ambiguity is whether the phrase *as a child* refers to Erickson or to the client, thus, the effect is a scope ambiguity which induces age regression on the part of the client.

Punctuation Ambiguity

In this book, we have identified punctuation ambiguity as the cases in which Erickson uses a sequence of words which is the result of an overlap of two well-formed Surface Structures sharing a word or phrase. For example, Erickson might say:

I want you to notice your hand me the glass

This ill-formed Surface Structure can be decomposed into two well-formed Surface Structures with the shared pivot word *hand*:[5]

I want you to notice your hand   Hand me the glass

All cases of punctuation ambiguity result in ill-formed Surface Structures. Our experience in using this technique is that it is very effective and that the client, typically, either responds immediately to the command given or stops processing with the normal linguistic processes almost immediately. The hypnotist may construct sentences using this technique by:

Step 1 — Identify the message you, as a hypnotist, desire that the client receive;

Step 2 — Check each of the words in the message to determine whether they are phonologically ambiguous;

Step 3 — Form two sentences, one of which has the phonologically ambiguous word as the last word in the sentence, the second, a command, in which the ambiguous word occurs as the first word in the sentence;

Step 4 — Delete the first word of the second sentence and say the entire sequence to the client.

You will help yourself to acquire this skill (as well as the others presented here) by generating a set of phonologically ambiguous words which occur naturally in your work. One set which we have found very useful are organ language (words which identify body parts and functions, e.g., *hand, shoulder*), phonologically ambiguous words such as those listed in Part II of this book in the section on ambiguity.

Lesser Included Structures

The linguistic analysis of Surface Structures claims that there is another level of representation available to native speakers/ listeners of the language — the meaning representation, or Deep Structure. For example, the Surface Structure:

I hope that you feel better

includes two complete clauses in Deep Structure, one of which corresponds to the sentence:

I hope X

and one which corresponds to the sentence:

you feel better

We refer to this last clause as a lesser included structure of the entire sentence. Erickson has succeeded in making extensive and skillful use of this pattern in his hypnotic work. There are three major types of lesser included structures: Embedded Questions, Embedded Commands, and Quotes.

Embedded Questions
In English, there are a number of predicates which, naturally, have as their objects a complete sentence which is characterized as

a question. For example, the predicates *wonder, ask, question, am curious, know, understand* — all take a *whether* complement clause:

> *I wonder whether* . . . .

> *I ask myself whether* . . . .

> *I am curious whether* . . . .

When a native speaker of English is asked the question:

> *Do you know where your knee is?*

he, typically, responds either *yes* or *no,* and the communication is complete at that point. However, when the native speaker of English hears the embedded question:

> *I wonder whether you really know where your knee is.*

since no response is asked for (no question was asked; therefore, there is no need to respond), he, typically, makes no direct response. Our experience is that clients do, however, respond covertly. In other words, when they hear an embedded question, they tend to respond internally as though the embedded question were asked directly. There are several ways in which the hypnotist can utilize this covert response. First, since he knows that the client is responding to the embedded questions covertly, he knows about a portion of the client's experience which the client is unaware that he knows about — a perfect situation for effective mind reading. Second, by skillfully selecting the question which he embeds, the hypnotist can lead the client in a direction which will accomplish the objectives of the hypnotic work. The following procedure will allow you to generate embedded questions:

> Step 1 — Identify the message which you, as a hypnotist, wish the client to receive;
>
> Step 2 — Form a question which will lead the client to the message which you wish him to receive;
>
> Step 3 — Embed the question within one of the verbs listed above to form an embedded or indirect question.

This technique is rendered much more effective if combined with presuppositions and analogical marking.

Embedded Commands

As a hypnotist, one of the ways to determine how responsive a client is at any given point in time is to present him with a command to respond in some way visible to you without the client's being aware that you have given such a command. Presenting the command in a covert way has all the other advantages which we have mentioned previously; e.g., avoids the authoritarian issue and, thereby, resistance; engages active participation on the part of the client at the unconscious level of behavior:

> Step 1 — Identify some message to which you, as a hypnotist, wish the client to respond;
> Step 2 — Form a command with the message;
> Step 3 — Find a Surface Structure which the command will fit into without making the result ungrammatical.

Again, the effectiveness of this technique is increased dramatically when it is combined with analogical marking. Examples of the result of this process are:

> *. . . a tomato can, Joe,* feel better *. . . .*

> *. . . people are able to* learn quickly *. . . .*

Quotes

In recounting our experiences to one another in verbal communication, we sometimes choose to present verbatim some of the conversation or verbal exchange which we had with a person in the course of our experiences. For example, in telling a story, we may say something such as the following:

> *. . . Yeah, and then he said to me, "Scratch your nose" . . . .*

The language material inside the quotes (marked by voice change in the auditory presentation) is quoted material. It is understood by the listener at the conscious level to be a command directed at someone in the story, not at the listener. However, the consistent effect which Erickson obtains with quoted material (as well as our own consistent experience with it) is the same as though he had delivered the command directly to the listener except that the listener responds unconsciously. This tendency depends upon the listener's tendency to commit an error of logical typing at the unconscious level — that is, to respond to a meta-statement (the quoted material) as though it were at a different logical level (see Bateson). This technique is extremely easy to use:

> Step 1 — Identify the message which you, as a hypnotist, desire the client to receive;
> Step 2 — Form the message into a command;
> Step 3 — Make up a story in which one of the characters says the command(s) emphatically.

Common to each of these three techniques is a dramatic increase in their effectiveness when they are combined with analogical marking. Erickson typically uses both his own movements and tempo and tonality changes to mark different portions of the Surface Structures he is uttering as a separate message. In this way, he is able to present several messages — to activate several Deep Structures simultaneously. Analogical marking of verbal communication and analogical communication more generally is a topic of Volume II of this series. We will leave a fuller discussion of the powerful techniques of Erickson until then.

The most basic strategy for analogical marking as it is used by Erickson can be presented here however:

> Step 1 — Identify the message which you, as a hypnotist, wish the client to receive;
> Step 2 — Make up a series of sentences which include as a proper subset all of the words which, if they were extracted, would communicate the message directly;
> Step 3 — Mark the subset of words included in the communication analogically (by tonal shifts, body shifts, tempo shifts, etc.) to communicate the included meaning.

Derived Meanings

As we stated before, when each of us uses a natural language system to communicate, we assume that the listener can decode complex sound sequences into meanings, *i.e.,* the listener has the ability to derive the Deep Structure meaning from the Surface Structure we present to him auditorily. In addition to the recovery of Deep-Structure meaning from Surface-Structure communication, we also assume the complex skill of listeners to derive extra meaning from some Surface Structures by the nature of their form. Even though neither the speaker nor the listener may be aware of this process, it goes on all of the time. For example, if someone says:

I want to watch Kung Fu tonight on TV

we must understand that Kung Fu is on TV tonight in order to process the sentence *I want to watch* . . . to make any sense. These processes are called presuppositions of natural language.

Another example of derived meaning is conversational postulate: If you answer the phone and someone says to you, "Is Jane there?" you are expected to derive the meaning that they wish to speak to her. This is part of our ongoing experience of processing language. It also offers a resource for hypnotists to give suggestions in an indirect manner.

Construction of Presuppositions

The formal representation of what constitutes presuppositions in natural language is as follows: Message **A** is a presupposition of Message **B** when Message **A** must be a true statement necessary for both Message **B** and the Message **Not B**:

A is a presupposition of B

if **B** implies **A**
and ~ **B** implies **A**

I want to watch
B
Kung Fu on TV tonight
A

I don't want to watch
Not B
Kung Fu on TV tonight
A

where ~ means negation

Both statements imply that Kung Fu is on TV tonight. Therefore, A is a presupposition of B and **not B**.

I want to know whether
B
you'll quit smoking on Sunday or Monday
A

I don't want to know whether
B
you'll quit smoking on Sunday or Monday
A

Procedure of Constructing Presuppositions

Step 1 — Identify the suggestion you, as a hypnotist, wish to make;

Step 2 — Form a sentence with the suggestion in it. Call this **A**;

Step 3 — Pick one of the syntactic environments from the Appendix on Presuppositions at the end of this volume. There are 32 from which to choose;

Step 4 — Imbed the sentence from Step 2 into the syntactic environment you chose from the Appendix.

The result will be a presupposition. Erickson uses presuppositions in almost every aspect of his work, and they are most useful and effective:

> *Will your unconscious mind let your conscious [mind] know what this terrible thing is in five minutes or in ten minutes?*

Construction of Conversational Postulates

There are two classes of conversational postulates. The first class is formally represented as follows:

A is a conversational postulate when **A** is a *Yes/No* question constructed from a presupposition, **B**

B is the sentence, "I want you to open the door," or "Open the door," **B** has the presuppositions:
(1) You can open the door.
(2) The door is closed.

So a conversational postulate can be constructed by changing (1) or (2) into a *Yes/No* question form.

(1) Can you open the door?
(2) Is the door closed?

The conversational postulate derived meaning is **B**, "Open the door."

Conversational postulate examples, first type:

command

(3) Can you focus your eyes on   *Focus your eyes on that spot.*
    that spot?

(4) Will your eyes close tightly?   *Close your eyes tightly.*

Construction procedures, first type:

> **Step 1** — Identify suggestion you want to give;
> **Step 2** — Make the suggestion a command;
> **Step 3** — Pick out one of the presuppositions of the command;
> **Step 4** — Form a *Yes/No* question from one of the presuppositions of the command.

The result will be a conversational postulate.

The second class of conversational postulates are Surface Structures such as:

> (1) There's no need to move.
> (2) You don't have to talk.
> (3) You can see her.
> (4) You may go now.

Examples (1) and (2) are slightly different in form from (3) and (4). The first two are examples of negative conversational postulates represented formally as:

> Any negation followed by a modal operator of necessity and then X is understood to mean **not X;**

> **Not X**
> *No need to move* then implies *don't move*
>
> *It isn't necessary to talk = don't talk*

The modal operator is dropped and the negation plus X are the derived meaning.

Examples (3) and (4) are positive conversational postulates which can be represented formally as:

> Any modal operator of possibility followed by X implies X
>
> *You can smile* implies *smile*
>
> *You may speak now* implies *speak now*

Both are similar in that they carry the same meaning with or without the modal operators.

Construction of negatives:

Step 1 — Identify suggestion;	Keep arm suspended in air after it has been lifted;
Step 2 — Form a command;	Don't put your arm down;
Step 3 — Embed command by inserting modal operator of necessity between negation and command.	Not necessary to put your arm down.

Construction procedure for positives:

Step 1 — Identify suggestion;	Open eyes.
Step 2 — Make command out of suggestion;	Open your eyes, Steve.
Step 3 — Imbed modal operator of possibility.	You can open your eyes, Steve.

Further examples of this class:

No need to remember	Negative: *no remember anything*
You can forget this.	Positive: *forget this*
It can be a boring task to remember.	Positive: *boring task to remember*
It's not necessary to hear anyone else's voice.	Negative: *no hear anyone else's voice*
You don't have to listen me.	Negative: *no listen*

Your unconscious minds can   Unconscious: *hear me*
hear me.

Conversational postulates are an extremely effective form of suggestion when used by Erickson (or by you). They utilize the processing of information at non-conscious levels in ways to which people are very used to responding. And, although they do not sound like commands, they are a form of command to which we all respond almost every day.

The common features of the two categories of presuppositions and conversational postulates are:

(a) They allow the hypnotist to instruct the client without directly stating the instructions;

(b) They allow the client to respond selectively without reducing the effectiveness of the hypnotist's induction or deep trance instructions;

(c) They depend for their effectiveness upon an additional processing on the part of the client — involving him even more actively in the process.

Summary of Part III

The linguistic patterns presented in a step-by-step manner in this part of Volume I constitute the basic foundations of Milton Erickson's use of language in his work with hypnosis. The next level of patterning is the way these lower level patterns are used in combination with each other to achieve the desired level of trance and the desired outcome of the suggested phenomenon (anastesia, control of pain, access to memory, weight loss, age regression, psychotherapeutic goals, etc.). Erickson's use of these patterns in combination demonstrates creative, consistent, and effective use at this meta-level of organization. The basic meta-patterns of:

(1) Pace and then lead
(2) Distract and utilize dominant hemisphere
(3) Access non-dominant hemisphere

have been presented already and are useful principles for organizing your own hypnotic work. There are an infinite number of choices of how the first order patterns may be put together. Erickson's creative use of these patterns in a large variety of contexts demonstrates his sensitive and ingenious use of these infinite complexities. The various ways in which all of these patterns can be put together, and how Erickson has put them together, are too numerous to mention in this first volume. However, there are some simple meta-patterning principles which will assist you in organizing your experience in combining these lower level patterns in a way which will most effectively assist you in achieving your desired purpose, while at the same time leaving you maximal room to use your own creativity to construct inductions which will fit your own style and needs as a practitioner of hypnosis.

Most Highly Valued Induction and Suggestion

The notion of most highly valued induction and suggestion is that the induction and suggestion which use the lower level patterns to achieve the maximal amount of:

(1) Pacing
(2) Distracting
(3) Utilization of dominant hemisphere functions
(4) Accessing of non-dominant hemisphere

with the least amount of words, at the same time being consistent with the client's model of the world. Any verbalizations meeting these criteria will be most highly valued. Of course, this depends upon the context and purpose of the hypnotic induction and suggestion. There are two principal ways to construct a highly valued induction and suggestion.

1. *Intersection of Unconscious Meanings*

The principle of intersection of non-conscious meanings is that inductions and suggestions will be most effective when the Deep Structure meanings that are activated (not the ones represented consciously) by transderivational search, ambiguity, lesser included structure, derived meanings, analogical marking, and causal modeling statements interact, i.e., all give the same suggestion. As a result, the suggestion is most likely to be accepted and acted upon by the client. For example:

> If one of the Deep Structures from an ambiguity is message **P**, one of the lesser included Deep Structures is **P**, one of derived Deep Structures is **P**, an analogically marked message is **P**, and a Deep Structure activated transderivational is **P**, then the unconscious meanings maximally intersect and message **P** will be accepted and acted upon by the client.

2. Maximal Direction

The principle of maximal direction is that the unified action of combining lower level patterns will serve to pace the client's experience while distracting the dominant hemisphere by utilizing the modeling processes of that hemisphere and, simultaneously, also serving to access the non-dominant hemisphere. This principle is stated as: If the hypnotist uses the level-one patterns to activate a set of unconsciously generated and accepted meanings represented by messages P_1, P_2, P_3, ... P_n for each pair of messages, P_2 and P_j, there is no conflict (they are consistent), then the overall effect is maximal direction. The set of unconscious messages reinforce one another and should proceed in an increasingly meaningful direction toward the desired goal; that is, P_j should not only not negate any other P_k, but P_1 should be the logical step leading to P_2. This is probably the most important factor in expediting hypnotic work.

The reader will have noticed that, following each of the patterns of Erickson's work which we extract in Part II of this volume, we have included the same short paragraph, with, in italic type, the expressions which were examples of the patterns which we had just finished describing. This paragraph, then, is an excellent example of the higher level patterning — the principles of the most highly valued induction and suggestion, especially intersection and maximal overlap. We repeat the same paragraph again for the convenience of the reader.

The writer immediately seized upon this last comment as the basis for the initial cooperation with him. He was told, "Please proceed with an account of your ideas and understanding, permitting me only enough interruptions to insure that I understand fully and *that I follow along with you.* For example, you mentioned the chair but obviously you have seen my desk and have been distracted by the objects on it. Please explain fully.

He responded verbosely with a wealth of more or less connected comments about everything in sight. At every slight pause, the writer interjected a word or phrase to direct his attention anew. These interruptions, made with increasing frequency, were as follows:

> And that paperweight; the filing cabinet; your foot on the rug; the ceiling light; the draperies; your right hand on the arm of the chair; the pictures on the wall; the changing

focus of your eyes as you glance about; the interest of the book titles; the tension in your shoulders; the feeling of the chair; the disturbing noises and thoughts; weight of hands and feet; weight of problems, weight of desk; the stationary stand; the records of many patients; the phenomena of life, of illness, of emotion, of physical and mental behavior; the restfulness of relaxation; the need to attend to one's needs; the need to attend to one's tension while looking at the desk or the paperweight or the filing cabinet; the comfort of withdrawal from the environment; fatigue and its development; the unchanging character of the desk; the monotony of the filing cabinet; the need to take a rest; the comfort of closing one's eyes; the relaxing sensation of a deep breath; the delight of learning passively; the capacity for intellectual learning by the unconscious.

Various other similar brief interjections were offered, slowly at first and then with increasing frequency.

Initially, these interjections were merely supplementary to the patient's own train of thought and utterances. At first, the effect was simply to stimulate him to further effort. As this response was made, it became possible to utilize his acceptance of stimulation of his behavior by a procedure of pausing and hesitating in the completion of an interjection. This served to effect in him an expectant dependency upon the writer for further and more complete stimulation. (1967, p. 33)

Clearly, the medical practitioner will have a different purpose in mind than psychotherapists, who will have a different goal than the dental practitioner, and so on. However, the notion of most highly valued induction will exist in each context. Faster inductions will make hypnosis a more practical tool for every practitioner and deeper trances, although not always required, will open new horizons for the application of hypnosis in other fields. The form of highly valued inductions will remain constant, although the content will vary in relationship to your purposes and the client with whom you are working. Explicit patterns of these inductions will be presented in Volume II. As we stated before, this work constitutes only a few of the many patterns of behavior used so effectively by Milton Erickson in his work with hypnosis. Although this work may represent only a part of what Erickson has to offer, the patterns presented here are effective in and of themselves. Study and experimentation in your own experience will reveal that the preceding patterns offer you a vast resource to enrich your skill in hypnotic activity and a foundation for you to further explore your own potentials. Volume II is on the way. The study of Erickson's work has been an incredible learning experience for us — we hope it will prove to be fascinating and useful for you.

FOOTNOTES FOR PART III

1. The name of this class of phenomena, *transderivational*, with its marvelous phonological ambiguity, refers to the process which our model claims the listener goes through to make meaning. Upon hearing a Surface Structure and recovering its associated Deep Structure, which has little or no obvious meaning relationship to the listener's ongoing experience, the listener activates additional Deep Structures, with their associated derivations, which are obtained from the original recovered Deep Structure by some specifiable formal characteristic. Thus, the listener searches across Deep Structures and their associated derivations at the unconscious level of language processing to extract some meaning relevant to his ongoing experience — therefore, *transderivational*. Transderivational phenomena were first proposed in liguistic theory by Postal, Perlmutter, and Grinder (see Lakoff, G., *Some Thoughts on Transderivational Constraints*, mimeograph, 1970).

2. The Deep Structure which we present here is a very crudely simplified version of what the actual Deep Structure is from a linguistic analysis. For example, the reader will notice that the words *learning* and *opportunities* are, themselves, complex; each of them is a nominalization (derived from a Deep Structure representation in which they originally occurred as predicates). Thus, while the actual Deep Structure from a linguistic analysis is much more complex, the processes which are being represented here in this simplified example apply to the more complex structure in the same way.

3. There is an excellent example of intonation ambiguity in this passage: Erickson first meta-comments

  . . . funny to talk about a tomato plant feeling good . . .

and then again comments:

  . . . isn't it Joe . . .

Depending upon the intonation pattern which the hypnotist uses here, the client will hear a simple tag question:

  . . . isn't it (pause) Joe . . .

or a direct meta-comment:

> *. . . isn't it Joe . . . .*

That is,

> *isn't it Joe whom I'm talking about feeling good.*

4. In the standard linguistic analysis, Deep Structure nouns may only be deleted (grammatically) if they either have another noun in the same Deep Structure which carries the same referential index (and is in certain specified structural relations to the one being deleted) or they carry no referential index in the Deep Structure representation.

5. This type of punctuation ambiguity is mentioned in Grinder and Elgin, 1973, under the name of Overlap Deletion, a technique sometimes employed in literary language and poetry.

Epilogue

This volume is the first in a series of studies of the patterns of hypnotic techniques employed by Milton H. Erickson. In this first volume, we have focused primarily on the verbal patterns which Erickson uses in his work. Furthermore, our emphasis here has been on the portions of his work dealing with the induction of trance and the use of suggestion for assisting the client in accomplishing the objectives of trance work. We intend to shift the emphasis of the future volumes to other patterns — the Table of Contents which we include for Volume II of *Patterns* will give the reader some notion of this future emphasis.

The patterns of Erickson's work which we make explicit in this first volume are neutral with respect to their application — that is, they are of equal value and potency in their medical, dental and psychotherapeutic forms. Common to the use of hypnosis in each of these three areas is that, during a trance induction and the subsequent trance work employing the powerful Erickson patterns which we have modeled in this volume, the client is assisted in achieving an altered state of consciousness in which communication between the hypnotist and the client occurs and dramatic and far-reaching changes may be initiated by the client without the awareness of the client's conscious mind. From our work both in therapy and in hypnosis we understand and accept the value of sorting or separating portions of the client's consciousness which assists the client in making the changes which he desires. However, in our work in both areas, we insist upon working with the client to integrate the changes made in one state of consciousness with his skills and resources in other states of consciousness, thereby leaving the client with a coordinated, unified and integrated model of the world on which to make choices which guide his behavior. In Chapter Six of *Magic I* and Part Two of *Magic II,* we go into great detail in presenting both examples and principles which underlie the integration of changes which clients succeed in making in therapy. Thus, what we wish to point out clearly to those who intend to use the powerful patterns which we have extracted and modeled from Erickson's work is that the use of these patterns includes the presupposition that the client may communicate and initiate changes of which one portion of his consciousness has no awareness; in other words, the use of these hypnotic patterns includes the disassociation of a portion of the client's model of the world. The use of these powerful techniques requires that the hypnotist assist the client in reintegrating his model fully before the hypnotic relationship is ended. In this way, the client truly comes to control his behavior and has available the choices which he entered the hypnotic relationship to secure for himself. Erickson has made this point over and over again in his work and writings — we endorse completely his statement:

> Another common oversight in hypnotic psycho-therapy lies in the lack of appreciation of the separateness or the possible mutual exclusiveness of the conscious and the unconscious (or sub-conscious) levels of awareness. Yet, all of us have had the experience of having a word or a name "on the tip of the tongue" but being unable to remember it so that it remained unavailable and inaccessible in the immediate situation. Nevertheless, full knowledge actually existed within the unconscious, but unavailably so to the conscious mind.
>
> In hypnotic psychotherapy, too often, suitable therapy may be given to the unconscious but with the failure by the therapist to appreciate the tremendous need of either enabling the patient to integrate the unconscious with the conscious, or, of making the new understandings of the unconscious fully accessible, upon need, to the conscious mind. Comparable to this failure would be an

appendectomy with failure to close the incision. It is in this regard that many arm-chair critics naively denounce hypnotic psychotherapy as without value since "it deals only with the unconscious." Additionally, there is even more oversight of the fact, repeatedly demonstrated by clinical experience, that in some aspects of the patient's problem direct reintegration under the guidance of the therapist is desirable; in other aspects, the unconscious should merely be made available to the conscious mind, thereby permitting a spontaneous reintegration free from any immediate influence by the therapist. Properly, hypnotherapy should be oriented equally about the conscious and unconscious, since the integration of the total personality is the desired goal in psychotherapy.

Milton H. Erickson, *Hypnotic Psychotherapy*, 1948, pp. 575 and 576

We are aware that simply pointing out the necessity of integration as the final step in the use of hypnosis is not adequate; rather, an explicit model of the way in which the hypnotist may assist the client in integration is required. This is the point of the references to the portions of *Magic I* and *II* and a portion of the focus of Volume II of *Patterns*. We wish to be clear here regarding integration — one of the advantages of the use of hypnosis in the therapeutic context is that through disassociation the client is able to cope with and initiate changes in portions of his model of the world which are so heavily laden with negative emotional associations that the client in the normal state of consciousness panics or feels overwhelmed. Thus, while integration in our model of hypnotic and therapeutic work is a necessary component, there is no need to require that the integration occur immediately; this would run counter to one of the most powerful advantages of hypnosis. Erickson, once again, states the case clearly:

However, the above does not necessarily mean that integration must constantly keep step with the progress of the therapy. One of the greatest advantages of hypnotherapy lies in the opportunity to work independently with the unconscious without being hampered by the reluctance, or sometimes actual inability, of the conscious mind to accept therapeutic gains. For example, a patient had full unconscious insight into her periodic nightmares of an incestuous character from which she suffered, but, as she spontaneously declared in the trance, "I now understand those horrible dreams, but I couldn't possibly tolerate such an understanding consciously." By this utterance, the patient demonstrated the protectiveness of the unconscious for the conscious. Utilization of this protectiveness as a motivating force enabled the patient subsequently to accept consciously her unconscious insights.

Experimental investigation has repeatedly demonstrated that good unconscious understandings allowed to become conscious before a conscious readiness exists will result in conscious resistance, rejection, repression and even the loss, through repression, of unconscious gains. By working separately with the unconscious there is then the opportunity to temper and to control the patient's rate of progress and thus to effect a reintegration in the manner acceptable to the conscious mind.

M. Erickson, *Hypnotic Psychotherapy*, 1948, p. 576.

NOW WWW WWW WWW W W W

Appendix

SYNTACTIC ENVIRONMENTS FOR IDENTIFYING NATURAL LANGUAGE PRESUPPOSITIONS IN ENGLISH

Our purpose in presenting the material in this Appendix is to indicate the scope and complexity of the natural language phenomenon of presuppositions. In addition, by listing some of the more common syntactic environments in which presuppositions occur, we provide an opportunity to practice for those students who are interested in sharpening their intuitions in recognizing presuppositions. The list of syntactic environments is not exhaustive, and we will not attempt to present any of the theories which have been proposed by different linguists, logicians, semanticists, or philosophers to account for presuppositions. Our objective, rather, is more practical.

At the present time, presuppositions are a major focus of study for a number of linguists, especially linguists who consider themselves Generative Semanticists. In compiling this list of syntactic environments, we have borrowed heavily from the work of Lauri Kartunnen. See the Bibliography for sources.

I. **Simple Presuppositions.** These are syntactic environments in which the existence of some entity is required for the sentence to make sense (to be either true or false).

(a) **Proper Names:** (*George Smith* left the party early.)
(there exists someone named *George Smith*)
where ⟶ means presupposes

(b) **Pronouns:** *her, him, they,* etc.
(I saw *him* leave.)
⟶ (There exists some male [i.e., *him*].)

(c) **Definite Descriptions:** complex noun arguments
(I liked *the woman with the silver earrings.*)
⟶ (There exists a woman with silver earrings.)

(d) **Generic Noun Phrases:** noun arguments standing for a whole class:
(If *wombats* have no trees to climb in, they are sad.)
⟶ (There are wombats.)

(e) **Some Quantifiers:** *all, each, every, some, many, few, none,* etc.
(If *some of the dragons* show up, I'm leaving.)
⟶ (There are dragons.)

II. **Complete Presuppositions.** Cases in which more than the simple existence of an element is presupposed.

(a) **Relative Clauses:** complex noun arguments, with a noun followed by a phrase beginning with *who, which,* or *that.*
(*Several of the women who had spoken to you* left the shop.)
⟶ (Several women had spoken to you.)

(b) **Subordinate Clauses of Time:** clauses identified by the cue words *before, after, during, as, since, prior, when, while,* etc.
(If the judge was home *when I stopped by her house,* she didn't answer her door.)
⟶ (I stopped by the judge's house.)

(c) *Cleft Sentences:* sentences beginning with *It* $\begin{Bmatrix} was \\ is \end{Bmatrix}$ noun argument.

> (*It was the extra pressure* which shattered the window.)
> ⟶ (Something shattered the window.)

(d) *Psuedo-Cleft Sentences:* identified by the form *What* ⟨Sentence⟩ *is* ⟨sentence⟩

> (*What Sharon hopes to do is* to become well liked.)
> ⟶ (Sharon hopes to do something.)

(e) *Stressed Sentences voice stress*

> (If it was *THE POLICE* Margaret talked to, we're finished.)
> ⟶ (Margaret has talked to someone.)

(f) *Complex Adjectives: new, old, former, present, previous,* etc.

> (If Fredo wears his *new* ring, I'll be blown away.)
> ⟶ (Fredo had/has an old ring.)

(g) *Ordinal Numerals: first, second, third, fourth, another,* etc.

> (If you can find a *third* clue in this letter, I'll make you a mosquito pie.)
> ⟶ (There are two clues already found.)

(h) *Comparatives: -er, more, less*

> (If you know bett*er* riders than Sue does, tell me who they are.)
> ⟶ (Sue knows [at least] one rider.)
> (If you know bett*er* riders than Sue is, tell me who they are.)
> ⟶ (Sue is a rider.)

(i) *Comparative as: . . . as x as . . .*

> (If her daughter is *as funny as* her husband is, we'll all enjoy ourselves.)
> ⟶ (Her husband is funny.)

(j) *Repetitive Cue Words: too, also, either, again, back,* etc.
(If she tells me that *again,* I'll kiss her.)
⟶(She has told me that before.)

(k) *Repetitive Verbs and Adverbs:* verbs and adverbs beginning with *re-,* e.g., *repeatedly, return, restore, retell, replace, renew,* etc.
(If he *re*turns before I leave, I want to talk to him.)
⟶(He has been here before.)

(l) *Qualifiers,* such as: *only, even, except, just,* etc.
(*Only* Amy saw the bank robbers.)
⟶(Amy saw the bank robbers.)

(m) *Change-of-Place Verbs: come, go, leave, arrive, depart, enter,* etc.
(If Sam has *left* home, he is lost.)
⟶(Sam has been at home.)

(n) *Change-of-Time Verbs and Adverbs: begin, end, stop, start, continue, proceed, already, yet, still, anymore,* etc.
(My bet is that Harry will *continue* to smile.)
⟶(Harry has been smiling.)

(o) *Change-of-State Verbs: change, transform, turn into, become,* etc.
(If Mae *turns into* a hippie, I'll be surprised.)
⟶(Mae is not now a hippie.)

(p) *Tactive Verbs and Adjectives: odd, aware, know, realize, regret,* etc.
(It is *odd* that she called Maxine at midnight.)
⟶(She called Maxine at midnight.)

(q) *Commentary Adjectives and Adverbs: lucky, fortunately, far out, out of sight, groovy, bitchin, innocently, happily, necessarily,* etc.
(It's *far out* that you understand your dog's feelings.)
⟶(You understand your dog's feelings.)

(r) *Counterfactual Conditional Clauses:* verbs having *subjunctive tense.*

(*If you had listened to your father and me,* you wouldn't be in the wonderful position you're in now.)

⟶ (You didn't listen to your father and me.)

(s) *Contrary-to-Expectation should:*

(*If you should* [happen to] decide you want to talk to me, I'll be hanging out in the city dump.)

⟶ (I don't expect you to want to talk to me.)

(t) *Selectional Restrictions:*

(If my professor gets *pregnant,* I'll be disappointed.)

⟶ (My professor is a woman.)

(u) *Questions:*

(Who ate the tapes?)

⟶ (Someone ate the tapes.)

(I want to know who ate the tapes.)

⟶ (Someone ate the tapes.)

(v) *Negative Questions:*

(Did*n't* you want to talk to me?)

⟶ (I thought that you wanted to talk to me.)

(w) *Rhetorical Questions:*

(Who cares whether you show up or not?)

⟶ (Nobody cares whether you show up or not.)

(x) *Spurious not:*

(I wonder if you're *not* being a little unfair.)

⟶ (I think that you're being unfair.)

Bibliography

I. General

Bach, E. *Syntactic Theory*. New York: Holt, Rinehart and Winston, Inc., 1974.

Bach-y-Rita, P. *Brain Mechanisms in Sensory Substitution*. New York: Academic Press, 1972.

Bandler, R., and Grinder, J. *The Structure of Magic I*. Palo Alto, Calif.: Science and Behavior Books, 1975.

Bandler, R., and Grinder, J. *The Structure of Magic II*. (forthcoming) 1975.

Bever, T. G. "The Cognitive Basis of Linguistic Structure," in J. Hayes (ed.), *Cognition and the Developments of Language*. New York: John Wiley and Sons, 1970.

Chomsky, N. *Syntactic Structures*. Mouton, The Hague, 1957.

Chomsky, N. *Aspects of the Theory of Syntax*. Cambridge, Mass.: MIT Press, 1965.

Chomsky, N. *Language and Mind*. New York: Harcourt Brace Jovanovich, Inc., 1968.

Dimond, S., and Beaumont, K. *Hemisphere Function in the Human Brain*. New York: John Wiley & Sons, 1974.

Dimond, S. *The Double Brain*. London: Churchill Livingstone, 1972.

Eccles, J. *Brain and Conscious Experience*. New York: Springer-Verlag, 1966.

Fillmore, C., "The Case for Case," in E. Bach and R. Harms (eds.), *Universals in Linguistic Theory*. New York: Holt, Rinehart and Winston, 1968.

Gardner, H. *The Shattered Mind*, Knopf, 1975.

Gazzainga, M. *The Bisected Brain*. New York: Appleton Century Croft, 1974.

Greene, G. "How to Get People to Do Things With Words," in *Papers From the 8th Regional Meeting of the Chicago Linguistic Society*. Chicago: University of Chicago, 1970.

Grinder, J. *On Deletion Phenomena in English*. Mouton, The Hague, 1974.

Grinder, J., and Elgin, S. *A Guide to Transformational Grammar*. New York: Holt, Rinehart and Winston, 1973.

Gruber, J. "Studies in Lexical Relations." Unpublished doctoral dissertation, MIT, 1965.

Haley,[1] J. *Advanced Techniques of Hypnosis and Therapy*. New York: Grune and Stratton, 1967.

Haley, J. *Uncommon Therapy*. New York: Grune and Stratton.

Horn, L. "A Presuppositional Analysis of *Only* and *Even*," in *Papers From the 5th Regional Meeting of the Chicago Linguistic Society*. Chicago: University of Chicago, 1969.

Jacobs, R., and Rosenbaum, P. *English Transformational Grammar*. Waltham, Mass.: Ginn/Blaisdell, 1968.

Jeffress, J. A. *Cerebral Mechanisms in Behavior*. New York: Hafner Co., 1967.

Kartunnen, L. "Remarks on Presuppositions," at the Texas Conference on Performances, Conversational Implicature and Presuppositions, March 1973, mimeograph.

Katz, J. *Semantic Theory*. New York: Harper and Row, 1972.

Lakoff, G. *Linguistics and Natural Logic*. Ann Arbor: University of Michigan, 1970.

Langacker, R. *Language and Its Structure*. New York: Harcourt Brace Jovanovich, Inc., 1967.

Levy, J. "Psychobiological Implications of Bilateral Asymmetry," article in *Hemisphere Function in the Human Brain*. New York: John Wiley & Sons, 1974.

Lyons, J. *Introduction to Theoretical Linguistics*. Cambridge, England: Cambridge University Press.

McCawley, J. "Lexical Insertion in a Transformational Grammar," in *Papers From the 4th Regional Meeting of the Chicago Linguistic Society*. Chicago: University of Chicago, 1968.

Plath, W., and Bever, T. *Specification and Utilization of a Transformational Grammar*. Bedford, Mass.: Air Force Cambridge Research Laboratories, July 1968.

Polya, G. *Patterns of Plausible Inference*. Princeton, N.J.: Princeton Univ. Press, 1954.

Postal, P. "On the Derivation of Pseudo-Adjectives," paper delivered to the 44th Annual Meeting of the LSA, 1969.

Postal, P. "On the Surface Verb *Remind*," in *Linguistic Inquiry*. (1; 1:37-120) 1970.

Ross, J. R. "On Declarative Sentences," in R. Jacobs and P. Rosenbaum, *Readings in English Transformational Grammar*. Waltham, Mass.: Ginn/Blaisdell, 1970.

Sapir, E. *The Selected Writing of Edward Sapir*. Berkeley: University of California Press, D. Mandelbaum (ed.), 1963.

Searle, J. *Speech Acts*. Cambridge, England: Cambridge University Press, 1969.

Weizenhoffer, A. *General Techniques of Hypnotism*. New York: Grune and Stratton, 1957.

Whorf, B. "Grammatical Categories," in J. E. Carroll (ed.), *Language, Thought and Reality*. New York: John Wiley and Sons, 1956.

II. Modeling/Formal Systems/Epistemology

Ashby, W. R. *An Introduction to Cybernetics*. Chapman and Hall, Ltd., and University Paperbacks, 1956.

Bateson, G. *Steps to an Ecology of Mind*. New York: Ballantine Books, 1972.

Boyd, D. *Introduction to Systems Analysis*. (in press) 1975.

Carnap, R. *The Logical Syntax of Language*. Totowa, New Jersey: Littlefield, Adams and Company, 1959.

Copi, I. *Introduction to Logic*. New York: Macmillan, 1961.

Herzberger, H. "The Logical Consistency of Language," in *Harvard Educational Review*, 35:469-480, 1965.

Hume, D. *Enquiry Concerning Human Understanding*. Oxford, England: Oxford University Press.

Korzybski, A. *Science and Sanity*. Lakeville, Conn.: The International Non-Aristotelian Library Publishing Company, 4th Edition, 1933.

Miller, G. A.; Galanter, E.; and Pribram, K. *Plans and the Structure of Behavior*. New York: Holt, Rinehart and Winston, Inc., 1960.

Newell, A.; and Simon, H. A. *Human Problem Solving*. Englewood Cliffs, New Jersey: Prentice-Hall, 1972.

Pribram, K. *Language of the Brain*. Englewood Cliffs, New Jersey: Prentice-Hall, 1971.

Russell, B. *Introduction to Mathematical Philosophy*. London, England: George Allen and Unwin, Ltd., 2nd Edition, 1921.

Schank, R.; and Colby, K. *Computer Models of Thought and Language*. San Francisco: W. H. Freeman and Company, 1973.

Tarski, A. *Introduction to Logic*. New York: Oxford University Press, 1941.

Vaihinger, H. *The Philosophy of "As If."* London, England: Routledge, Kegan and Paul, Ltd., 1924.

---

1. References labeled "(Milton H. Erickson) 1967" refer to Haley (ed.), 1967.

BOOK LIST
Meta Publications Inc
P.O. Box 565
Cupertino, CA. 95015

Thinking About Thinking .... $ 9.95
Joseph Yeager (paper)

The Master Moves $14.95
Moshe Feldenkrais

Magic in Action $14.95
Richard Bandler

Roots of Neuro-Linguistic Programming $22.00
Robert Dilts (hardcover)

Applications of Neuro-Linguistic Programming $22.00
Robert Dilts (hardcover)

Meta-Cation: Prescriptions for Some Ailing Educational Processes .. $12.00
Sid Jacobson (hardcover)

Meta-Cation: Volume II $12.00
Sid Jacobson (hardcover)

Phoenix—Therapeutic Patterns of Milton H. Erickson $14.00
D. Gordon & M. Myers-Anderson (hardcover)

Neuro-Linguistic Programming $24.00
Dilts, Grinder, Bandler et al Limited Edition (hardcover)

The Elusive Obvious $20.00
Moshe Feldenkrais (deluxe edition)

Patterns of Hypnotic Techniaues of Milton H. Erickson, M.D. .... $ 9.95
Bandler and Grinder
Volume I (paper only)

Patterns of Hypnotic Techniques of Milton H. Erickson, M.D. $17.95
Bandler, DeLozier, Grinder
Volume II (hardcover)

Provocative Therapy $12.00
Farrelly & Brandsma (hardcover)

Gestalt Therapy and Beyond .... $ 9.95
Marcus (hardcover)

Changing With Families .... $ 9.95
Bandler, Grinder and Satir (hardcover)

The Structure of Magic, Volume 1 .... $ 8.95
Bandler and Grinder (paper)

The Structure of Magic, Volume II .... $ 8.95
Bandler and Grinder (paper)

Practical Magic $12.00
Stephen R. Lankton (hardcover)

Therapeutic Metaphors $12.00
David Gordon (hardcover)